In Community With Readers

Transforming Reading Instruction with Read-Alouds and Minilessons

Lynsey Burkins and Franki Sibberson

I0127872

Routledge
Taylor & Francis Group
NEW YORK AND LONDON
A Stenhouse Book

Cover photo by Karla Detwiler (Banks Photography)

First published 2025
by Routledge
605 Third Avenue, New York, NY 10158

and by Routledge
4 Park Square, Milton Park, Abingdon, Oxon, OX14 4RN

Routledge is an imprint of the Taylor & Francis Group, an informa business

Library of Congress Cataloging-in-Publication Data
Names: Burkins, Lynsey, author. | Sibberson, Franki, author.
Title: In community with readers : transforming reading instruction with read alouds and minilessons / Lynsey Burkins and Franki Sibberson.
Description: New York, NY : Routledge, 2024. | Includes bibliographical references and index. | Identifiers: LCCN 2024017042 (print) | LCCN 2024017043 (ebook) | ISBN 9781625316509 (paperback) | ISBN 9781032680804 (ebook)
Subjects: LCSH: Oral reading. | Group reading. | Reading (Elementary) | Lesson planning.
Classification: LCC LB1573.5 .B87 2024 (print) | LCC LB1573.5 (ebook) | DDC 372.41--dc23/eng/20240515
LC record available at https://lccn.loc.gov/2024017042
LC ebook record available at https://lccn.loc.gov/2024017043

ISBN: 978-1-625-31650-9 (pbk)
ISBN: 978-1-032-68080-4 (ebk)

DOI: 10.4324/9781032680804

Typeset in Chaparral Pro
by KnowledgeWorks Global Ltd.

This is the book I want for all teachers of reading. For those who know that teaching is really the work of deeply listening to and loving all kids. Franki and Lynsey show you their evolution as longtime teachers and center the kids in each teacherly decision. Before you begin your next year of teaching, start here.

—**Nawal Qarooni,** educator and author of *Nourishing Caregiver Collaborations: Elevating Home Experiences and Classroom Practices for Collective Care*

In Community With Readers invites us into a beloved reading community and supports us in planning whole-class reading instruction that centers freedom, love, and standards. Burkins and Sibberson show us how to shift the power dynamics in our instruction to co-create understanding and unpack standards alongside our students. They help us learn how to read standards with criticality, recognizing our biases and the impacts of systemic oppression. They provide classroom examples, step-by-step guides, planning ideas, and questions to view the standards through a lens of possibilities rather than limitations. This book is a call to action to cultivate joyful readers who are critical thinkers, compassionate listeners, truth seekers, and citizens who advocate for justice. This book is what teachers need, want, and aspire to create for their students every day.

—**Clare Landrigan,** literacy coach and co-author of *It's All About the Books: How to Create Bookrooms and Classroom Libraries That Inspire Readers*

Within these pages, Lynsey and Franki use artifacts from their and their students' learning to share the why, what, and how of nurturing a beloved reading community. Their words show respect and care for a beloved teaching community, making this text an addition to my "menu of mentors" for those who are either new to the field *or* new to the practice of teaching with and learning from children.

—**Keisha Smith-Carrington,** Supervisor of Humanities and co-author of *Read-Alouds with Heart: Literacy Lessons that Build Community, Comprehension, and Cultural Competency*

Imagine a classroom where teachers and students joyfully and intellectually co-create a "beloved reading community" where all learners are invited, as one student put it, to "come join our family." Masterful teachers Lynsey Burkins and Franki Sibberson have crafted a magnificent resource that provides us numerous tools, routines, strategies, and plans for co-constructing with students the deep questioning, analyzing, and listening skills that lead to authentic conversations around terrific texts. Intentional instruction and responsive teaching at its finest!

—**Regie Routman,** teacher and author of
The Heart-Centered Teacher: Restoring Hope,
Joy and Possibility in Uncertain Times

Rooted in a pedagogy of listening and reflection, Franki and Lynsey exemplify how to cultivate and sustain a beloved reading community where children's voices are honored as they co-construct meaning collectively. This book is a reminder of the marvelous brilliance that readers bring to our school community and the power of collective thinking.

—**Stella Villalba,** language and literacy
educator and consultant

No matter where you are in your journey as an educator, *In Community With Readers* will leave you inspired. You'll walk away eager to begin or continue pursuing the love and freedom that we know reading offers when experienced alongside those we find ourselves in community with.

—**Antonia Adams,** educator and book
blogger @BlackGirlThatReads

What shines from every page of this book is a deep respect for children—their experiences, their opinions, and their inner lives. Lynsey and Franki create spaces where young readers can find intellectual and emotional safety and the freedom to be themselves. Many conversations about young readers do not include their voices. This book reminds us all that children's voices should be the loudest in the room.

—**Donalyn Miller,** reading advocate and author

To Kassia for your dedication and commitment to lifting the voices of children, teachers, and classroom communities.

Contents

Foreword by Gary R. Gray, Jr.   ix

INTRODUCTION
••••••••••••••••••
Centering Community—The Important Role
of Whole-Group Reading Instruction   1

CHAPTER 1
••••••••••••••
Building Identity, Independence, and Agency
for Readers through Whole-Class Instruction   11

CHAPTER 2
••••••••••••••
Shifting Power and Control in Minilessons
and Read-Aloud   31

CHAPTER 3
••••••••••••••
Getting to Know the Standards   63

CHAPTER 4
••••••••••••••
Getting to Know Books   85

CHAPTER 5
••••••••••••••
Getting to Know Your Students by Listening
with Love and Intention   111

Contents

CHAPTER 6
••••••••••••••

A Close Look at a Minilesson Cycle 133

CHAPTER 7
••••••••••••••

A Close Look at a Read-Aloud 165

CHAPTER 8
••••••••••••••

Planning Intentionally for the First Eight
Weeks of School 191

Appendices 235
References 238
Credits 241
Index 243

Foreword

Dear Readers,

Gloria Ladson-Billings writes, "A culturally relevant pedagogy is designed to problematize teaching and encourage teachers to ask about the nature of the student–teacher relationship, the curriculum, schooling, and society" (1995, 483).

These words are beautifully reflected in the work of Lynsey Burkins and Franki Sibberson. Once you start to explore the pages of *In Community With Readers*, you will be reminded of the importance of this concept. Lynsey and Franki's willingness to reimagine reading in the classroom not only inspires but also challenges our current thinking around reading communities and their potential to foster liberation. As a reader, you are asked to take a deep dive into your practices and discover new ways to empower young minds, allowing children to take the lead on a transformative journey towards a vibrant community of readers.

The primary focus of this book is on returning power to the students and enabling them to take charge of their own learning experiences. Rather than advocating for a complete overhaul of your current approach to teaching reading, *In Community With Readers* offers small but powerful adjustments that can make your existing practices even more meaningful for students. The tools in between the pages promote choice, freedom, identity, agency, and love. Lynsey and Franki provide explicit guidance on how to transform student dialogues into meaningful learning experiences aligned with standards and offer various approaches to documenting and monitoring student progress. Additionally, this book goes above and beyond by offering comprehensive planning ideas for the first eight weeks of reading conversations. I urge you to utilize these ideas to establish a foundation for literacy classrooms that foster a sense of community and camaraderie among readers. By embracing Lynsey and Franki's recommendations, you will witness a shift in classroom dynamics, with student ownership and empowerment taking center stage. Each student will have the freedom to contribute to the community in ways that align with their individual needs and assets.

Lynsey and Franki exemplify Gloria Ladson-Billings's message as they encourage educators to reconsider traditional practices in whole-classroom reading. They advocate for dismantling instructional norms and placing students at the center, empowering them to drive learning conversations through dialogue and critical thinking. By disrupting power dynamics in the classroom and fostering thoughtful exchanges, they create an environment where literacy discussions become a trusted space. Within this supportive framework, students can rely on one another for learning, cultivating a sense of freedom and love. This approach restores power to students, allowing them to use their voices and ideas to shape their very own understanding.

This is a gift y'all.

A gift that gives access to the authors' years of practical experience in reading instruction with children. The resource emphasizes the significance of "listening with love and intentionality," as Lynsey and Franki would affirm, and reinforces the importance of having a deep familiarity with the books educators read in their classrooms. Truly, this resource is a labor of love that will remain a cherished companion throughout your professional educational journey for years to come.

Lynsey and Franki know reading; they know kids.

They understand that being mindful of not only *what* they teach but *how* they teach can have a significant impact on students. They know that there is no such thing as a perfect lesson or unit plan. They explain their past mistakes and draw from the lessons they have learned, showing teachers how they have reimagined their learning spaces.

I can't stop smiling, and neither will you after reading *In Community With Readers*.

This book will leave you feeling motivated to make a change, as it is a powerful resource that evokes excitement about literacy and inspires reflection on your teaching practice. It's all about empowering and prioritizing those who are most important—the learners themselves. It comes as no surprise that Lynsey and Franki, who have dedicated so much to education, have created yet another book that will continue to empower students, educators, and myself. I couldn't resist going back to my own lesson plans and making adjustments, knowing that these shifts directly impact learning and provide immediate benefits. Lynsey and Franki's approach enables students to leave their classrooms with skills they can immediately apply in the outside world.

It's a gift that all educators need in their stack.

Enjoy, y'all.

Enjoy every bit of it.

Gary R. Gray Jr., educator and author of *I'm From*

Reference

Ladson-Billings, Gloria. 1995. "Toward a Theory of Culturally Relevant Pedagogy." *American Educational Research Journal* 32 (3): 465–491.

Introduction

Centering Community— The Important Role of Whole-Group Reading Instruction

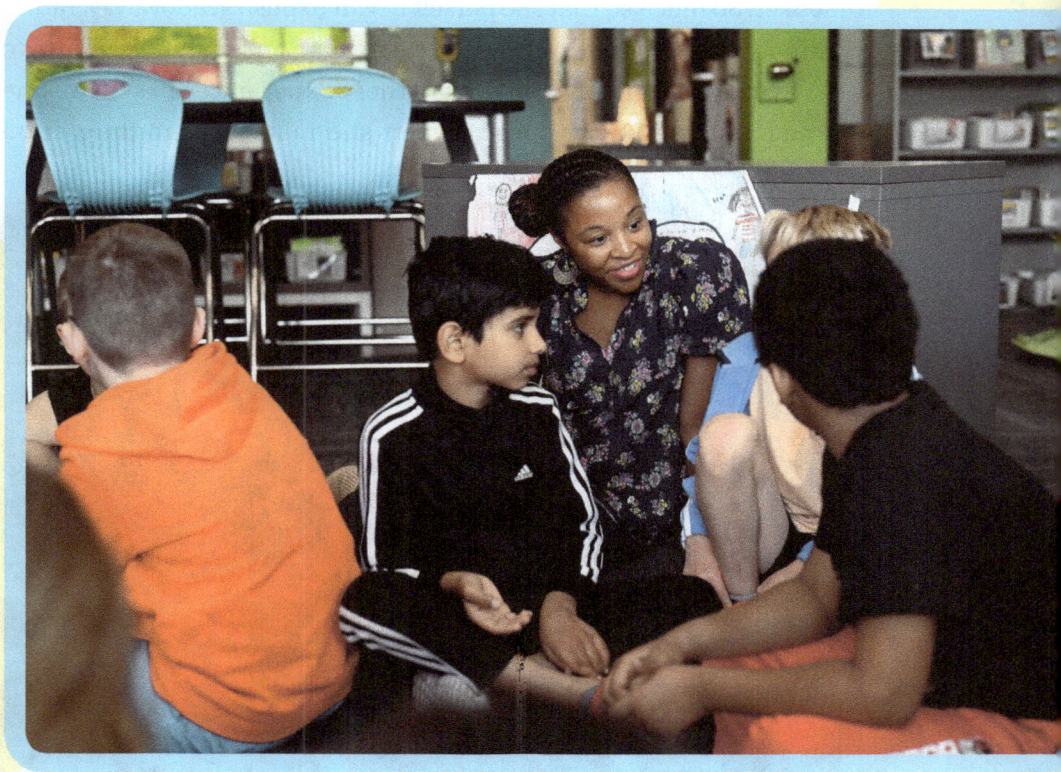

Lynsey's Story

As a child, Lynsey never fully understood what her mom meant when she would tell her over and over again, "Lynsey, take school seriously. Our ancestors died for our right just to learn to read." Eight-year-old Lynsey heard these words, noticed that she was in the "slower" group for reading, and felt the books she read in school were not interesting. She also felt confused as she noticed no one around her had brown skin and kinky hair like hers. Lynsey didn't know at the time that her identities as a reader and as a human were tightly connected to her relationship with school and especially literacy. Day after day Lynsey began to realize that the conversations she was having at school and the materials that were used for instruction looked and felt vastly different from her lived experiences as a Black girl. The books she was given to read at school never felt like home. Lynsey always felt like an onlooker. So much so that she herself began to push school away, rather than continue to feel pushed away by the curriculum and materials in front of her.

Lynsey still vividly remembers these experiences in school. She later learned what her mom meant when she talked about their ancestors.

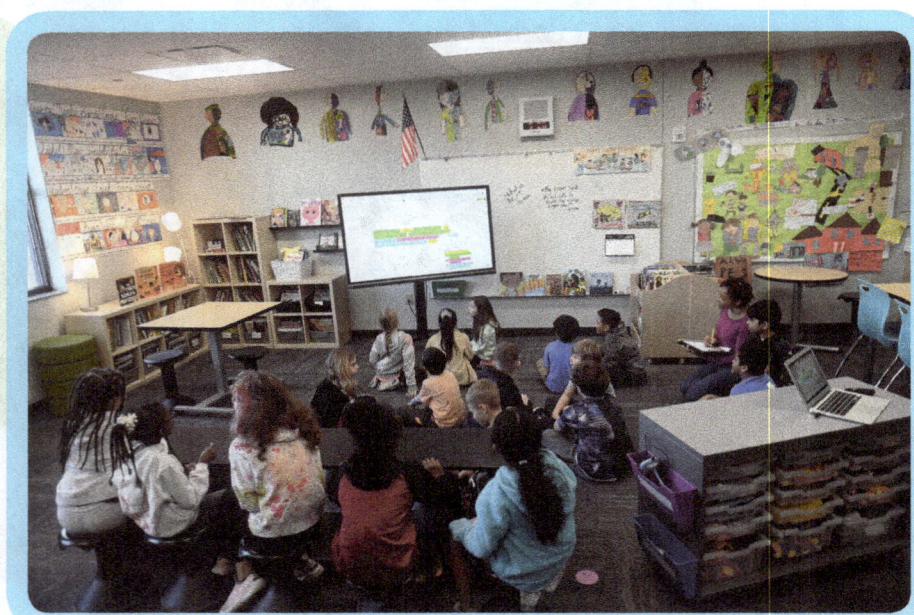

Figure I.1   *Lynsey sits with the reading community as they gather for the reading minilesson.*

There was a reason it was a crime to teach her enslaved ancestors to read and write. The enslavers knew all too well the power of literacy and freedom it conveys. Now as an adult and a teacher, Lynsey has worked for decades to create a literacy classroom that values the identities of each and every one of her students. The work of Paulo Freire, Vivian Vasquez, Mariana Souto-Manning, and Gloria Ladson-Billings have informed her beliefs and practice from the beginning of her career. She views the reading workshop as a time of freedom, choice, identity, agency, and love.

Franki's Story

Franki's journey to this work is a bit different. Franki has always been committed to student choice and student agency. This is why she has been such an advocate for the reading workshop throughout her entire career. Thanks to people like Regie Routman and Nancie Atwell, she realized early in her career the power of the structure and the ways that the reading workshop gives each and every student choice and independence.

Reflecting on her career as a classroom teacher, she realizes she's fought hard against any system that took choice and agency away from children. If you ever sit next to Franki during a staff or district committee meeting, you know she is vocal against levels and testing and rewards and punishment. She has argued multiple times over the years against a mandated read-aloud list, points and prizes for books read, and taking choice away from our most vulnerable readers.

Peter Johnston's work in *Choice Words* has been instrumental in Franki's growth as a teacher. From Peter Johnston she learned about the power of her language as a teacher and she began to ask herself whether the language she used in her teaching supported student agency or whether it demanded student compliance.

But as a white woman who has always had the privilege of seeing herself represented in books and who has always felt a sense of identity and agency as a reader, she has realized that there was a lot she was missing when it came to the teaching of reading. Until recently, for example, she did not understand the role that love and freedom played in her work as a reading teacher. The work of Dr. Ernest Morrell, Dr. Gholdy Muhammad,

Dr. Mariana Souto-Manning, Lorena Germán, Dr. Valerie Kinloch, and Dr. Carla Shalaby has been instrumental to her new understandings of teaching and learning.

Franki now understands why it is not enough to give children choice in the books they read and to embed their thinking into our teaching. The focus of her work, which has always been on reading and understanding how to best meet children's needs as readers, is still important, but it can't stand alone. She has learned that this work must stand alongside the commitment to love and freedom as a right for every child.

Our Story Together

Although we've both been on our own individual journeys as teachers, we've also been lucky to be on this journey together. We've had each other to think alongside over the past eighteen years. For much of this time, we've taught together, often in the same building, sometimes across the hall from each other and sometimes just a few doors apart. Over these eighteen years, the two of us have grown a relationship of thinking together. The power of our relationship has been centered in love for one another and for our students. It is anchored in the joy of deeply questioning and reflecting on our practice. Our trust in each other has allowed our thinking to continuously evolve together and individually. This rich relationship has taken us on a journey of inquiry around student learning that includes a study of community, identity, joyful learning spaces, and intellectual integrity. Our beliefs and practices around whole-class reading instruction have grown and changed over the years because we've done a lot of talking and thinking and reading together.

Because we've been committed to thinking and learning together, we've come to a shared understanding about what we believe about whole-class instruction. We both want students to feel free to bring their whole selves into the work of reading. We want students to be free in the space of whole-group reading instruction by providing choice, helping them claim their agency, and most of all listening to them as an act of love.

Recently in Lynsey's classroom, she was reading *I'm From* written by Gary R. Gray, Jr. and illustrated by Oge Mora, a picture book that beautifully explores the identities from which the author comes. As Lynsey was reading aloud she got to the page that said, "And the other kids. Can I touch your hair? You don't sound Black! Do you play basketball?"

Almost immediately, Lily jumped in, "Mrs. Burkins, can you stop here, please stop here?!" The class turned towards Lily because they all knew she had something to say. "People put their hands in my hair a lot and I don't like it. My mom says that I need to tell them to quit."

Lily, a Black girl with beautiful curls, continued, "My mom even got me a shirt that says don't touch my hair."

A moment of silence filled the air until MacKenzie, a Black girl with colorful gorgeous dreads, added, "Lily, that used to happen to me until I had to keep saying...my hair is not for you to touch. My mom taught me that too."

The class, clearly interested in this conversation, began talking, asking questions, and making comments. Lynsey allowed time for her students to process these ideas. A couple of minutes passed and MacKenzie got up from the meeting area and went to grab a book in the classroom library. As she walked back towards the group with a copy of *My Hair*, written by Hannah Lee and illustrated by Allen Fatimaharan, she announced, "This all reminds me of this book. Can I read it to the class tomorrow?"

"Absolutely," Lynsey affirmed, as she picked up the picture book and continued to read *I'm From*.

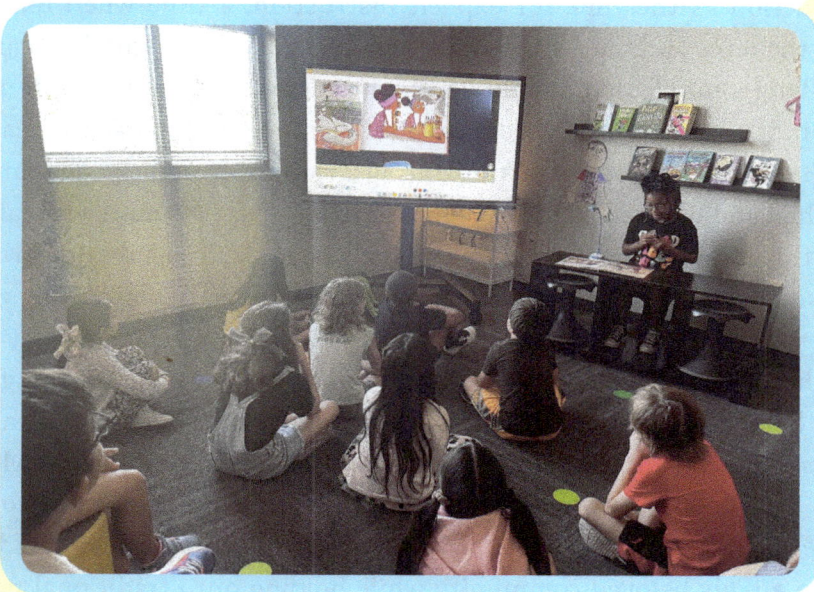

Figure I.2   *MacKenzie reads to the reading community the following day.*

As you read this book, we hope that you see the teaching moves we share through the lens of freedom, choice, agency, and love. Every teaching move is intended to cultivate free students. Learning to read and think in order to understand our world is freedom. Literacy is the type of freedom that can't ever be taken away from the individual. That is why, calling on the words and power of bell hooks, we create the beloved reading community centered on love and freedom.

We have come to believe that whole-class reading instruction has the power to harness the collective knowledge of the reading community. And it is the collective knowledge that will ultimately foster independent readers and thinkers as they move through their literate lives. It is bell hooks' definition of "beloved community" that now anchors our work. She writes, "Beloved community is formed not by the eradication of difference but by its affirmation, by each of us claiming the identities and cultural legacies that shape who we are and how we live in the world" (1996, 221).

We are committed to creating this type of beloved community during the reading minilesson and read-aloud time of each day, as these are the two times we come together as a whole class, a community of readers. For years, we have read and listened to experts who viewed whole-class instruction as the time for explicit instruction, a time when teachers took the reins and taught the skills that needed to be taught. We learned how long a minilesson should be, the right way to structure each minilesson, where we should sit during a minilesson, and that as the teacher we should do most of the talking during this time. However, the more we watched and listened to the students in front of us, the more we realized that this idea of teaching went against all we understood about learning. It also created a power dynamic that we just weren't comfortable with. We realized that if we wanted our students to have voice and agency during these instructional times, we had to push back against the things we were being taught about what made effective minilesson and read-aloud times. Once we let go of some of the traditional thinking around whole-class instruction, we discovered the power in being responsive to our students, rather than scripted in our teaching. We realized we could not create a truly beloved community while holding onto traditional power structures in the classroom.

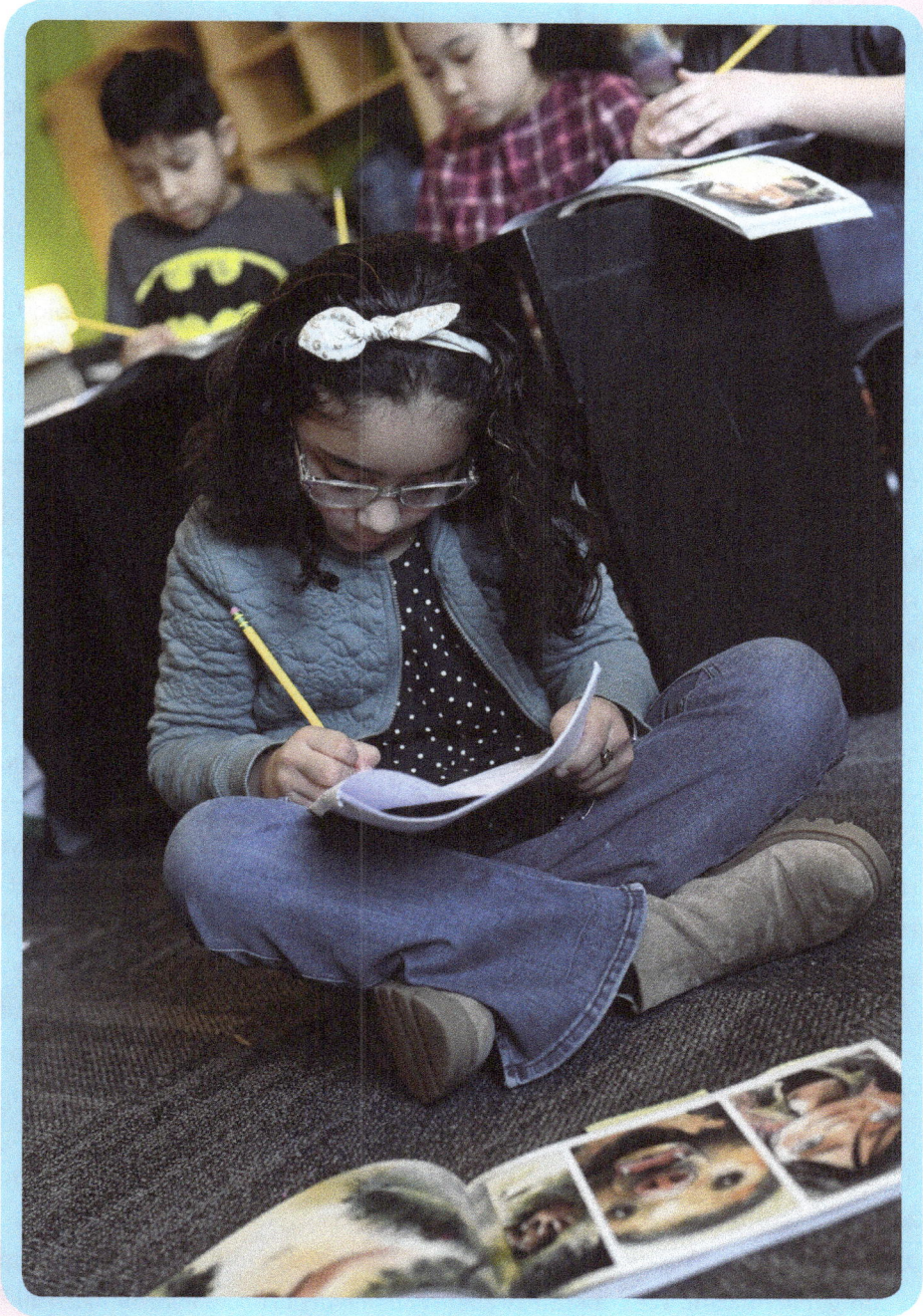

Figure I.3 *Readers prepare to share their knowledge with the community during read-aloud.*

How This Book Is Organized

As part of this journey, we've learned the power of both our individual and collective thinking. We write this book with one collective voice in hopes that we can share the intricate weaving of our thinking. We view this book as a window into how we have come to reimagine whole-group reading instruction over the years.

Through our journeys we've learned that minilessons and read-aloud times are so much more than structures. In Chapter 1 we'll discuss these important times of day and how they can and should work together. We'll explore the ways that whole-class reading instruction can anchor your literacy classroom in grades 3–6.

Minilessons and read-aloud lean upon intentional planning and thoughtful considerations. It also requires us, as teachers, to shift power in the classroom. In Chapter 2 we will examine teacher decisions and the ways we can evolve our teaching by making small power shifts in the classroom.

We believe strongly that all of our work in whole-class instruction must be both intellectual and joyful. We want our reading community to be a joyful place where students use their intellect to grow together as readers. Reading itself should be joyful, but there is nothing like watching a reader or a group of readers unlock all the pieces a text has to offer and witness that joy in new understandings. In Chapter 3, we'll dig into our commitment to fully understand the standards and to helping our students make sense of them in meaningful and satisfying ways.

As teachers, a critical part of being responsive to our students and building a joyful reading community is knowing books. This is an important component of being responsive to the reading community's needs during whole-group instruction. In Chapter 4, we'll explore the importance of being a teacher reader and carefully choosing the best books to share with the young readers in front of us. Over the years, we have consulted with each other on an ongoing basis about what makes a book the right choice for whole-group reading instruction. We constantly ask: *What elements do we look for in a book? How do we decide which authors to lift up? How does authenticity play a role? What parts of the text allow for community discourse? How can this particular book support our readers? What challenges does this book pose?*

We quickly learned that we could not be responsive without taking a listening stance as educators. As teachers, this is one of the most powerful shifts we can make. In Chapter 5, we explore the ways this shift toward listening as action research versus listening to merely gather information allows us to be responsive. This listening stance ensures we keep our intellectual reading community joyful and our planning intentional, because readers can always anticipate their voices reflected in all the learning that takes place.

As we grew our practice towards a community-centered approach to whole-group instruction we began to reflect on the steps we took to move forward in our teaching. This type of instruction and/or pedagogical shift does not happen without planning and intentionality before the school year begins and beyond. In Chapter 6, we look closely at one cycle of mini-lessons and in Chapter 7 we take a close look at a cycle of read-aloud lessons. We capture our big-picture planning as well as the teaching moves we make along the way.

Finally, in Chapter 8, we'll give you a glimpse of what whole-class instruction might look during those first important weeks of school in order to make all of this possible.

Community at the Center

We each stand on the shoulders of so many brilliant educators who have come before us and we continue to learn from educators who share their stories generously through professional writing. It is easy to lose our grounding in this time of high-stakes testing and deficit-model thinking. The way we have been able to stay grounded is to constantly learn from others in the field. We believe that, as teachers, we are constantly learning, and it is our hope that this book is another step in your professional journey. We hope that this book provides an anchor for you to reflect on your practice and to grow in ways that lead you to new strategies for more effective whole-class instruction that center love and joy.

This book is centered on the questions in the list below. These questions are ones we have asked ourselves and each other often over the last decade of our teaching and we hope they are helpful to you as you read our story.

How did you come to the work of being a teacher of reading?

How do you center love in your teaching each day?

Whose shoulders do you stand on?

Who do you learn from?

Who do you learn with?

Whose voices do you raise?

What are your core beliefs about children and learning?

How have you evolved in this work?

What do you cause trouble for?

What's next in your journey as a teacher?

Figure I.4 *The reading community works together to understand the important ideas in the text during the reading minilesson.*

CHAPTER 1

Building Identity, Independence, and Agency for Readers through Whole-Class Instruction

A Glimpse into the Beloved Community

As Lynsey was rereading Jacqueline Woodson's book *The Other Side* to her third-grade class, Tania remarked, "Look what Jacqueline Woodson writes, 'Someday somebody's gonna knock down this old fence, yeah someday.' I don't think she's just talking about the fence." The class, gathered together on the carpet for the minilesson, began to think and talk together about Tania's idea:

Mahir: No, it's like a metaphorical fence maybe.

Brian: What does that mean?

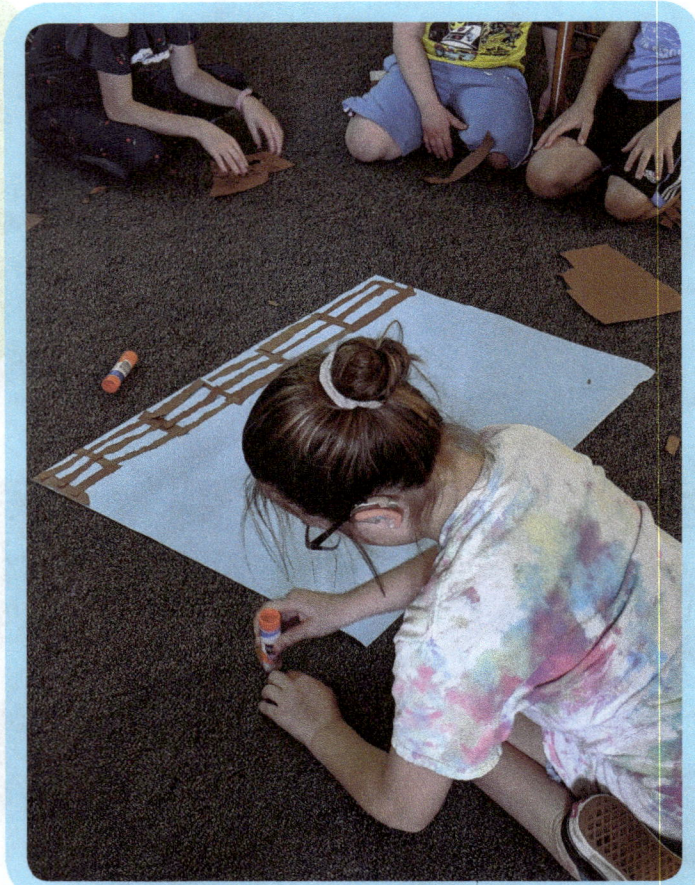

Figure 1.1 *The reading community works together to create a representation of what they feel are fences in our world.*

Tania:	Like maybe the fence is really white and Black people being kept apart.
Meghan:	That's called segregation.
Lynsey:	If Jacqueline Woodson is using the fence as a metaphor, are there other fences in our world that could be knocked down?

This conversation didn't end here. Instead, Lynsey invited further conversation by amplifying the words of her students and building future minilessons from Tania's words.

Conversations like this one happen daily in our classrooms during minilesson and read-aloud time. We spend time creating routines so that our students in grades 3–6 come to whole-class instruction understanding the power of collective thinking and knowing that their words matter. We have come to think of our whole-class instruction time as a set of invitations and conversations. In our planning, we know the standards, we know our students' strengths and challenges, and we carefully select the books we share with children. We plan for the ways the books we use will support

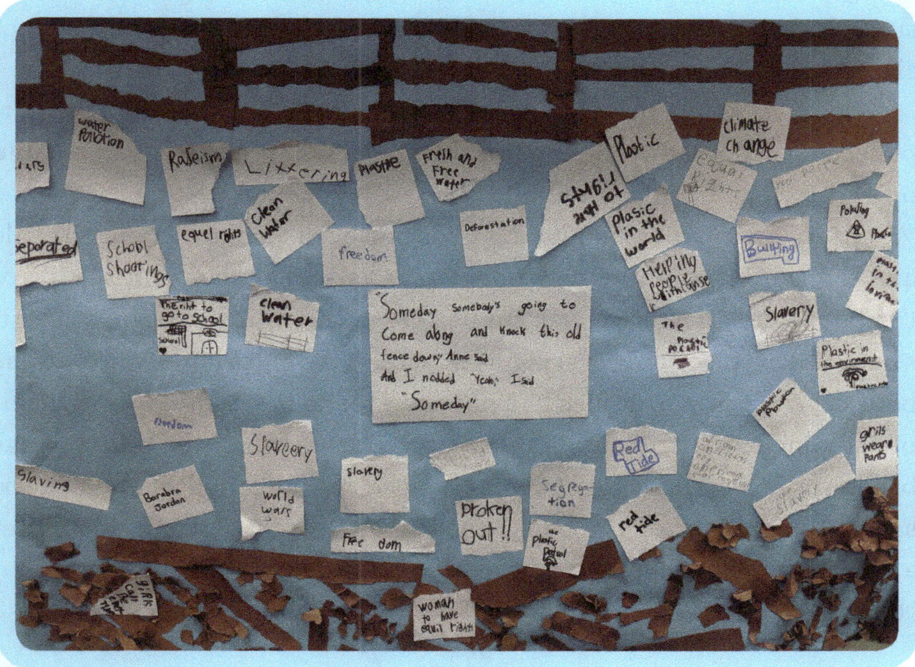

Figure 1.2 *The representation of breaking down fences created by the reading community.*

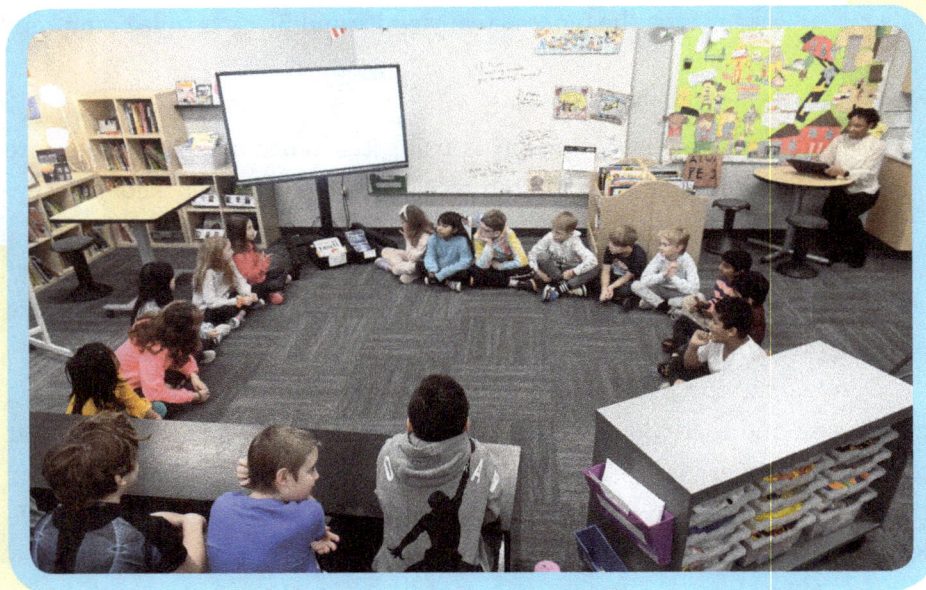

Figure 1.3 *The reading community thinks together about a text while Lynsey captures their thoughts during the reading minilesson.*

this group of students as they grow as readers. But we are never exactly sure which direction the learning will go because we are purposely responsive in our daily work.

Because we are open to where the learning will go, we are often surprised and delighted by the insights our readers share and it is easy to build on those ideas from students. While reading *Harbor Me*, by Jacqueline Woodson, fifth graders in Franki's class had been thinking about the title and the word "harbor." One student asked whether the main setting of the book, the classroom, was connected to the word harbor because it seemed like a place that everyone felt safe. Although Franki had read the book several times, this idea had not occurred to her. But in this moment of listening to her student, Franki realized the depth of the thinking was brilliant. This student's comment changed the direction of the conversation for the rest of the book. The discourse and learning was better and deeper because Franki believed in read-aloud that builds on student thinking.

Whole-class reading instruction has the power to harness the collective knowledge of the reading community that will foster independent readers and thinkers as they move through their literate lives. We believe that in order to achieve this type of community, there has to be a shift in power. There has to be a shift from the traditional power of teacher-led minilessons and read-aloud to community-centered lessons. We want our students to have clear and present voice and agency during these instructional times. This shift in power allows us to be responsive to our students rather than scripted in our teaching.

Why Does Whole-Class Instruction Matter?

Lynsey can remember some years ago, early in the year teaching third grade, when a student who knew it was time for the reading minilesson audibly groaned and said, "Do we *have* to do a minilesson? I just want to read." His words were then followed by others protesting the same thing. At the end of the day, Lynsey couldn't get those words out of her mind. She wondered: *Why do they feel this way? What purpose do they think the minilessons serve? Can they see themselves in the learning? Are the lessons supporting their independent reading? Who is interacting during the minilesson? Who is silent, and what does this silence mean?* This experience was pivotal in Lynsey's journey to clarify for herself and her students just *why* whole-class teaching matters.

This conversation in Lynsey's classroom was so impactful that Lynsey and Franki have reflected on it for years. We've had to ask ourselves to think hard about the reasons we make the instructional choices we do when it comes to whole-class reading instruction. And we've had to be honest with ourselves about the unintentional messages we were sometimes giving to our students during whole-class instruction. We continuously ask ourselves: *How do students view our whole-class instruction time? How can we make sure it is relevant to each*

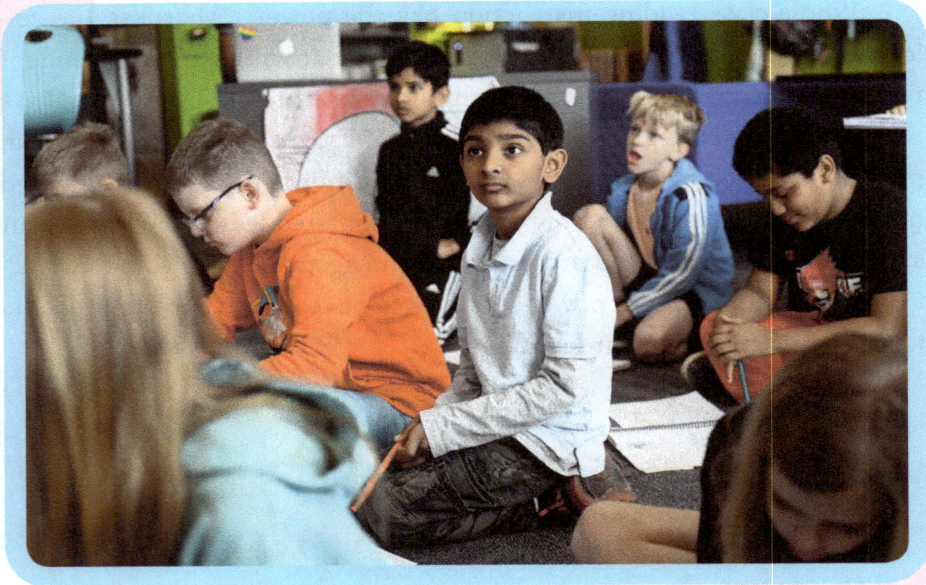

Figure 1.4 *The reading community thinks together about a text during the whole-group read-aloud.*

and every student? How can we shift our practices so that our readers see the power of whole-class instruction? Most importantly, we had to answer the question for ourselves: Why do we spend so much time on whole-class instruction?

What Is the Beloved Reading Community?

Recall that writer, feminist and social activist bell hooks wrote, "Beloved community is formed not by the eradication of difference but by its affirmation, by each of us claiming the identities and cultural legacies that shape who we are and how we live in the world" (1996, 221). While hooks wasn't writing specifically about reading instruction, or even teaching, her words illustrate why we believe in the power of whole-class reading instruction. hooks' words remind us each day that creating a beloved community anchors our work as teachers.

This quote also reminds us how critical the role of whole-class reading instruction is in developing independent readers who are part of a community of readers. Our goal is to create a beloved community so that when students take their reading skills to their independent reading, they have the collective wisdom of the reading community with them. Whole-group reading is about freedom, choice, agency, and—most of all—love. When our readers come together as a whole group, as a beloved community, they grow as readers, yes, but also as learners and as human beings. Being part of a beloved community means being part of a community that cares for and values each member's voice, a community that comes together to learn and grow. We believe strongly that it is this beloved community that allows our students to become readers who think deeply about their reading, are confident to share their thinking and who value the perspectives of others.

Figure 1.5 *A reader shares their thoughts with the reading community during a reading minilesson.*

The Power of Whole-Group Instruction

There is something special about grades 3–6. Most of our students have learned to read by this point in their education. But we don't give credence to the myth that in grades K-3 children learn to read and in grades 3–6 they read to learn. It's a simple way to think about reading but one that is harmful to our readers, especially our readers in grades 3–6. Instead we know that every reader continues to grow for a lifetime and that grades 3–6 are critical learning years for our young readers. We know that whole-class instruction is where our readers learn the skills needed to understand complex text and to grow as independent readers.

In grades 3–6, we have seen the magic that happens with the combination of the minilesson and the read-aloud. In the minilesson, we often share a picture book or other short text—something that can be shared in one sitting. During this minilesson time we are able to work on a skill or strategy across a whole text. Read-aloud, on the other hand, is a time in which we typically read a longer novel or other text that takes weeks to read. It is within the read-aloud time that our 3rd–6th graders can transfer those important skills learned in minilessons to longer texts. Our 3rd- to 6th-grade readers who have recently moved to chapter book reading learn how the strategies and literary techniques they learned when reading picture books can be transferred to longer, more complex texts.

When a student says during a read-aloud of *Ghost* by Jason Reynolds, "Oh, no. Is this going to be one of those books with a big surprise like *Spencer's New Pet*?" you know that they are beginning to see the ways literary elements work and understand that they appear in stories no matter the format, length, level, or media form. This connection between minilessons and read-aloud is both natural and powerful for readers.

Another reason whole-class reading instruction is so valuable in grades 3–6 is because the texts students read become much more complex as they move up through the grades. Think for just a moment about some of the different skills readers use as they make their way through more complex texts:

Some Skills Readers Use as They Read Increasingly Complex Text

In Fiction	In Nonfiction
→ Holding onto the plot across a longer book	→ Using evidence from the text to support thinking
→ Inferring events in a plot	→ Reading information with depth and moving beyond a focus on facts
→ Keeping track of multiple characters and dialogue	
→ Noting the changes in setting	→ Figuring out more complex vocabulary
→ Understanding characters' internal and external conflicts and following their changes over time	→ Utilizing more complex text features for deeper understanding
→ Seeing metaphor and symbolism	→ Understanding how the author's perspective can affect meaning
→ Being patient with longer introductions before the action begins	→ Paying attention to important details
→ Thinking about theme and big messages	→ Dealing with sections of text that are less interesting
→ Recognizing various complexities in text structure: flashbacks, elapsed time, different chapters focus on different characters, changes in perspective, etc.	→ Attending to changes in thinking and understanding

And on top of all this, whether the text is fiction or nonfiction, readers have to constantly monitor for meaning and know how to clear up confusion.

The teaching we do during minilessons and read-aloud is connected, but it's also different. In both contexts the invitations we offer and conversations we have are meant to support students as independent readers, and the tools and routines we use in each structure overlap. Both are responsive to where students are as readers each day. But it's the way we go about the teaching and the texts we use that make minilessons and read-alouds different from one another.

Comparing Minilessons and Read-Aloud

Whole-Class Minilessons	Whole-Class Read-Aloud
• Texts might be one short book, sets of books, a picture, a quote, a piece of digital media, a photograph, a poem, an excerpt from a book	• Texts are novels
	• Longer stretches of time (a novel might be read over several weeks)
• Pre-planning to break down grade-level standards into specific teaching points and match them to texts	• Multiple teaching points over the course of one novel
	• Tools are offered for student annotation
• Tightly structured time mostly focused on a specific teaching point	• A variety of notebook options are available for writing and sketching
• Led by the teacher with student engagement	• Charts are created to capture whole-class thinking
• Charts are created to capture whole-class thinking	• Application and practice of skills and strategies previously learned
• The teaching point and the invitation to try it are very explicit	• Synthesis of many skills used in a longer, more complex text
	• Norms for conversation allow for student-centered dialogue

Minilessons and read-aloud work together in important ways. In grades 3–6, students are in or beyond the transitional stage of reading and they are learning to read longer, more complex texts. Minilessons invite students to try a new strategy or skill, while read-aloud time invites students to use those skills in a longer, more complex text over time.

In both structures, students learn to rely on the support of the community to grow as individual readers—but this doesn't happen by accident. As teachers, we have to commit to creating a culture of conversation and spend a lot of time early in the year building trust in the community. Of course, the work doesn't end after these first six weeks. If we want students' talk and understanding to deepen across the year, we have to develop routines and tools to support this talk and use them consistently.

In both minilesson and read-aloud time we want readers to make sense of what they are reading as it relates to the world around them. When we come together as a whole class, we teach students to ask themselves questions such as:

* What messages is the author sending me through their text?
* Do these messages make sense based on what I see in my world?
* Are the stories I'm reading and the people/characters in them reflective of my world? Do they feel true?
* Whose story is this—and who's telling it?
* Whose voice is missing from this story?
* What do I believe or not believe when reading the text?
* Who in the text has power and who doesn't? How do I know?

Teaching our students to ask important questions as they read is essential. We want them to experience reading as a joyful act, and also as a *critical* one that helps them to understand the power structures of their world.

Finally, whole-class instruction invites intellectual conversations so that each student has access to rigorous and joyful reading experiences. As Dr. Kim Parker states in her book *Literacy is Liberation*, "Literacy best happens within a community because students are able to take in, respond, and learn in relation to each other. Literacy has a social function" (2022, 51). In these communities our students learn to see the power of discourse and to understand the power of their own thinking and the power of their words. No matter their independent reading level, these two routines give

Whole-Class Instruction: A Visual

Know Books ↔ Know Our Students ↔ Know the Standards

Know Our Students → Responsive Planning

"Beloved community is formed not by the eradication of difference but by its affirmation, by each of us claiming the identities and cultural legacies that shape who we are and how we live in the world."

bell hooks

Responsive Planning → Whole-Class Instruction

Read Aloud

Longer book read over time (usually a chapter book)

Whole-Class Instruction

Minilesson

Book that can be read in one sitting (often a picture book, short article, or poem)

Independent Reading

Small-Group Instruction

Individual Conferences

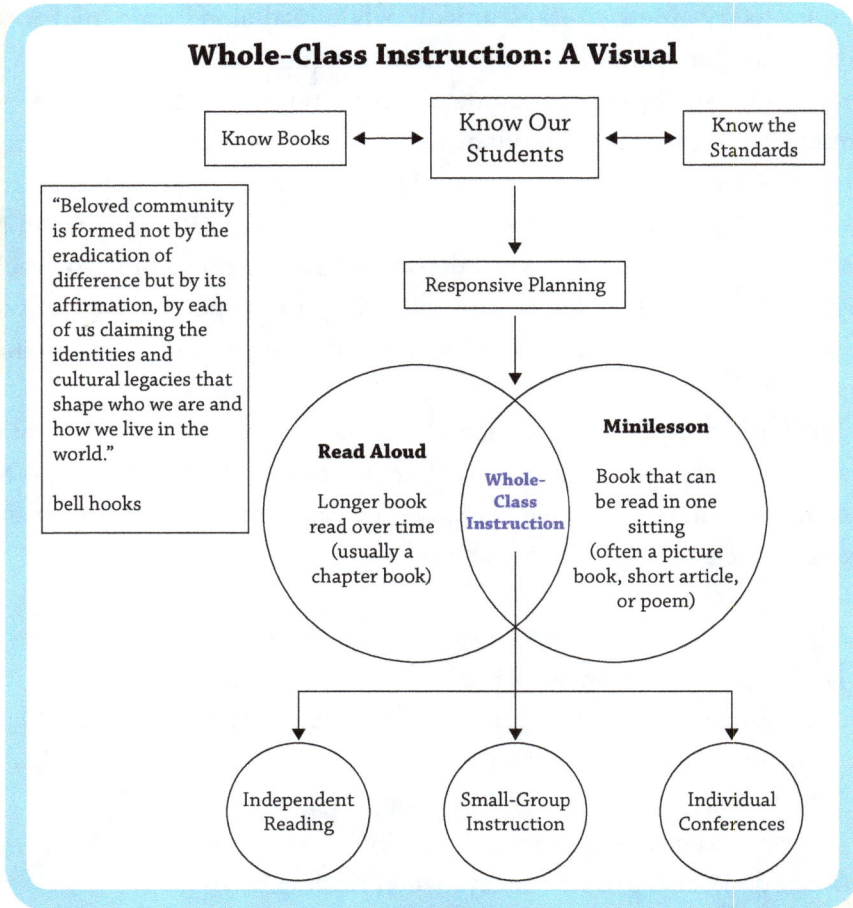

Figure 1.6   *A visual of how whole-class instruction shapes reading workshop.*

students access to rich experiences around complex texts on a daily basis. We know that students have varied reading identities in their independent reading. We know that they have different tastes, strengths, and challenges as readers. We can and should design our whole-class instruction with access points for every member of the collective community.

Whole-class instruction is essential because it gives the reading community time to think, learn, and practice these new skills together. As teachers, we skillfully facilitate, and each student brings their unique reading experiences and abilities to the conversation where they learn not just new reading skills, but also the value of learning from and with each other. When big questions come up in the life of the classroom or in our students' lives, we can bring in fiction and nonfiction texts that help build understanding and empathy and explore them together. When students learn to listen to the ideas of others, they begin to see new ways to approach a text and new ways to think about their reading. They become stronger readers *because* of the community.

Whole-Class Instruction and Independent Reading Go Hand-in-Hand

Had you asked us years ago, we would have told you that independent reading time was the core of our reading workshop. We always had minilesson and read-aloud time as part of our day but we didn't think it was quite as important as independent reading time and conferring. We hate to admit it, but we pretty much just checked minilesson time off our list as something that was part of reading workshop, a part where we imparted knowledge to students. Although we still believe strongly in the power of time for daily student-chosen, independent reading for every reader, we have come

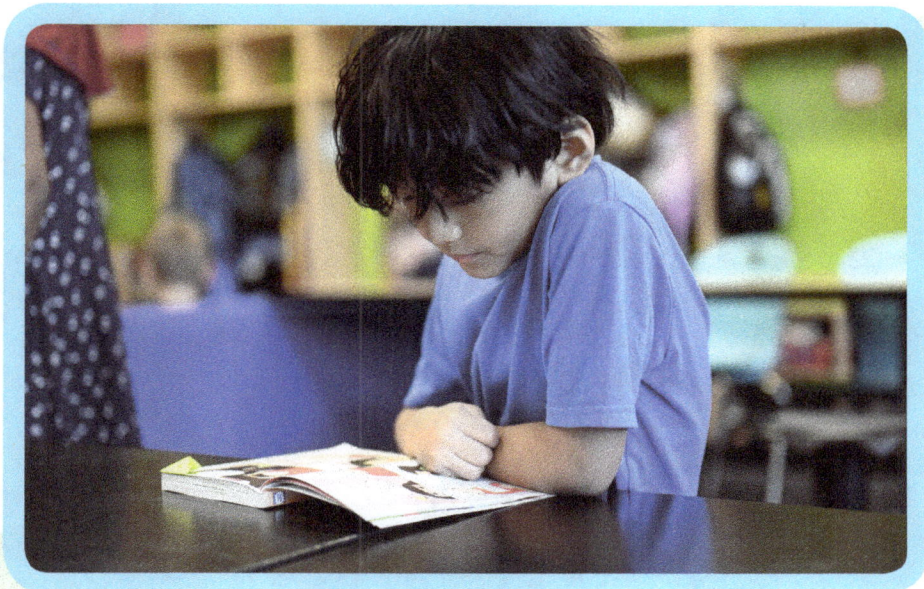

Figure 1.7 *A student reads during independent reading time.*

to realize that without coming together as a community for whole-class instruction, independent reading time would not be so powerful. It is the whole-class instruction that supports children in growing as independent readers. But the whole-class instruction time is only powerful and impactful now because we have rethought the things about it that weren't working for our students in the past. We have learned that we can't have independence without responsive whole-class instruction.

Whole-Class Instruction Is Rooted in Collective Thinking

Carla Shalaby, author of *Troublemakers: Lessons in Freedom from Young Children*, writes, "I am an educator, and as an educator it is my job to insist on every child's right to a classroom experience that daily honors her, reveres her smarts, engages her curiosities and ensures her dignity" (2017, xv). This quote has stayed with us long after first reading Shalaby's book. Above almost everything else, we charge ourselves with insisting on every child's right to an intellectual space where they feel seen.

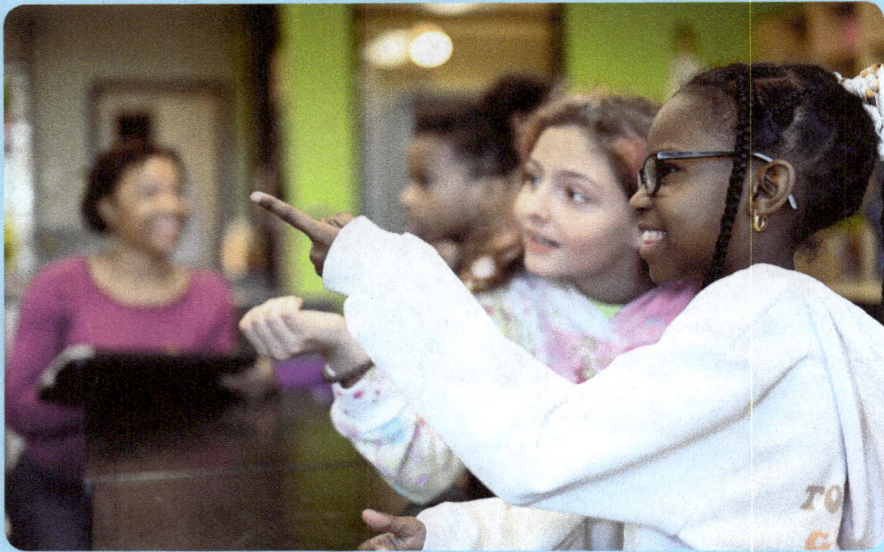

Figure 1.8 *Reading community members work together during the reading minilesson.*

To insist on every child's rights to an intellectual space where they feel seen is what we charge ourselves to cultivate. Whole-group instruction should always be rooted in the idea that we bring the whole group together because we believe in the power of their collective thinking and voice. Collective thinking empowers each member of the community.

We came to this understanding because we questioned our own rationale. We made this necessary shift in our "why" from teacher-directed to community-driven whole-group reading instruction. In addition to questioning the rationale, we've also both spent a lot of time studying our whole-class teaching and paying attention to what was and wasn't working. We noticed when our time with students in these lessons felt purposeful and engaging, and when it didn't. We've tried a variety of different teaching strategies we've learned in our professional reading as we searched for how to make the most of our time in our lessons.

Over time we have learned that if we want our whole-class teaching to feel relevant and purposeful to our students, there are concrete actions we can take. We have to be so intentional when we invite students to join conversations and to try new skills and strategies in their reading lives.

As we plan and implement our whole-class teaching, we...

* share our goals openly, honestly, and often with students, making sure we discuss what *they* would like this time to look and feel like.
* listen closely to students as they interact in lessons, noting the power dynamics and addressing them with teaching when we see a need.
* watch what students are trying to do and become as readers and plan with this in mind.
* familiarize ourselves with the kinds of reading our students enjoy, but also read widely so we can introduce them to new authors and genres.
* honor students' conjectures and experiences with texts and build teaching from their wonderings, questions, observations, and interests.
* invite students to teach minilessons, sharing their personal expertise and learning.
* listen to our students' feedback about whole-class teaching and how it is and isn't working for them—both collectively and individually.
* use conferring time to listen and find patterns in student strengths and needs.

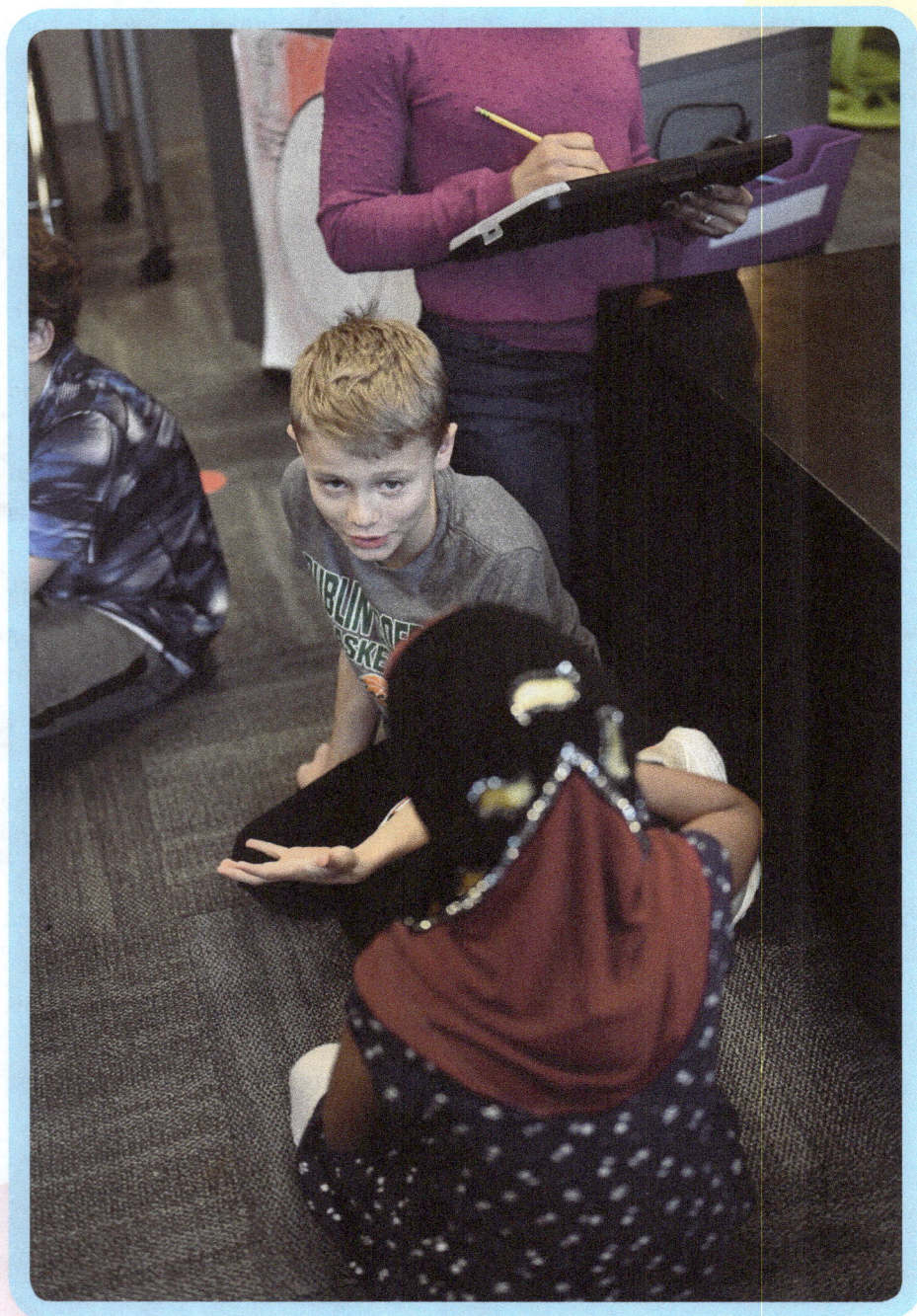

Figure 1.9 *Lynsey listens and takes notes on what readers say during the reading minilesson.*

When Do We Gather for Whole-Class Instruction?

We've both spent years figuring out how to make the most of this important teaching time, especially when so many of the conversations about whole-class instruction in our professional development were focused on explicit teaching, teacher-directed talk, and standards as a checklist.

Through much reflection, we've come to realize how important it is that 1) we are very clear about our goals for whole-class instruction, and 2) our students understand those goals and take part in planning for whole-class instruction. When we keep our goals and our students at the forefront of our planning, it helps us ensure that our whole-class teaching is purposeful and that it supports every reader in our care.

The whole-class reading community convenes twice a day to learn together. There is a minilesson which typically happens before students begin their independent reading and there is also a read-aloud which occurs during a separate part of the day and involves a longer piece of literature being read aloud by the teacher. In both of these instructional times the community works together to acquire the skills and strategies they need to grow as literate individuals.

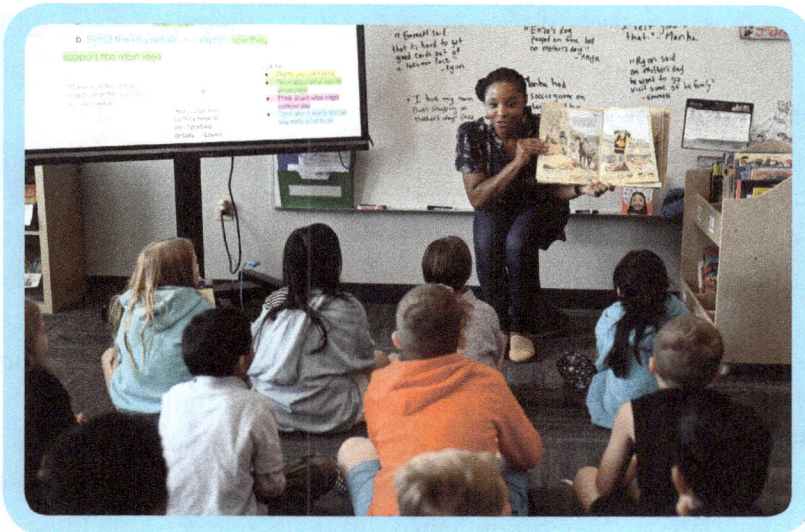

Figure 1.10 *The reading community gathers for whole-class instruction.*

Why Do We Make Time for Both Read-Aloud and Minilessons?

Towards the end of a minilesson cycle in Lynsey's room, in which her third graders were studying how readers use questions to understand the story better, the reading community began a new chapter book during the read-aloud time. As Lynsey was reading aloud *Odder* by Katherine Applegate, Tyse signaled that he wanted to offer the group his thoughts:

Tyse:	Mrs. Burkins, can you highlight those words right there? (*Tyse walked toward the interactive board placing his finger next to the digital text that was being projected.*)
Lynsey:	Sure, Tyse.
Roman:	Oh man, I was thinking that was deep too!
Sofia:	Tyse, why do you want that highlighted?
Tyse:	I'm wondering what humans did to make Odder so scared?
Sofia:	Yeah, like why would she know to be afraid?

The class immediately broke out into so many side conversations that one student had to say loudly, "Hey, can we have one conversation?" At the end of the conversation the group decided that they were going to keep track of all the things that author Katherine Applegate writes about the humans in *Odder* and try to see if that helped them figure out the answer to Tyse's question.

Lynsey knew that this strategy of tracking ideas across a book was one way the group had handled a similar question during the reading of *The World's Loneliest Elephant* during a previous minilesson. As is often the case, young readers are able to transfer the skills they learn in short texts to longer, more complex texts when they have daily minilesson and read-aloud routines.

We believe our students learn best in community and we come together for whole-class reading instruction two times each day: once for a minilesson before students go out to read independently, and once for a read-aloud. Here are two sample schedules that show you how these times fit into a full day's schedule:

Sample 3rd-Grade Daily Schedule	Sample 5th-Grade Daily Schedule
9:00–9:15 Slow-Start Buddy Reading	9:10–9:25 Class Meeting
9:15–9:30 Conversation Circles	9:25–10:10 Science/Social Studies
9:30–10:10 Math Workshop	10:10–11:30 Math Workshop
10:10–11:00 Art, Music, PE, Library	11:30–11:45 Word Study
11:00–11:30 Continue Math Workshop	11:45–12:30 Art, Music, PE, Library
11:30–12:00 Read-Aloud	12:30–1:15 Lunch/Recess
12:00–12:15 Word Study	1:15–2:05 Reading Workshop
12:15–1:00 Lunch and Recess	**1:15–1:25 Minilesson**
1:00–2:00 Reading Workshop	1:25–2:00 Independent Reading/ Small-Group Time
1:00–1:15 Minilesson	2:00–2:05 Reading Share
1:15–1:55 Independent Reading/ Small-Group Time	2:05–2:50 Writing Workshop
1:55–2:00 Reading Share	**2:50–3:20 Read-Aloud**
2:00–3:00 Writing Workshop	3:20–3:30 Closing Meeting
3:00–3:35 Content (Science or Social Studies)	3:35 Dismissal
3:40 Dismissal	

Whole-Class Instruction as Invitations and Conversations

We believe that whole-class reading instruction should…

* be designed so individual readers can thrive, with many access points so readers can grow from where they are.

* lead readers to independence and agency, building on their strengths and responding to their needs.
* invite readers to try out new skills, strategies, behaviors, and ideas on increasingly complex texts and with the support of their teacher and their peers.
* create a space where powerful, co-constructed meaning-making happens because a diverse group of readers *learns* how to think, talk, listen, and reflect together as a community.
* invite readers to ask deep, meaningful questions as they read together and examine power, inequities, and issues of social justice.
* allow readers to see and experience the many possibilities when living their lives as readers.

We are passionate about our whole-class reading instruction. We believe it is these two times in each day that are the heart of our reading workshops. Our readers learn the power of community and the power of their own thinking during these times. We know that when whole-class time is strong, the entire reading workshop time better supports every reader. Throughout the rest of the book, we'll dig deeper into our journey—the ways we plan, the things we've changed, and some things that work for us when being responsive to our students.

CHAPTER 2

Shifting Power and Control in Minilessons and Read-Aloud

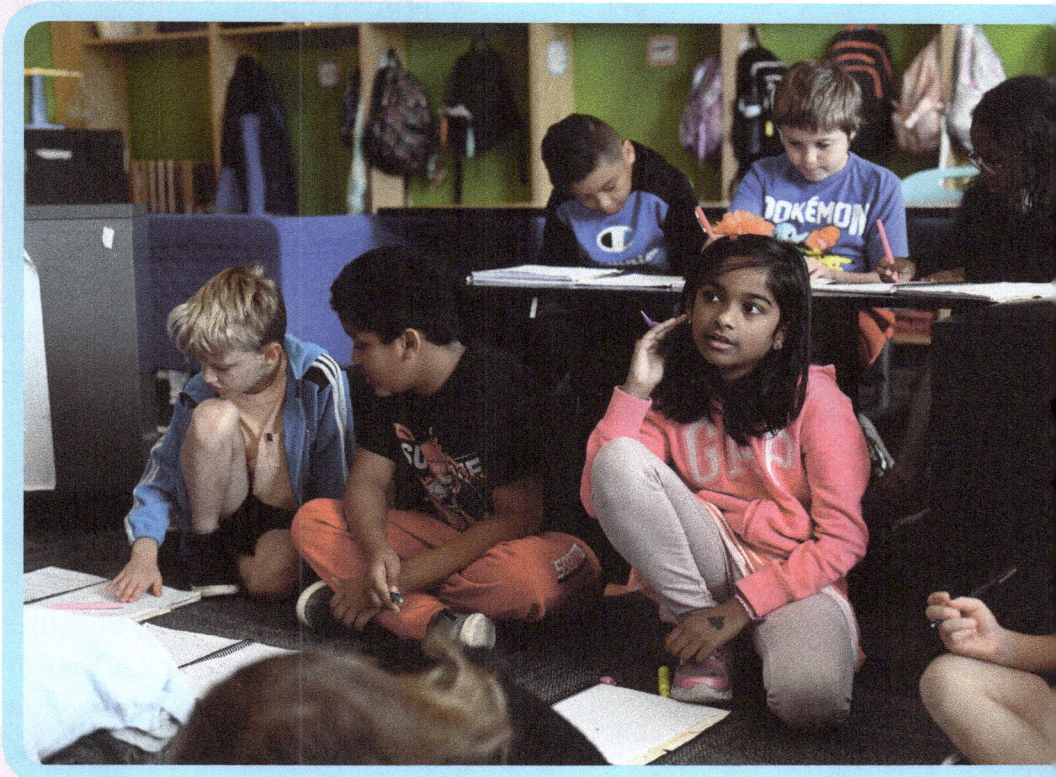

Years ago, after several visitors had been in her classroom, one of Franki's fifth graders announced: "I don't really understand why all these people come in to watch us and to watch Mrs. Sibberson. We don't really *do* anything. All we really do is read and talk about books." At first Franki was a little upset, but then she realized that, for this student, the minilesson and classroom read-aloud time just felt like talk. Of course, that's what Franki wanted—for her students to feel like the whole-class instruction each day was really just conversations within a community of readers, for these times to be authentic, sort of like a great book club.

Franki and Lynsey have talked about this comment for years. Franki knew the time and energy she put into planning—into knowing her students, knowing the standards, and knowing books—but she also knew that she wanted students to feel empowered and to be part of authentic experiences. Before this comment, Franki wasn't intentional about this power shift in the classroom but this comment helped both of us think about the ways that we can plan intentionally *and* shift power and control. We realized the more we talked about this conversation that we wanted our students to be even more empowered. We wanted them to be part of charting the course, we wanted their interests and their knowledge to intersect with our planning and help drive it. Before this comment, Franki hadn't been intentional about sharing power with her students. She hadn't yet invited her students to be part of the planning and she hadn't been intentional about sharing the ways she was building curriculum around their words. Franki's student's insight helped both of us think about the ways we can plan intentionally and shift power and control.

Teaching is revolutionary work. This can only be true if we intentionally shift power and co-create learning with students. As we have evolved in our thinking about this idea, we have leaned on the words of Paulo Freire who wrote that, "A revolutionary leadership must accordingly practice co-intentional education" (2000, 69). Freire was a Brazilian philosopher and an expert in the field of literacy as a humanizing practice. His work and writing illuminate what we believe to be true—that the work of literacy educators is critically tied to the work of freedom, liberation, being fully

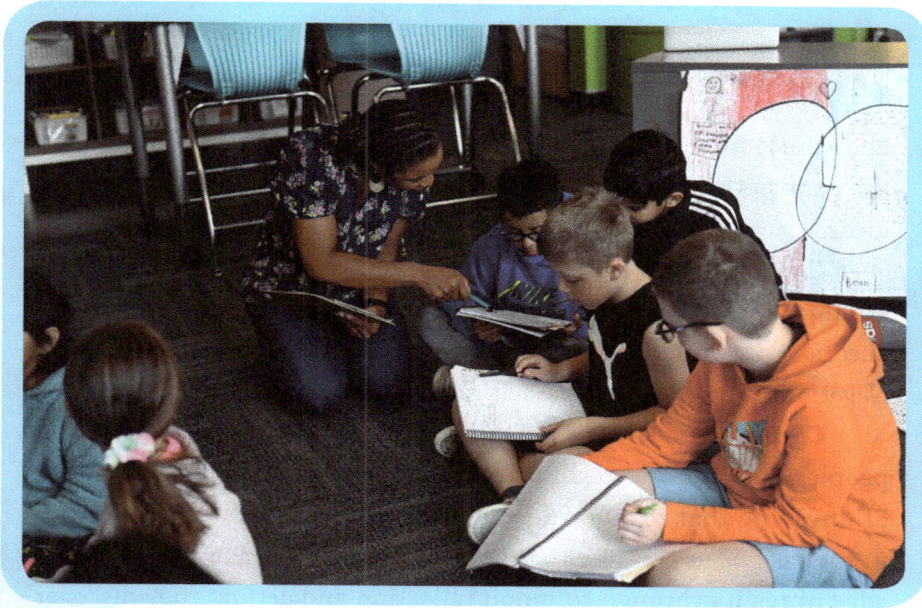

Figure 2.1 *Teacher and students doing the work of learning together.*

human and justice. Freire reminds us that any type of educational relation-ship in which learning is the intended outcome should be *co-intentional—* teachers and students should be doing the work of learning together. In a co-intentional relationship between teachers and students, it is not teachers who are saving students, it is teachers and students who together are both the teacher and learner actively constructing knowledge together. Building on this idea, we also trust in the words of Mariana Souto-Manning, who said in an interview that, "we educators must understand that there is more expertise distributed in a community than in any one person and position ourselves and our students as teachers and learners" (Ferlazzo, 2020).

Over the years, we have worked relentlessly to create a reading work-shop that is joyful and authentic and one that is focused on growing readers. And we want to make sure we are *co-creating* this space with our students. The changes we've made in our whole-group instruction have been gradual, but when we look back, they have added up.

A Note on Language

Let's pause for a moment to define a few important terms and call on the words of those from whom we've learned about these words and ideas.

Critical lens: "A critical perspective suggests that deliberate attempts to expose inequity in the classroom and society need to become part of our everyday classroom life" (Vivian Maria Vasquez, *Negotiating Critical Literacies with Young Children*, 2004).

Co-intentional lens: "Teachers and students (leadership and people), co-intent on reality, are both Subjects, not only in the task of unveiling that reality, and thereby coming to know critically, but in the task of re-creating that knowledge. As they attain this knowledge of reality through common reflection and action, they discover themselves as its permanent re-creators" (Paulo Freire, *Pedagogy of the Oppressed*, 2000).

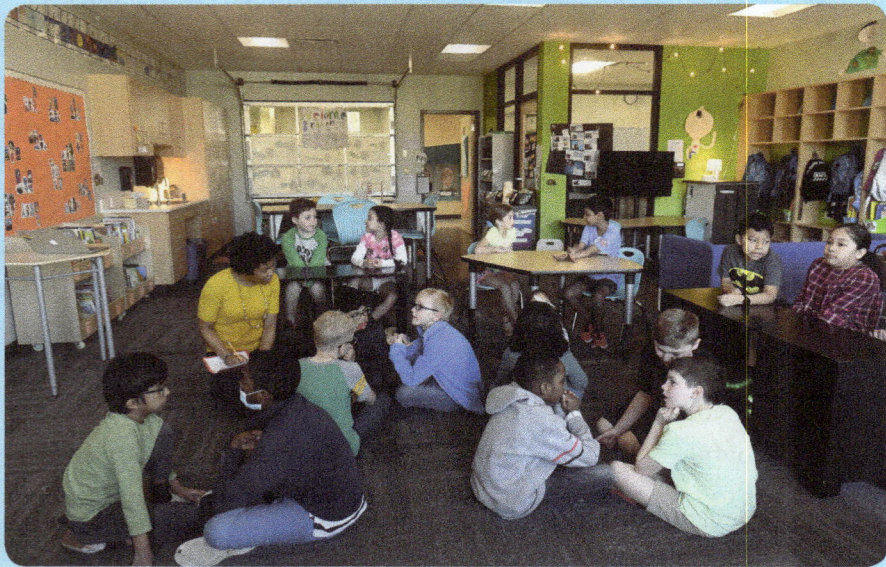

Figure 2.2 *Lynsey's third-grade classroom is designed for joyful authentic literacy.*

A Close Look at the Shift in Power

This year, Lynsey used the book *The Teachers March!: How Selma's Teachers Changed History* for a minilesson. Her class had previously read *The One and Only Ivan* during read-aloud and they were very interested in learning more about protests that have created change. Because Lynsey knew that the nonfiction standards were coming up in her district's year-long curriculum plan, she jotted down the comments children made about protests and thought about books that could extend that conversation while also meeting the nonfiction reading standards she was responsible for teaching. Lynsey gathered five books about protests and decided to show her students the covers of these books. The students were most inquisitive about the title and cover illustration of *The Teachers March!*. As they examined the cover and front matter, Lynsey jotted down some of their comments:

> "Why are there toothbrushes on the end papers?"
> "Oh my goodness the teachers even marched!"
> "Did something happen with the toothbrushes?"
> "Is this a real story?"

Based on the level of energy, comments, and questions around this book, Lynsey knew exactly where the community wanted to start. She knew that the third-grade informational standard (RI.3.3 *Describe the relationship between a series of historical events, scientific ideas or concepts, or steps in technical procedures in a text, using language that pertains to time, sequence, and cause/effect.*) would allow her to engage students in a study that they were interested in *and* focus on the reading skills and strategies they needed to access this standard.

In the past, this lesson would have been a bit different. We may still have used *The Teachers March!*, but instead of using it because the class was interested, we would have used it because we thought it was a good book to teach the standard. We would still have created a text set of books that focused on protests, but we would have determined the

Standard: RI.3.3 Describe the relationship between a series of historical events, scientific ideas or concepts, or steps in technical procedures in a text, using language that pertains to time, sequence, and cause/effect.

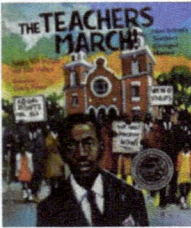

RI.5.6 Analyze multiple accounts of the same event or topic, noting important similarities and differences in the perspectives they represent.

> Oh my goodness the teachers even marched! -Hunter

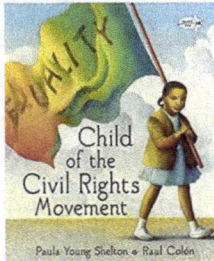

Reading skills and strategies:
- Use text evidence to sequence events
- Use text support to track information around language
- Use the strategy of compare/contrast to describe relationships

Additional Texts:

- *We March* by Shane W. Evans
- *Let the Children March* by Monica Clark-Robinson
- *The Youngest Marcher* by Cynthia Levinson

Figure 2.3 *Lynsey and Franki used a similar set of texts to think about a third-grade standard and a fifth-grade standard.*

order that we'd read them based on the books and not on the children in front of us.

These shifts in our teaching have been subtle, but powerful. We have learned how important it is to listen to our students as the foundation for instructional planning. The chart below shows the changes in our teaching that have impacted student learning.

The small powerful shifts we'll talk about in this chapter have changed the power dynamic in the classroom. We've been more and more intentional about our own commitment to community, our role as a teacher, balancing the power dynamic within the intellectual community, and the idea of freedom. We want every child to feel part of a community of readers and to be excited to think and talk with others about what they read. We want our whole-class instruction time to feel authentic and joyful, just like the best book clubs. We want every reader to understand and experience the power of collective thinking as a way to shape how they see themselves and their world.

Our Teaching Then	Our Teaching Now
We started from scratch when we began a new unit or cycle of minilessons. We started with the standard and built lessons from there.	We start with the students in front of us. We listen with our ears open for ways that we can connect student thinking to the standards that we are responsible for teaching.
We'd do a K-W-L chart or other activity to get students thinking about what they knew about a topic.	We make the connection to past conversions visible to students so they realize that, as a community, we've explored this idea and will dig a little deeper. We connect new learning to students' words in conversations and writing.
We create a text set with three to four books and a goal for each book.	We create a Menu of Mentors, a stack of four to six books that we might use. We know we won't use all of the books and we know that the order of the books used will be determined daily based on student engagement and response.
We shared these books from the text set in the order we determined before we began.	We listen closely to the ways students respond to the first minilesson to determine which book would best scaffold our readers.

The Physical Space and How It Has Evolved

The first thing we do when setting up our classrooms is decide where we will hold our whole-group instruction. We believe this community space is the most important physical space we create, so we design the whole room around it. This hasn't always been the case. We used to set up other areas in our classroom

Figure 2.4   *While most students sit on the floor during whole-class instruction, there are other seating options that serve as borders to the space where some children choose to sit. The goal is for everyone to find a comfortable space where they can participate as a valued member of the community.*

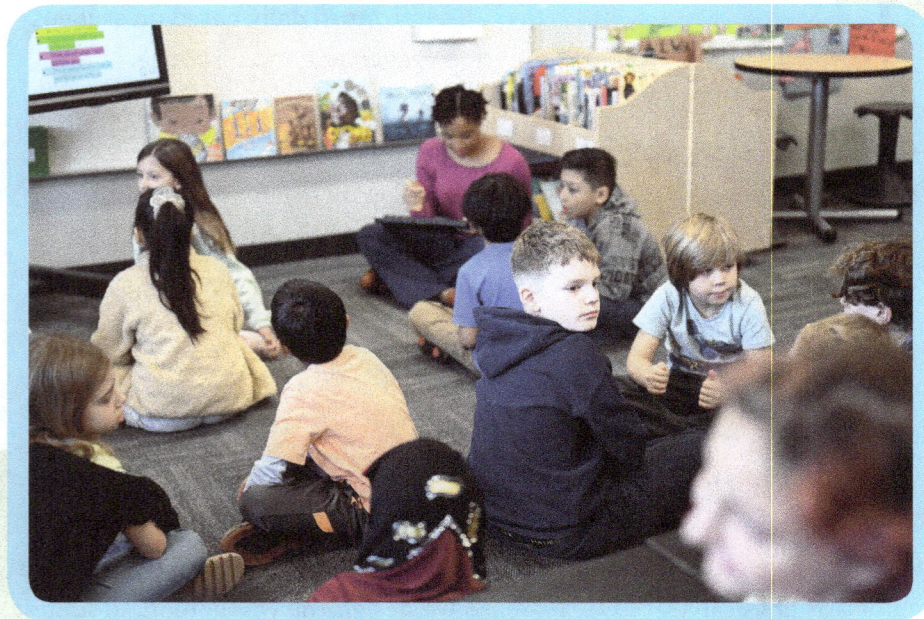

Figure 2.5   *Lynsey and her third graders in their meeting space.*

Figure 2.6 *The space designated for whole-class instruction is large enough for times when the entire class sits in a circle for discussion.*

first but since we believe strongly in the power of the whole-class community and since the size and location of the whole-class space is so critical, we now decide on that space first. This meeting area has space for readers to sit comfortably when they're all together. This space anchors community thinking, providing opportunities for whole-class conversations as well as partner talk.

Centering the Text

A move Lynsey has made recently is to be intentional about not centering herself in whole-class instruction. Rather than setting up a chair in the front of the whole-group space to share books during minilessons or read-aloud, Lynsey moves around in the back of the space while the text is centered on a large screen in the room. This shift has been a powerful one as the students, the text, and the conversation are the things that are centered.

Centering Students' Words

A goal we have for each day is ensuring that our voice as the teacher is not the most important voice in the room. We want our students to know that every voice in our community is equally important and that everyone's voices are valued. We learn together that we cannot grow individually without the collective thinking that happens each day.

Figure 2.7 *Lynsey teaches from the back of the whole-group space.*

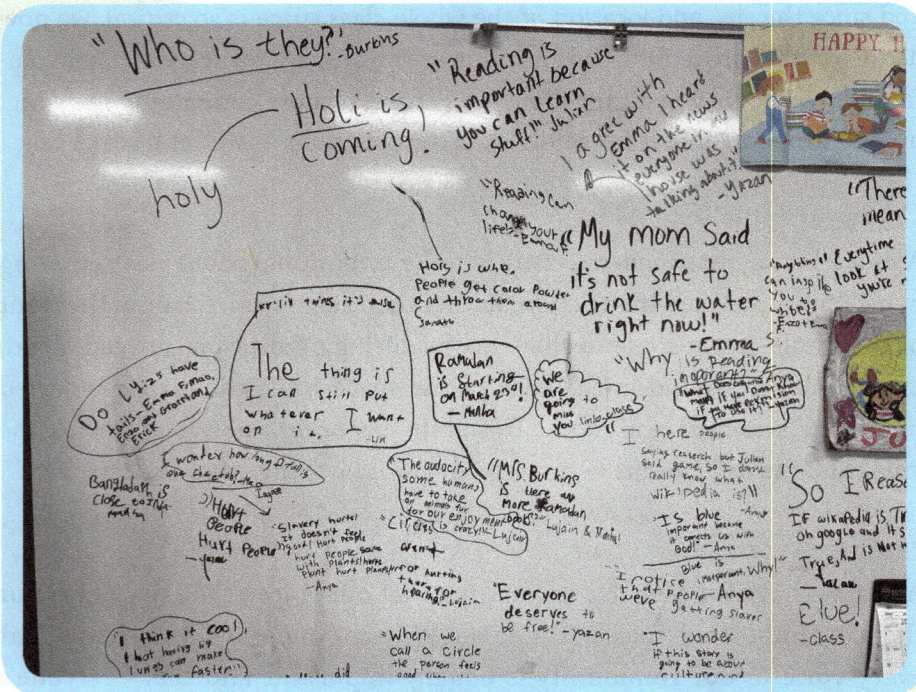

Figure 2.8 *The whiteboard in Lynsey's classroom is filled with students' words.*

One way we make this intention clear to students is to visibly amplify students' words. In the past we often used charts to capture students' thinking, but over the past few years Lynsey began using the classroom's central whiteboard to highlight students' words across the week. She begins each week with a blank board and as she hears something a child says that seems important to capture, she adds the words to the wall along with the student's name. Early in the school year after she begins this routine, students, themselves, also start adding quotes they hear to the board. The whiteboard is full by the end of the week and the words have been referred to over and over throughout the week. Students know that their words matter.

The Ways Our Language Has Shifted

During the read-aloud of *Dragons in a Bag*, several of Lynsey's students became interested in the next book in the series. They had seen the cover of the second book in the series, *The Dragon Thief*, and were using it to think about where the bigger story of the series was going. But much of this excitement around book two took them away from the thinking about *Dragons in a Bag*, the book they were in the midst of reading. Instead of responding the day that the class was a bit "off topic," Lynsey started the read-aloud the next day with a quick lesson. She said:

> I know that many of you are excited about the next book in this series and you are curious about the whole series. This is what series book readers do. Today let's work together to look for the key evidence in *this* book that helps us understand what is happening in the story better. How do you think we should do that?

Lynsey typed the group's ideas as she listened to see if there was something she could add that would help the reading community. Lynsey noticed that the community didn't mention keeping track of the actions of the main character, a skill that can help readers make sense of the plot and character actions in a story. She invited the students to find a way to keep track of the actions in their reading notebook to see if that helped with their thinking and evidence from the current book in the series. Lynsey acknowledged and affirmed what her readers were doing and found a way to build upon it. In past years Lynsey might have said something like, "Readers, let's focus on book one," as an attempt to refocus the community. The difference between the two approaches lies within the agentive possibilities. Lynsey's new approach:

* noticed and named a strategy that readers do,
* provided affirmation to the reading community,
* allowed space for the conversation to grow.

It usually takes several weeks to work your way through a read-aloud of a single-chapter book, and students learn that their role in the read-aloud sessions is to be honest and authentic with their thinking including

---

≷ Tip Box ≷

During whole-class teaching, students are talking and thinking together in ways we invite them to try out later in their independent reading. Here are three tips for making your teaching more *conversational* and *invitational*:

* Try shifting your language from, "Today I'm going to teach you…" to "Today we're going to think about…" Creating a conversational structure is a challenge if students believe the teacher delivers the learning.
* Make the informal invitation to try a new skill or strategy relevant so students know it can help them achieve their own goals and growth as readers. Know and be okay with the fact that children may not take you up on the invitation and that's okay! A particular invitation might not be right for a student at this moment, but might be perfect for them later.
* Create a visible representation of the learning so students can revisit it. This could be an anchor chart, a digital chart, or a quick image used during a minilesson.

any confusion or disagreement. We want our teacher language to encourage students to:

* Question
* Make connections
* Debate ideas
* Study the text and look closely at the author's words
* Record their own thinking
* Weave their thinking with the thinking of the group

Shifting Our Minilessons

Much of our early learning about minilessons taught us that the minilesson should be short and focused—ten to fifteen minutes max—so students had plenty of time for independent reading. We'd choose a minilesson topic based on a standard, select a book, and make a plan. While we still follow these steps, we've changed a bit of our thinking within each of them.

From Text Sets to Menu of Mentors

The Menu of Mentors approach to choosing texts is a more recent shift in power we've made. We have always been excited to read and find new texts for instruction and to curate these texts by topic or by literary element to create text sets. In the past, this practice involved us, as teachers, doing the work of reading and studying great texts. It's a joyful experience but one in which we held all of the power in choosing books we'd use in minilessons. The process lacked the voices of the reading community as collective curators of texts we read together. As we slowed down to listen to what was happening during our day we realized that students are often recommending books for us to read to the class. Whether it is during a reading conference, "Can you read this one to everyone?" or during share time, "I think the class should hear this book," or during a read-aloud, "Do protests really help?", students are often suggesting books or ideas they want to explore. As we strive to be co-intentional about the time we have in whole-class instruction, we asked ourselves, "How can we use these recommendations as part of the co-intentional planning of minilessons?"

Now instead of curating a text set, we curate a set of possibilities. A set of books that we think will work together in a certain way in our teaching. We have come to call this new set of texts a Menu of Mentors. We create the Menu of Mentors around a certain standard or idea. We know the books on the menu well, and it includes books we find as teachers as well as books that students suggest. When students notice that the books they recommend show up in minilessons, they begin to read and recommend with more purpose and joy. Our role as teachers is to read and study the books so that we know the types of conversations the books naturally invite and the ways the books will connect to previous and future learning.

As the skillful facilitator we can begin to ask these questions of ourselves and our students:

* Where would this book fit in our learning journey?
* Would this book fit best when we read informational text, fiction, or poetry?

A Recent Menu of Mentors on Character Development

Many of these titles are available in both print and digital formats:

Brave Molly by Brooke Boynton-Hughes

A Plan for Pops written by Heather Smith and illustrated by Brooke Kerrigan

My Teacher Is a Monster! by Peter Brown

All the Way to the Top written by Annette Bay Pimental and illustrated by Nabi H. Ali

The Oldest Student written by Rita Lorraine Hubbard and illustrated by Oge Mora

My Fade Is Fresh written by Shauntay Grant and illustrated by Kitt Thomas

The Box, a short film directed by Eliott Belrose, Carole Favier, Loïcia Lagillier, Aloïs Mathé, Juliette Perrey, and Joran Rivet

* What are you most excited about when you envision the class reading and talking about this book?
* How has this book moved you?
* What do you think the class might learn from this text?

More recently we noticed students really enjoying digital shorts. We have started using these short, powerful narratives told through video as part of our Menu of Mentors. We treat these digital shorts as texts to also be studied alongside print texts.

From "What Will I Teach Next?" to "What Does the Community Say They Need Next?"

The structure of our curriculum, probably like most of yours, encourages us to continually ask, "What will I teach next?"—it's a standardized system. Along the way, we've learned to balance the rigidity of the curriculum with our desire to create an environment in which we could be free to listen and respond to what the community says they need next while still making sure curricular needs are embedded. Co-creating learning with students means blending the needs of the learners with the knowledge, skills, and strategies they are charged with learning. To do this we look at our learning standards as endless opportunities. The standards are there, we know them, but the texts we use to teach them are dependent on what our students are saying they need. The topics that they want to investigate together, the themes they are interested in, and the text structures they are begging to understand better can all be explored through the context of our standards. We know the end goal but every class meets that goal by following a different path. So, our question has expanded from "What will I teach next?" to include "What are the topics and ideas students are excited to think about?" and "What standards best support the direction the community is going?"

These are some questions we ask ourselves as we end each unit cycle:

* When we think about the next standards we are required to teach, what do students already bring to that new literacy content? What do they already know and do as readers?
* What have I heard or seen from students that lets me know where to go next in our learning?

* How can we use topics students are interested in to create these literary experiences?

These are some questions we ask the group as we end each unit cycle:

* Based on what we just learned together, what literacy learning might be next for us?
* What information can we find about this topic to help us learn about it?
* Has anyone seen anything in the classroom library that can help us?

From Isolated Lessons to a Connected Cycle of Lessons

Another shift we've made in our minilesson planning lies in the way we intentionally connect our lessons. Of course we've always tried to connect our minilessons to students' prior learning. But we are now more intentional to also connect to previous thinking and learning the class has done *together* in previous unit cycles. Sometimes we look at a chart the class has worked on the previous day, an annotated piece of text we studied together weeks ago, a quote of something important said by someone in the class, a picture—really, anything that connects today's learning with something the class has learned before is key to our planning. Once we have the connection, we make sure our students are aware of the connection.

We Know Our Standards So We Are Constantly Looking and Listening...

Making the connections between minilessons explicit for our students is critical work. It ensures we aren't just teaching a random string of lessons, checking isolated skills off as we go, but rather that our minilessons build on one another, adding up to our goal of creating stronger, more engaged readers. Over time, students come to expect these connections and they rely on them to build bridges in their learning.

A commitment to connected teaching is especially critical to planning. In many ways, minilessons can best be described as extended conversations that unfold over time. As we plan, we are always thinking about how *this* lesson fits with the ongoing conversation our classroom community is having. We continuously ask ourselves questions like these:

* Why am I teaching this? How does it fit into the bigger picture? What's the connection?

* Are my students' identities, interests, and learning strengths and needs represented in the lesson?
* What have my students done that shows me they need this lesson?
* What evidence do I have that this lesson is the next best step for most learners?
* What are the big goals I have for students around this skill/strategy/ behavior? What will it look like when I see they are "getting it"?
* Which texts could I use that will naturally invite conversation around this big idea?
* How will I provide space for students to enter at their own level?
* What are students already able to do around this skill/strategy/behavior?

How Does the Power Shift Happen?

A couple weeks after winter break in Lynsey's third-grade classroom, students were gathered in the meeting area, hanging on every word as two of their peers shared during the writer's workshop. "Listen everyone, animals are dying in our oceans. Do you want to know why?" Anya had everyone's attention.

Emma added, "And it's because of what humans are doing." The class erupted. You could hear lots of students just asking why and others looking shocked and confused. When the pair shared the slides they created as part of the informational writing unit, Lynsey noticed she was taking so many notes that she could hardly keep up. As she listened, Lynsey realized that the share time had shifted from a traditional writing share to a conversation with all students involved. Lynsey's notes were messy but she saw a pattern in their conversation that showed how interested and passionate the class was in their classmates' ideas. They were becoming interested in the ways plastic in the ocean impacted the world and they wanted to know more.

Then Emma and Anya moved to their last two slides that were focused on action and the community decided together that they want to learn more about this issue and help. Lynsey wrote in her notes, "call to action," "students asking where they can learn more," and "Mrs. Burkins, can we learn more about this?" At this point Lynsey knew that the topic of ocean conservation had sparked a community interest and passion and that the upcoming reading informational unit in the reading workshop would fit this interest beautifully. Listening to students in order to inform instruction is a shift in power that helps move us from teacher-directed instruction to co-created reading instruction.

Starting with the Standards

Like most teachers, we have curriculum and standards that we are required to teach. To help Lynsey honor the voices of the reading community and teach state-mandated standards *and* district curriculum, she created a planning and documentation tool to support a co-creation approach to minilessons. This tool lets her see the state standards for the district unit in one place and her kids' voices alongside them. Lynsey puts her students' quotes on the thinking tool to begin the process of co-creating the next series of reading minilessons around what students are eager to learn about. She lovingly refers to this planning and documentation tool as a "messy sheet," an idea she developed from the thinking of Clare Landrigan and Tammy Mulligan's work *Assessment in Perspective* (2013).

Using the Planning and Documentation Tool

"Wait, Mrs. Burkins, I have something to say," Annabelle confidently asserted, while listening to the informational text *Blue: A History of the Color as Deep as the Sea and as Wide as the Sky*. Lynsey immediately paused as the community moved their gaze from the book to Annabelle.

Annabelle:	I notice that the color blue is so much more than a color...it has a deeper meaning?
Yazan:	Can you say more, Annabelle?
Emma:	Yeah, tell us more about what you mean by deeper.
Annabelle:	Like I noticed that people trick others by giving them blue cloth then they take them and hurt them and how they trade other people.
Anya:	You mean get them and sell them?
Annabelle:	Yes, that's terrible.
Erick:	There are also other ways blue is more than a color.
Julian:	Can we go get our reading notebooks and write things down while you read?

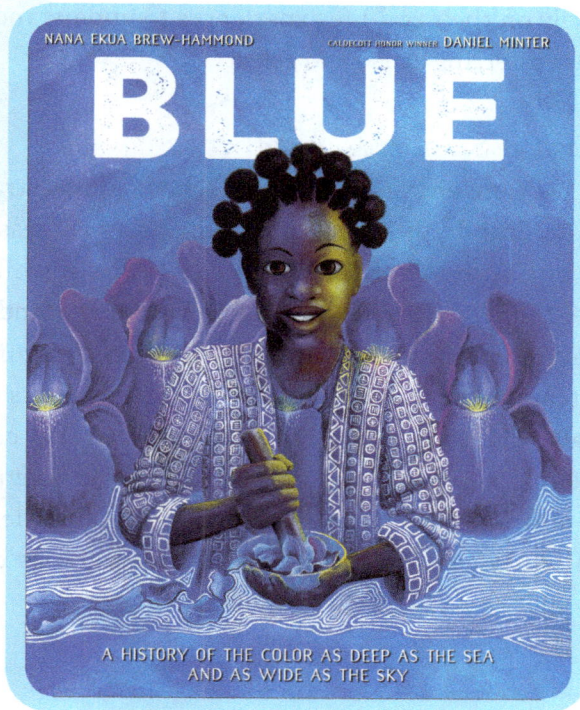

NANA EKUA BREW-HAMMOND   CALDECOTT HONOR WINNER DANIEL MINTER

BLUE

A HISTORY OF THE COLOR AS DEEP AS THE SEA
AND AS WIDE AS THE SKY

Lynsey nodded: "Whatever will help you as a reader, please do it." Lynsey watched as her entire class got up, grabbed their reading notebooks and tools to write with, and came right back to the meeting space. Noting the excitement around this text, Lynsey immediately grabbed a copy of the planning and documentation tool that she created in anticipation of a new unit with the standards for that unit already printed on it [Figure 2.9]. She began her own notetaking alongside the students.

Lynsey knew this conversation would tell her a lot about what her readers already knew and understood about how to think through a text like *Blue*. Her focus was on capturing students' thinking in order to use it for planning an upcoming unit. This is what Lynsey learned about her students by using the documentation tool. Students were:

* noticing interesting words that were new to them
* starting to form explicit questions related to the content of the text
* making attempts to explain historical events

* relying heavily on their real-life experiences to understand the text
* ready to start inferring cause and effect

Understanding the Standards Together

Some time ago we were encouraged by our school administration to post the Ohio Learning Standards in the classroom during our lessons. It never seemed quite right. A chunk of words posted next to us while we taught. Then, soon after the request to post the Ohio Learning Standards, we had professional development time to "unpack" the State Learning Standards in grade-level teams and create related "I can" statements for students to recite. This also did not seem right. We recognized that creating these "I can" statements had more to do with an increased national focus on accountability and testing than our students' actual understanding of goals for learning. We also recognized that whoever was doing all the

---

Reading Theme: Real Life Reading

"All these cultures wanted blue for different reasons." Ryan

Reading Informational Text

Key Ideas and Details
RI.3.2. Analyze informational text development.
• a. Determine the <u>main idea</u> of a text.
• b. Retell the key details and explain how they support the main idea.

Integration of Knowledge and Ideas
RI.3.7. Use information gained from illustrations (e.g., maps, photographs) and the words in a text to demonstrate understanding of the text (e.g., where, when, why, and how key events occur).

"Can we go back to the page with the hands and the kids flying, what does this illustration mean?" Manha

"I think the picture with the woman singing is showing us that it was wrong to trade people just to get the color blue." Sanath

"Why was it ok to hurt people for the color blue?" Enzo *"Why did everyone want blue?" Julian* *"Why was blue so important?" Lujain*

Craft and Structure
RI.3.5. Use text features and search tools (e.g., key words, sidebars, hyperlinks) to locate information relevant to a given topic efficiently.

Integration of Knowledge and Ideas
RI.3.9. Compare and contrast the most important points and key details presented in two texts on the same topic.

"What does iris mean?" Brianna *"Lapis lazuli is in Roblox." Garrett*

Reading Literature

Craft and Structure
RL.3.4. Determine the meaning of words and phrases as they are used in a test, distinguishing <u>literal</u> from <u>nonliteral</u> language.

"What does luxury mean?" Emma

Reading Foundational Skills

Phonics and Word Recognition
RF.3.3. Know and apply grade-level phonics and word analysis skills in decoding words.
• b. Decode words with common Latin suffixes.

Figure 2.9 *Lynsey uses a planning and documentation tool to capture students' thinking around* Blue *as it relates to the standards in an upcoming unit. We will expand further on this tool in Chapter 6.*

studying was also doing all the learning. We worked to become masterful at knowing and understanding the learning standards so that we could achieve our true goal of co-creating an understanding of the standards alongside our students. We no longer accepted just having standards posted, but rather decided that standards would be a living part of our learning process as we worked to think about them together as a class. We began the process of "unpacking" the reading standards as a community.

The process of unpacking the standard looks the same each time the community comes together to do this work. The reading community looks at the language of the standard and begins to think about:

* Words you do not know
* What you do understand
* What is confusing
* Words that let you know what to do

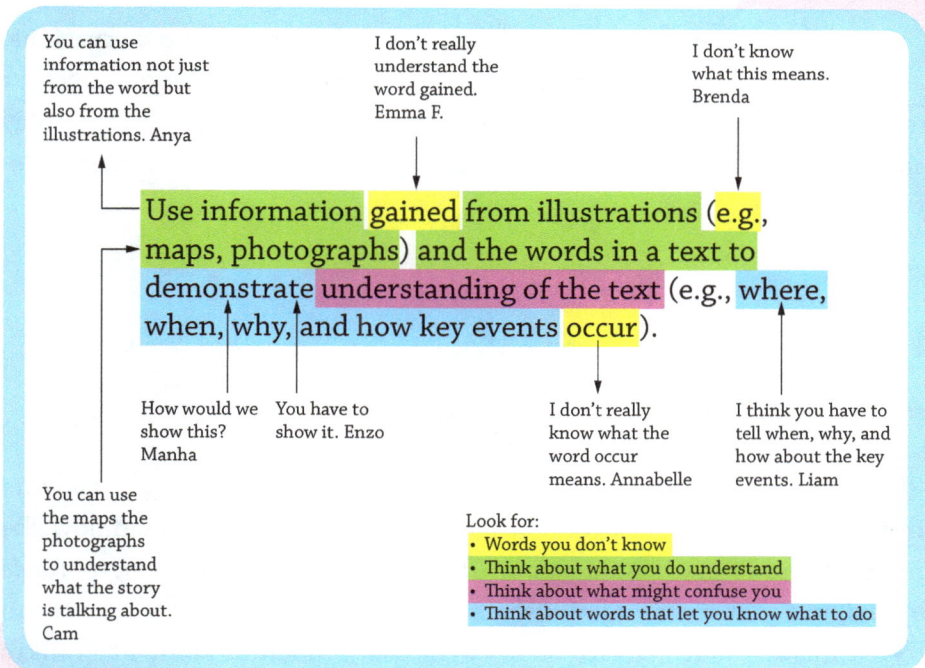

Figure 2.10 *One of the Ohio Learning Standards annotated by Lynsey's third-grade class during a reading minilesson.*

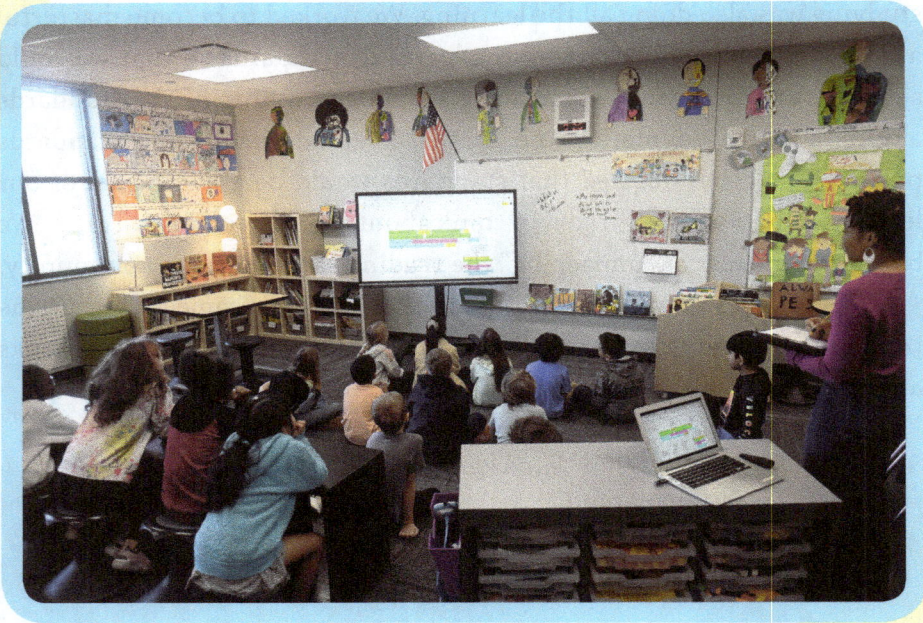

Figure 2.11 *Lynsey's third-grade class works together to annotate an Ohio Learning Standard during the reading minilesson.*

Through a series of turn and talks, idea charting, group discussions, and rethinking opportunities, the learning standard is unpacked together over a series of days. This process allows students to access what they should do as readers during whole-group instruction and in their independent reading lives.

What Read-Aloud Time Looks Like and How It Has Evolved

Recently, Franki reconnected with one of her former fourth-grade students from twenty-plus years ago. As they chatted, Jaclyn mentioned how she remembered Franki reading aloud *The True Confessions of Charlotte Doyle* by Avi and that it was a book she still loves to this day. It is always fun to reminisce about favorite books with past students. Many of Franki's students are grown and are parents themselves. She sometimes hears from a past student who is a new mom sharing a book with her child that she remembers from the classroom. We've always known that read-aloud time is a favorite time for students but these conversations, years (often decades) later, remind us of the power of the classroom read-aloud. There is nothing like sharing an incredible story together over time.

Franki started really thinking differently about the possibilities of read-aloud through learning with friend and colleague Mary Lee Hahn. In her book *Reconsidering Read-Aloud* Hahn writes:

> Read-aloud may look like an ordinary event in a typical class-room, but it feels extraordinary when the teacher who is reading is aware of the power of the book and the importance of her role in not only reading to her students but leading them through the book—using read-aloud as a teaching time.
>
> (2002, 1)

It was Mary Lee who helped Franki see that read-aloud time was more than the sharing of a good book. Instead it is a powerful teaching time that centers students and is responsive to their needs as readers.

Although our read-aloud time has evolved over time and we've learned to be more intentional, we never want to lose the emotional aspect of read-aloud that makes it such a positive experience for children. We are committed to a read-aloud time that is joyful and engaging for every child. So as we learn more about how to support growing readers during read-aloud, we also still want students to feel compelled to find us in twenty years and share their great memories of read-aloud.

Previewing a Book: The Power Shift

We have found that spending time previewing a read-aloud book invites in-depth and thoughtful conversations throughout the read-aloud experience and also helps us, as teachers, listen to our readers to see how they are entering the text. Previewing also gives us the opportunity to build on our students' thoughts and insights. We often spend two entire read-aloud sessions previewing a chapter book before we actually begin reading! To preview we might:

* Look at the cover and talk about the title
* Talk about the author and their work
* Read any blurbs from folks endorsing the book

* Look up reviews of the book online
* Read the inside flap
* Read the table of contents
* Read the first page

When we first started making book previews a regular part of our read-aloud routine, it was really about setting readers up for understanding. We knew that as readers ourselves, we never entered a book without reading the inside flap, thinking about the author, and studying the cover. We knew that building a habit of previewing would help our readers enter a book with strong thinking that would enable deeper comprehension.

However, the more we previewed books together with our students, the more we learned about all *they* were bringing to a text. The more we listened to children, the more we realized that the book preview serves as an important tool for us, as teachers. Even though we always choose a chapter book because of what we know it offers our readers, we also know that the preview allows us to embed our students' thinking into the conversations and learning from the start.

One way the routine of previewing has evolved in our classrooms is in the way we use it to focus discussions based on both the standards and our students' noticings. We have realized that following one big idea across a longer text is key to reading complex texts with depth. So we might hold onto a question such as "How is this character changing?" or "How are we, as readers, making sense of this unfamiliar setting?" across an entire text.

We never know when we preview a book together which things will capture the interest of our readers or which things the community will spend time thinking about. So we are always listening for those things that spark the most conversation and questions when we preview a book. And we are always listening for connections to the standards we know as teachers. We can then build on those throughout the book.

One year, in Franki's fifth-grade class, the class previewed the new read-aloud book *Harbor Me* by Jacqueline Woodson. As usual, the class looked at all of the pieces of the book available to them—the front cover, the inside flap blurb, the author information, the dedication, and the first page. Franki's class was particularly interested in the dedication which reads, "For Lena and Alana, who harbor so many/And for my family, who harbors me," and wondered about the meaning of the word "harbor" and its connection to the title (2018, front matter).

The students wondered who Lena and Alana were and whether this dedication was made because the story somehow connected to the people mentioned. Franki had chosen this book because of the rich characters. She knew the book would invite conversations about the ways characters change over time. But when she heard this conversation, she realized there

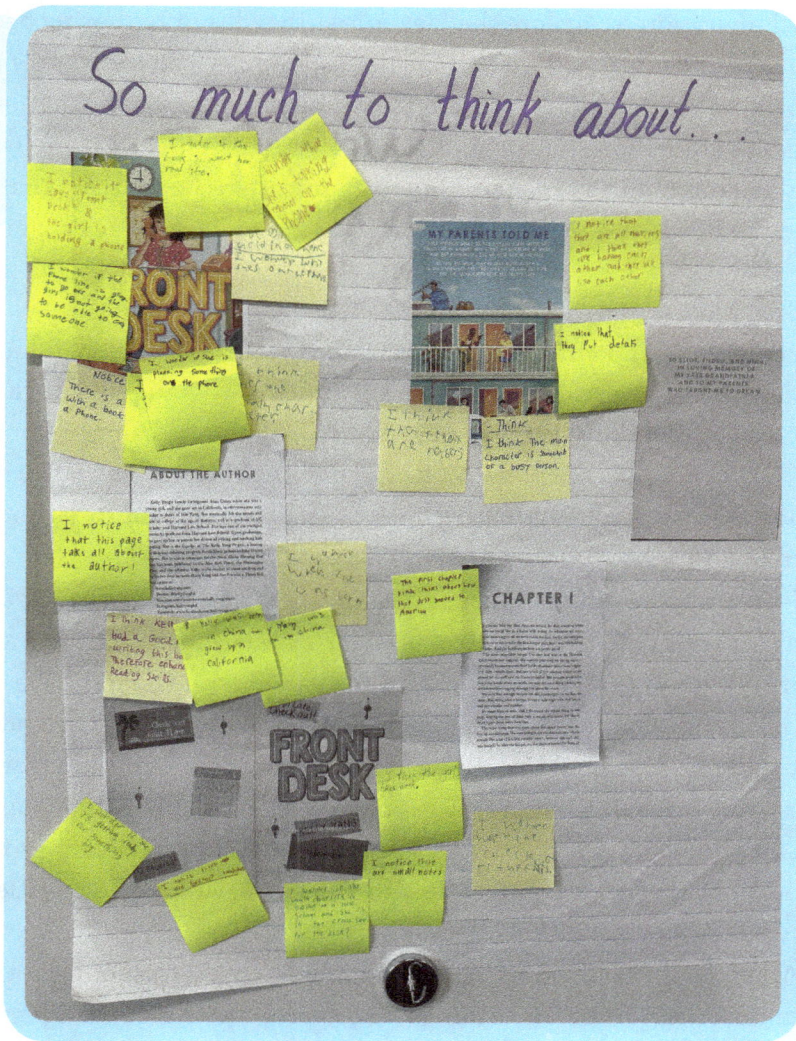

Figure 2.12   *This chart shows the thinking a group of fifth graders did after a preview of* Front Desk *by Kelly Yang and how their thoughts were captured so they could be built upon throughout the reading.*

was an opportunity for another conversation across the book. She realized that her students could learn the power of words, metaphor and title when thinking across an entire book. She knew this conversation (if they continued it) could help them think deeply about the theme of this book and the way the title was a type of metaphor. In response to her students' interest, she made sure to enlarge the dedication page, and have it displayed on the board once they began the read-aloud. Placing this dedication on the board served as a reminder of the class's initial conversation as well as a visual invitation to explore the idea more. The idea of harboring became an anchor for so many conversations the community had across this read-aloud. These conversations had a clear connection to so many important fifth-grade standards. Throughout the book, students learned the ways a word's meaning can be expanded, how authors often choose titles that connect to the theme of the book, and the idea of a single word as a metaphor.

Annotations: The Power Shift

As readers grow and change, our previewing becomes more sophisticated and readers take more ownership of this process. It is important that we value student thinking over any agenda we may have had for the read-aloud. We definitely choose books because of the skills and strategies that will most likely come up naturally, but our students constantly surprise us by thinking in ways that we couldn't have predicted.

In the middle of fifth grade, Franki's students were beginning a new read-aloud, *The Girl Who Drank the Moon* by Kelly Barnhill. This was a favorite of Franki's and she was excited to share it with children. She chose the book for several reasons. The book was longer than any they had read before and she knew holding on to longer stories was important for fifth graders. She knew fantasy was a genre they had not yet read aloud that year and she knew the characters were strong and several changed over the course of the story. Franki knew there were several opportunities for learning and growth through reading this book.

After the initial preview, the class thought together about the things that caught their attention—things in the preview that made them stop and think—things that they predicted would be things they'd continue to think about throughout the entire book. Because they had experience reading complex books together, they felt confident in their thinking.

As they began the read-aloud, Franki noticed many students were setting up their notebooks in a way that would allow them to focus on one or more of the ideas that had come out during the previewing process. Franki asked students if they wanted to collect their collective thinking around these ideas from the preview on a board as they read. Students were eager to do so, and together they created a board that captured the big ideas with space for the community to add new ideas (via sticky notes, sketches, etc.) throughout the read-aloud. Because many of the readers in the class were big fantasy readers, much of the thinking they had after the preview connected to their understanding of the genre. Headings on the board were:

* Fantasy: Unfamiliar Setting
* Fear of Standing Up for What is Right

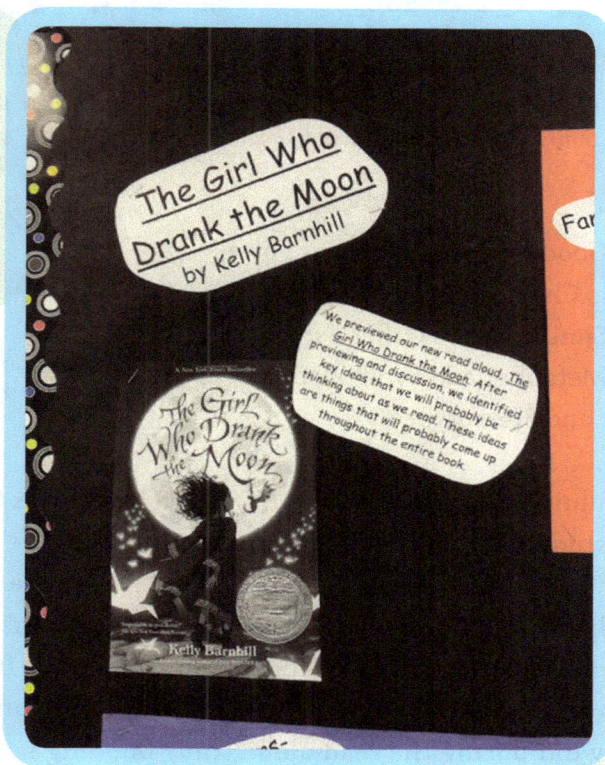

Figure 2.13   *Franki's fifth graders created a display of ideas that came out in their preview of* The Girl Who Drank the Moon *that they wanted to continue to track throughout the read-aloud.*

Figure 2.14 *The display featured themes and ideas the group noticed in their preview of* The Girl Who Drank the Moon *with plenty of space for adding new thinking throughout the read-aloud.*

* Fantasy: Good vs. Evil—Who Has Power?
* Characters Changing Over Time
* Fantasy: Similarities to Other Fantasies
* Fantasy: Metaphor and Symbolism
* Character and Stereotypes

As the community read *The Girl Who Drank the Moon* over the six-week read-aloud, students added new ideas to the board. The preview set the stage for the kind of thinking the class did across the book. There was definitely overlap in the types of conversations Franki had hoped would happen and those that did happen, but by opening it up and giving power to students, they were in control of the thinking and documenting they did during the read-aloud, thus building both skills and reader agency.

Over the years, the power shift that has happened when we think about annotations in both minilessons and read-aloud has been critical.

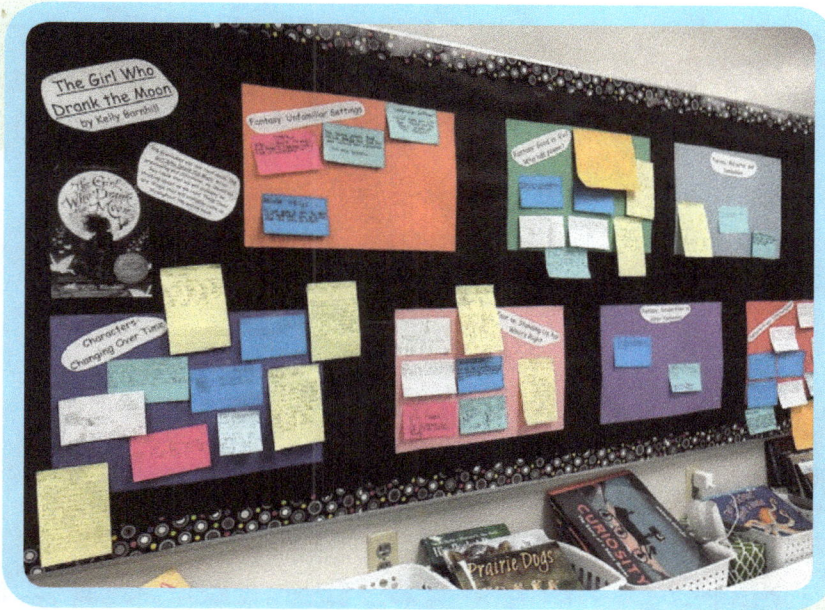

Figure 2.15   *This is the board at the midway point of the read-aloud as children added ideas as they read.*

It was our previewing routine that pushed us to think more deeply about student agency in annotation.

Student Ownership of Annotations

Once we've previewed the book, we often set kids up for deeper conversation by giving them time to focus on their individual thinking before we start the read-aloud. Some students may predict that the main character will learn something, so much of their annotation will focus on that. Others may find the idea of the plot to be confusing, so they decide to keep track of events. Others may focus on the details in the text that come up over and over.

Once the community has previewed a book together, students begin to use what they've learned during this time to focus their thinking and talk. And when children focus on what is interesting and relevant to them, collectively we think about so many things! We capture this early thinking in a variety of ways for students to refer to throughout the read-aloud.

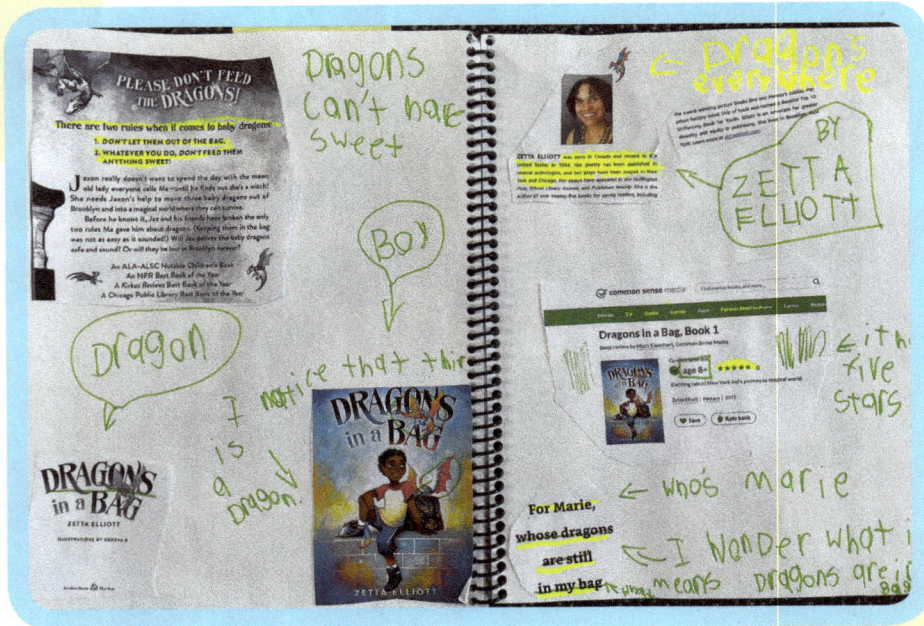

Figure 2.16   *Students work independently to preview an upcoming read-aloud of Dragons in a Bag by Zetta Elliott before the class meets together.*

During a fifth-grade reading of *The Girl Who Drank the Moon* by Kelly Barnhill, the list of things that individual students followed across the book included:

* Good vs. Evil—Who has the power here? Do the same people keep the power?
* How is _____changing?
* How is this book similar/different to other fantasies I've read?
* What symbolism is used in this book? Why is the author using it?
* What does the title mean?
* What parts of this setting are most important to the story? Why?

The Evolution of Reading Notebooks

Lynsey and Franki have always provided reading notebooks for students. We've always been committed to writing about reading and writing as a way of making sense of things. Years ago, our reading notebooks were lined spiral notebooks with designated sections for different kinds of recording.

The sections changed a bit year-to-year according to the grade we were teaching or the ways we hoped students would think about their reading but the notebooks often included a space for Read-Aloud, a space for a Reading Log, and a space for Reflections.

Over time, we've let go of the ways we think kids will use the notebook and instead we hand them a blank unlined notebook. We have learned that a blank notebook allows readers to organize their thinking in the way that works for them. This gives readers the opportunity to sketchnote, glue items into the book, create charts, graphs, and more. For example, when Franki's fifth graders read *Rump*, the blank, unlined paper in their reading notebooks allowed them to paste in images of the cover, table of contents page, and inside flap, and respond to this preview material in ways that made sense to them. The more we've let go of our control of the notebook, the more possibilities our students have discovered.

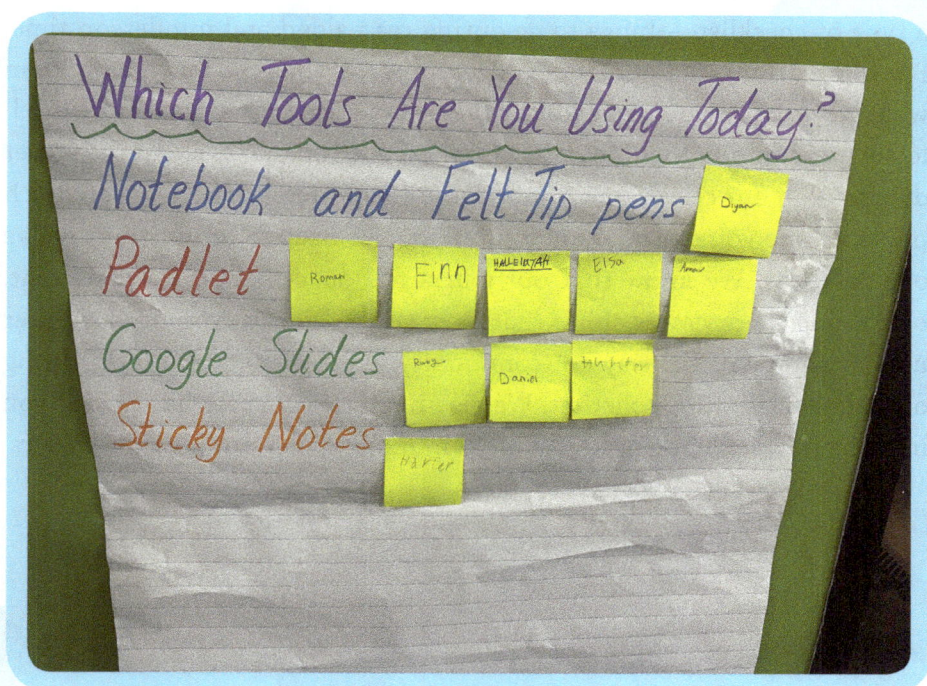

Figure 2.17   *Students decide which annotation tool they will use when capturing thinking for the new read-aloud book.*

Although we still provide reading notebooks, we know that some students will choose to capture their thinking in different ways. Some students will choose to have a copy of the book and use sticky notes to capture thinking. Others will choose a digital tool such as Padlet to keep track of their thinking. We've had to remind ourselves that finding the tool that works for each reader is an important goal in itself, and asking every child to use the same tool isn't always the best idea. We've had to remember that our goal is for students to grow as readers, and as such we want them to be empowered to choose the tools that will support them best.

Looking Ahead

In the following chapters, we explore more of the specifics behind whole-class instruction and the instructional moves we make. We know that without the beliefs we hold about power in the classroom and the intellectual community, the moves we describe in the next few chapters could become a type of checklist—things to *do* during read-aloud and minilesson time. But our teaching and our students' learning are about so much more than what we do. If we are true to our beliefs about the importance of an intellectual community then we must be honest with ourselves about the power dynamics in our classrooms. Once we see something that gives too much power to one voice or one way of thinking, we need to rethink and evolve our practices. We know that our journey is ongoing and we hope that, by sharing these power shifts that have worked for us, you have a better understanding of the way our community looks, sounds and feels during our whole-class time together. We also hope this chapter has helped you imagine the kind of beloved reading community you want for your readers.

CHAPTER 3

Getting to Know the Standards

One afternoon Franki was reading *Sweep: The Story of a Girl and Her Monster* by Jonathan Auxier to her fifth-grade class. She read the line, "If we all could just ignore the way other people looked, then we could see who they really were." Just as Franki finished reading this sentence, Sam spoke up:

> I am wondering what the author really means by the word monster [in the title]. At the beginning I thought the monster was the actual monster but the more we read, I wonder if monsters are what you look like or what is on the inside because Mr. Crudd seems to be the real monster.

A few students nodded and responded and we added this idea to a chart we were using to keep track of our thinking as we read.

Blair immediately went back to the cover of the book and to the subtitle. She said, "I've been thinking the monster in the book is Charlie because of the title and the picture on the cover, but Charlie is so kind and good. Could there be more than one kind of monster?"

The class continued to wrestle with the meaning of the word "monster." They thought through the characters in the book as well as the multiple meanings of the word monster. They asked each other questions and formulated theories by referring back to the text. During their five-minute read-aloud conversation, Franki's students used several skills and strategies named in their grade-level standards simultaneously. They were able to:

* quote accurately from a text when explaining what the text says explicitly and when drawing inferences from the text. (RL.5.1)
* determine a theme of a story, drama, or poem from details in the text, including how characters in a story or drama respond to challenges or how the speaker in a poem reflects upon a topic; summarize the text. (RL.5.2a)
* determine the meaning of words and phrases as they are used in a text, including figurative language such as metaphors, similes and idioms. (RL.5.4)

* read and comprehend literature, including stories, dramas, and poetry, at the high end of the grades 4–5 text complexity band independently and proficiently. (RL.5.10)

Note: While the standards that appear throughout this book are Ohio's Learning Standards (2017), many of these same skills and strategies are also part of state standards throughout the country.

As they read *Sweep*, Franki's students were fully engaged in their read-aloud conversation and meeting multiple standards. This was not an accident. Franki set clear teaching goals for whole-class instruction, with the read-aloud and standards in mind, and her students valued this time to think together.

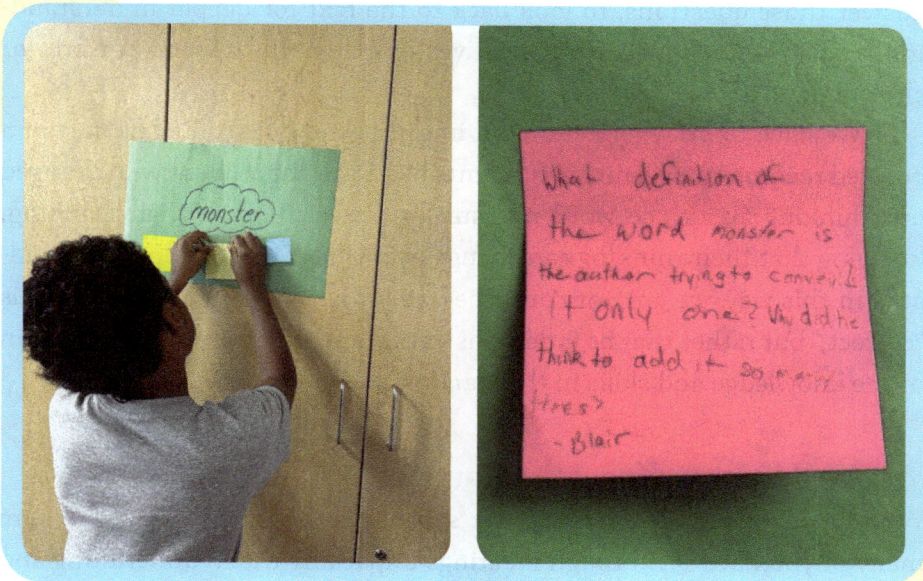

Figure 3.1 *After a student questioned the meaning of the word "monster" in the book* Sweep, *Franki and her students created a quick poster. Readers used sticky notes to share their evolving thinking about this word and idea as the class continued to read the book. As students had new ideas or read something that added to their thinking about "monsters" (during read-aloud or at some other time during the day), they would add a sticky note to the poster. As the class continued reading the book over the next several weeks, they revisited the poster periodically together as a community.*

The Role of the Standards in Whole-Class Reading Instruction

We know that these whole-class conversations are possible when we, as teachers, know our standards well and study them with a critical lens. That means we make sure *not* to view them as a checklist of isolated knowledge and skills. We also make sure *not* to think about the standards as separate from the students in front of us each year and what they bring to the learning.

When we think about the bigger goals of literacy, such as developing independence and responding to and understanding various perspectives, we want each child to bring their whole self to these standards. We want every child to be empowered to ask questions as they read, to answer those questions, to look back to the text for deeper understanding, and to truly hear the perspectives of others in order to confirm or change their thinking.

We have to put every standard in the context of reading as part of a beloved reading community so students like Sam (the student who changed our thinking about the word monster) are free to share their thinking, knowing that their thinking can change over time. When we look at standards in this way, we are not concerned about whether Sam's statement is "correct," but rather that he is demonstrating authentic use and application of the knowledge and skills in the standards in order to make meaning.

What It Means to *Know* the Standards

We have all spent time reading our state learning standards. We're sure many of you have sat through meetings unpacking them: underlining and labeling verbs and nouns, doing all the work that is done just to "understand" and "know" them. But we think truly knowing the standards is about so much more than simply underlining verbs and sorting them into categories.

We have colleagues who can tell us the number of a standard. But that is not what we mean here by *knowing* the standards. We study the standards so that we can use them in humanizing ways. We don't read the standards with the test in mind. We read the standards with the readers in mind.

We use the standards as starting points so we can reach higher and protect the learning that we are co-creating with our students. Vivian Vasquez in her book *Negotiating Critical Literacies with Young Children* says it best when she writes, "As the classroom teacher, I made sure that I understood what was expected of me through the mandated curriculum in order to demonstrate to parents, colleagues, and administration that our negotiated curriculum surpassed the required curriculum" (2004, 27).

Our reading standards are all about encoding and decoding texts, analyzing texts, studying craft and structure of texts, and reading for sustained periods of time. Since we understand and know these standards, we are free to select the texts we use to teach them. We can create the units, we can group and pace standards in ways that are responsive to our learners' needs, and we can pace them however our students need. In an interview for *EdWeek*, Mariana Souto-Manning helped us further understand how to link the learning in the classroom with the learning standards when she wrote:

> Learn the standards and use them strategically to justify your teaching. While we may think of standards as constraining our teaching, we believe that it is important to really get to know, to study the standards not only for our grade level but for two or three grades above. This allows us to strategically link the rich learning that is taking place in our classroom to the standards for our grade level and beyond. Instead of starting from standards, we have found it helpful to start with the children—their stories, identities, interests, communities, and questions.
>
> (Ferlazzo 2020)

Standards hold tremendous power in schools. They are often used not just to dictate what we teach, but how we teach it, for how long, and what materials we use to do so. As teachers, we can take back some of this power that is often given to standards by knowing what they say and what they do not say. We can take back the power so that we can share this power with students, using standards as a foundation for the learning we co-create with them, alongside texts they want to read and topics they want to discuss.

View the Standards Through a Co-Intentional Lens

It is the responsibility of the teacher to view whole-class reading instruction through the lens of both each individual reader's development as well as the whole group's development as a community of readers. The read-aloud and reading minilessons are times in which the reading standards are applied. During these whole-group learning times the reading standards are not just delivered to students as if the children were empty vessels, they are instead negotiated, practiced, and learned as a reading community.

When we know our standards well, we can build on all the thinking our students do naturally during read-aloud and minilesson time. Franki's fifth graders realized that the title of *The Turtle of Oman* by Naomi Shihab Nye might refer to the main character in the book instead of the actual turtles because, in the words of one of her students,

> The word "turtle" is in the title, not "turtles." If the author was talking about the actual turtles, she would have said more than one. Since it is "turtle," I think she means the character is Aref and he does sometimes go into his shell.

Franki knew this comment would change the trajectory of the conversation and she knew this conversation showed evidence that her students were meeting several standards at once (RL.5.1 Quote accurately from a text when explaining what the text says explicitly and when drawing inferences from the text; RL.5.2 Analyze literary text development. a. Determine a theme of a story, drama, or poem from details in the text, including how characters in a story or drama respond to challenges or how the speaker in a poem reflects upon a topic; and RL.5.4 Determine the meaning of words and phrases as they are used in a text, including figurative language such as metaphors, similes, and idioms). By knowing the standards well, we can use them in a way that goes beyond a checklist of isolated skills and be more responsive to our students.

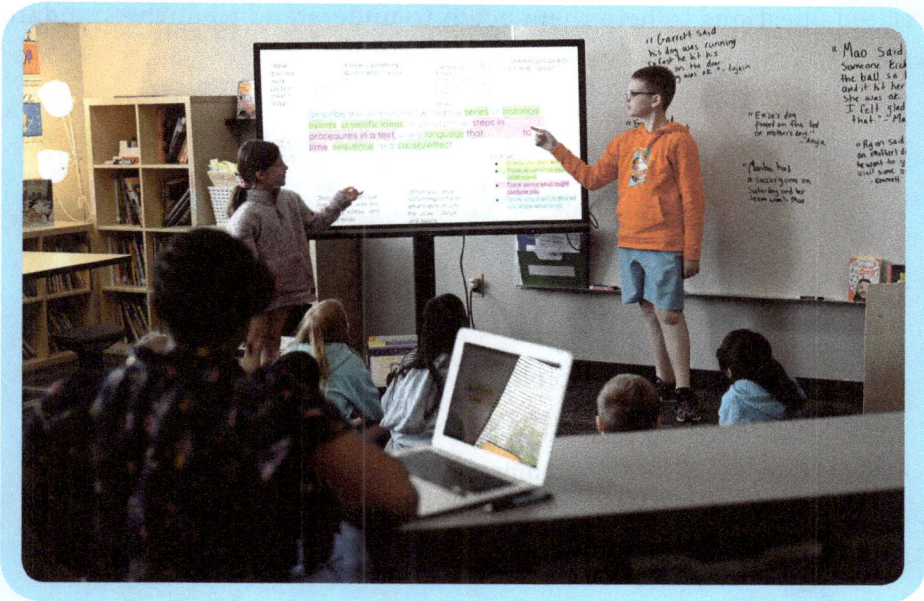

Figure 3.2 *The reading community works toward negotiating, practicing, and learning the standards together.*

This type of educational relationship in which learning is the intended outcome should be *co-intentional*, meaning that teachers and students do the work of learning together. This is why invitations and conversations are so important—because co-intentional teaching centers both teacher and student in the intellectual work of reading. We offer many invitations to our students and pay close attention to those that elicit authentic conversations.

Teachers have the power to use the standards as a tool rather than just a mandated list of what to teach. However, in order to do this, we need to commit to spending time intentionally negotiating how the standards can be used for critical thinking. We push back on the idea that we use the standards with the sole purpose of testing.

In order to truly understand the standards, we ask ourselves the questions below with a teacher lens. Then we ask students a set of related questions to help them begin to understand what the standard says:

Questions I Ask Myself as the Teacher	Questions I Ask My Students
• How do I, as the teacher, understand this standard?	• How do you currently understand this standard?
• What do you notice and wonder about this standard?	• What do you notice and wonder about this standard?
• What biases or misinterpretations might I have as I read this standard?	
Note: Sometimes we bring our own biases to how we understand and interpret a standard. These biases are often unintentional and are largely dependent on our own lived experiences in this world.	
• How will I engage students in understanding the standard together as a reading community?	• What do you need to know to understand this standard better?
• How will I look for evidence that the community understands and learns the standard?	• What do you understand about what this standard is asking us to learn?
• What do I think the reading community might already know or be ready to learn around this standard?	• How will you know that you have learned this standard?

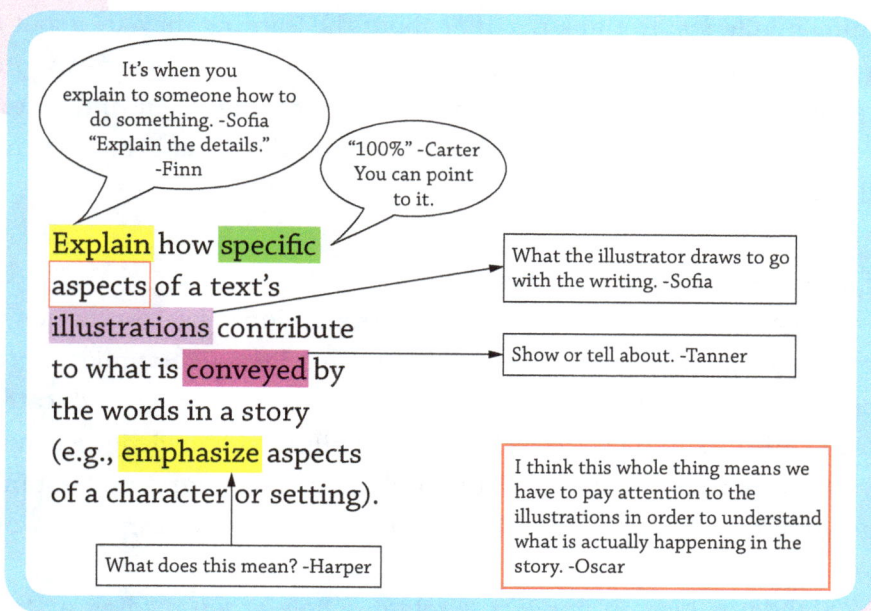

Figure 3.3 *The reading community builds understanding of the standard together.*

After studying the standards on her own, Lynsey's students also work together to co-create meaning around what the standard is asking them to do as readers. Students continually revisit their thinking as they read books together and learn how to use these skills as readers. By the end of the unit, students use their initial thinking and the thinking they revised along the way to demonstrate that they can apply this reading skill in their independent reading and their talk in the beloved reading community. Figure 3.3 is an image of the community's collective thinking around the standard on the first day of exploration together.

The power of the co-intentional lens is that it leads to creating meaning together. As teachers, we do the pre-work of reflection around critical questions (like those in the table) in order to deeply know the standards. Then we are better able to facilitate the conversation around the standards with the students to begin the process of co-creation. The point where the teacher gathers the beloved reading community during the whole-group reading minilesson to think together about the learning they are about to engage in together is where the co-intentional meets the co-creation of meaning. The students and the teacher work together in an intellectual conversation to understand the specific reading skills and behaviors they will develop.

Read Standards with a Critical Lens

In her work with young readers and writers, Sonia Nieto reminds us that "language is never neutral" (2016). This idea also applies to the language of standards. High-stakes testing has encouraged educators to think of the standards as a checklist of skills and knowledge we must cover rather than thinking about the literacy behaviors, understandings, and knowledge that equip students to be active learners in our world.

Standards play an important role in whole-group reading instruction, however, when we consider them through a critical lens. To read a standard critically we must think about the standard as a power structure and possible barrier to the literacy learning and reading community. We want the standards to empower students so that whole-group learning time can propel readers into their independent reading lives. Oftentimes we anchor our read-alouds and minilessons with a standard or a grouping of standards so reading them critically is vital to shifting the power in the classroom.

When looking at your standards:

1. First, think of what the standard says, implies, and doesn't say.
2. Next, think of other standards that naturally align with the thinking the community will be trying to reach.
3. Then, think of what your students already know and understand and ways these standards grouped together can push their understanding forward in a whole-group reading experience.
4. Make connections to whole-class instruction across the year.

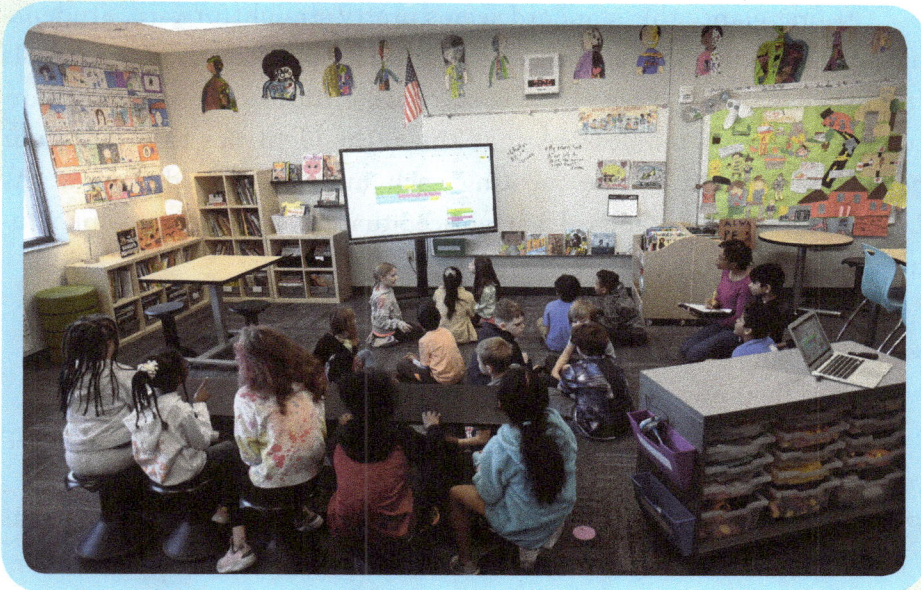

Figure 3.4 *The reading community thinks about what they notice and wonder as they analyze a reading learning standard together.*

Let's take a look at one example of how we might read the standards with a critical eye. During the first few weeks of the school year, Lynsey noticed that her third graders were hesitant to share their thoughts and were focused on "correct answers" in all of their discussions around books. They seemed to rely on her, as the teacher, to guide the thinking around texts they read during a minilesson or during read-aloud time. Lynsey knew that it was critical for this group to be empowered as readers so she dug into Ohio Learning Standards for English Language Arts Standard RL.3.1.

Key Ideas and Details

RL.3.1 Ask and answer questions to demonstrate understanding of a text, referring explicitly to the text as the basis for the answers.

At first glance this standard seems pretty straightforward. Students have to read a text and ask/answer questions using key ideas and details from that text. But if we read the standard critically, we see the opportunities to design minilessons that affirm the identities that shape our beloved community while meeting each individual child's needs. As Lynsey studied this standard, she noticed that underlying it are opportunities for students to:

* notice questions they have as they read/are read aloud to,
* notice their own thinking as they read/are read aloud to,
* be able to record/voice their noticings and wonders in a whole-group setting,
* recognize the types of noticings and questions that help them as readers,
* go back into the text to support the thinking they have,
* listen to the thinking of others in order to understand different perspectives,
* change their thinking/understanding based on evidence in the text and conversation with other readers.

By breaking down a standard and thinking about all the behaviors and strategies readers must practice in order to be competent with the standard, we can then plan our minilessons and read-aloud in ways that reflect the students in front of us. A list, like the one above that Lynsey created, allows teachers to think through and plan individual minilessons and read-alouds.

   Lynsey used the list she created alongside her knowledge that these students tended to rely on asking questions rather than answering them to reflect on this standard. Here is what her thinking looked like:

Steps for Planning with Standards in Mind	Lynsey's Thinking About This Standard	Tips for Doing This Work
First, think of what the standard says, implies, and doesn't say.	**Says** → Ask questions as you read → Use evidence in text to support thinking **Implies** → Each student's questions are valued → There is no single right answer → Reasoning is more important than correct answers **Doesn't say** → Students must answer end-of-text questions → The teacher must ask the questions → Whose perspective is valued when asking and answering questions → Students must answer multiple choice questions	Think about reading with a critical lens. Let go of the traditional way of reading the standards and the way you know it shows up during standardized testing. It is important to read the standards with the goal of supporting students in becoming intellectual citizens instead of only preparing them for a grade-level test. Don't get stuck in literal interpretations of the standard. This could limit your ability to other possible interpretations. Instead think, "How can every student in my classroom show their brilliance when engaging with this standard? What do I know about the histories of my students that would help me broaden how this standard is interpreted?" Read the standard with the goal of making sure there is an access point for every student.

(Continued)

Steps for Planning with Standards in Mind	Lynsey's Thinking About This Standard	Tips for Doing This Work
Next, think of other standards that naturally align with the thinking that the community will be trying to reach.	RL.3.1 Describe characters in a story (e.g., their traits, motivations, or feelings) and explain how their actions contribute to the sequence of events.	Think about studying yourself as a reader through the lens of the standard you will be teaching. When was the last time you used the skill or strategy the standard is referring to? What did it look like for you?
	RL.3.4 Determine the meaning of words and phrases as they are used in a text, distinguishing literal from nonliteral language.	Now, thinking about all the skills and strategies your students are already bringing to this standard, what might the skills, strategies, and thinking in this standard look like for students in the text that they are reading? How might their individual brilliance stand out and be documented as knowledge and ways of understanding what they read?
	RL.3.6 Distinguish their own point of view from that of the narrator or those of the characters.	
	RL.3.7 Explain how specific aspects of a text's illustrations contribute to what is conveyed by the words in a story (e.g., create mood, emphasize aspects of a character or setting).	
	RI.3.1 Ask and answer questions to demonstrate understanding of a text, referring explicitly to the text as the basis for the answers.	

(Continued)

Steps for Planning with Standards in Mind	Lynsey's Thinking About This Standard	Tips for Doing This Work
Then, think of what students already know and understand and ways these standards grouped together can push their understanding in a whole-group reading experience.	At this point in the year, Lynsey's students were focused on the "answering" part of this standard and they relied on others (especially the teacher) to pose the questions.	Go back to any notes you have from students' previous learning. Look for evidence of strengths and challenges around the standards for this specific group of children. Craft a map of where you think they might be headed using the standards as a guide. Take a look at Lynsey's note-taking tools and strategies for doing this work. 
Make connections to whole-class instruction across the year.	Lynsey knew that supporting students to monitor their thinking while reading, and helping them understand that asking questions was just as valuable as answering them would be the important work of the next several weeks.	Think about the big learning and unlearning that students will have to do in order to use this standard in authentic ways. **Big Learning** → Being literate means what you read is never neutral. → Reading for meaning requires multiple ways of understanding texts.

(Continued)

Steps for Planning with Standards in Mind	Lynsey's Thinking About This Standard	Tips for Doing This Work
	This also seemed like a good place to make sure that each and every child's thinking is valued. As Lynsey planned minilessons and read-alouds for her class, she chose books with multiple entry points so that every member of the community could access the learning. Lynsey also ensured she was selecting a variety of books that had characters, themes, and settings that represented the lives and interests of the children in the classroom.	**Unlearning** → I read something and I consider just my perspective. → I read something and believe everyone else understands it the way I do.

This planning practice allows us to look at the standards in a way that holds us accountable to every child in front of us. When we read the standards in this way, we see all that is possible and how these standards can and should be used during whole-group reading opportunities.

Amplify and Anchor Student Learning with the Standards

It was toward the end of the school year and Lynsey's students were used to having conversations around our reading learning standards. On this particular morning the class was engaged in a reading literature standard around perspective. The entire reading minilesson was designed as a conversation for the reading community to make sense of the standard together. The students knew their role was to talk and discuss. They also knew that Lynsey's role was to listen and capture. They loved Lynsey's role because they loved to see their own words highlighted and how she would capture those words in writing.

The class gathered together in their meeting area as Lynsey put a standard up on the screen and gave a few minutes for everyone to read the standard on their own. Since students had their reading notebooks with them, some jotted things down as they did a first read. After a few minutes Lynsey asked if anyone wanted to start the conversation around the standard. The students jumped in right away.

Jordan: (*Begins to read the words on the slide aloud.*)
Tyson: I don't understand what any of it means.
Craig: I'm sure you know something, Tyson.
Ruby: Remember we can look for words we don't know. Let's turn and talk and see what words we don't know.

(*The class turns and talks, then comes back together to share words they don't understand from the text.*)

Ruby: Who wants to share?
Alania: I don't know "distinguish." (*Lynsey highlights the word in yellow.*)
Garrett: I don't understand "perspective." (*Lynsey highlights the word in yellow.*)

The community continued to talk as a whole group and in partners as they thought about the standard in front of them. Lynsey noticed that, despite his protest that he didn't "understand what any of it means," the community wasn't going to let Tyson forget what he *did* know. They immediately asked Tyson a series of questions to help him make sense of what he did and did not know. It was at this moment when Lynsey truly felt the power of being co-intentional about co-creating the learning together. It was the reading community's full intention to do this thinking together. They knew that the power was in the beloved reading community and that their words and thoughts would be amplified and anchored as the work of the community.

Look for:
- Words you don't know
- Think about what you do understand
- Think about what might confuse you
- Think about words that let you know what to do

I don't understand what any of this means. -Tyson

I think it means... manners. -Sanath

Perspective means it's someone's point of view. -Ruby

Put down what you know about something. -Craig

RI.3.6 Distinguish their own perspective from that of the author of a text.

I understand perspective -Imani

I have an example if you are thinking of one thing it's your and the other persons is theirs. -Dallas

The key details in the book. -Anya

What the text says. I don't know how to explain. -Haylee

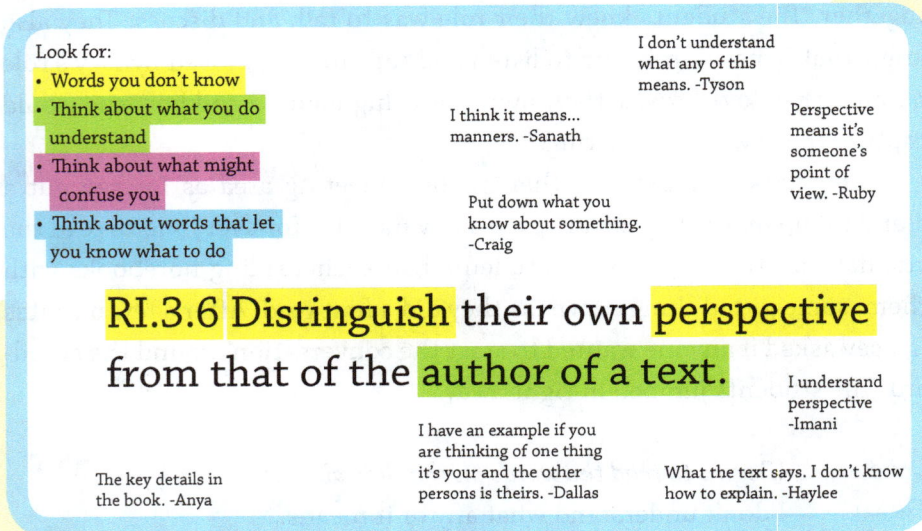

Figure 3.5 *The reading community builds understanding together around the standard.*

The standards should be used as a way to create access to the learning by anchoring what the students already know and understand to the standard. This way of engaging with standards amplifies students' voices and helps them see how their learning evolves as the minilessons and read-aloud progress.

We, as teachers, need to read and study the standards in a way that positions every child as a reader. And as Lynsey's story illustrates, readers do not use one standard at a time. Students and teachers bring all that we know about literacy into each standard we engage with, including our own lives as readers. Readers ask questions as they read, but we never ask questions without doing other things as readers as well.

Keep Track of Students' Learning as it Relates to the Standards

How do we make sure that we are helping children grow in the skills named in the standards *during* their reading and not merely assessing it at the end of their reading? What does it mean for students to implement a skill *during* reading? Here are some tips for keeping track of students' learning as they engage with texts:

*   Consider the ways you keep track of student learning. Try recording how you see students using reading skills, strategies, and behaviors during their varied reading experiences. Charts and quick anecdotal notes work well for this.

*   Assessing learning throughout the year and across standards is critical to students understanding how they are engaging in texts. Consider the question posed earlier in the chapter: How will you know that you have learned this standard? Use the beloved reading community's answers to this question as natural assessment points throughout the learning.

*   Application of reading skills, behaviors, and strategies is a high priority. Supporting readers in making their thinking visible to the beloved reading community strengthens the intellectual learning community and emphasizes the importance of learning with and from each other. As the teacher, making sure students have a dedicated time each day to share supports this goal. The teacher's role during the sharing time is to be the recorder so that the reading community has a visual documentation of how reading skills, strategies, and behaviors look in the community.

Planning and Documentation Tools

We have created planning and documentation tools that help us get to know the standards and begin planning. These planning tools allow us to use what we know about the standards alongside what we know about our students to plan daily instruction.

Figures 3.6 and 3.7 are two forms we rely on to keep track of what we learn about our students as it connects to the standards. We use these pages to jot observations, keep track of words they say, and record notes on possible confusions. Once we have taken these notes, we look for patterns across them to help determine where we might go next with whole-class instruction.

Our standards planning and documentation tool [Figure 3.6] allows us to keep the standards we are working on at the forefront of our thinking.

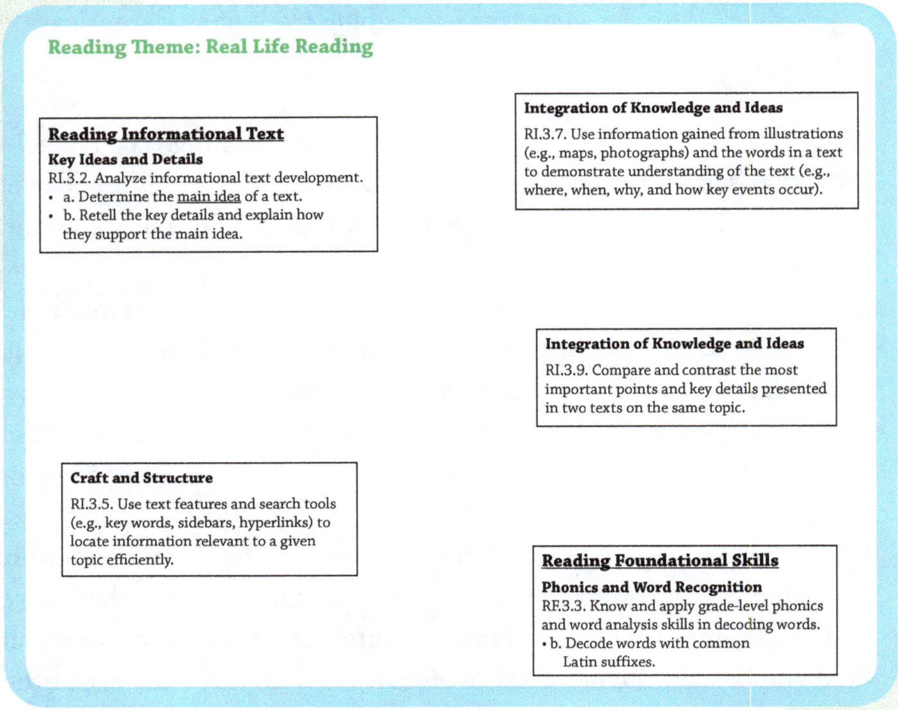

Reading Theme: Real Life Reading

Reading Informational Text
Key Ideas and Details
RI.3.2. Analyze informational text development.
• a. Determine the main idea of a text.
• b. Retell the key details and explain how they support the main idea.

Integration of Knowledge and Ideas
RI.3.7. Use information gained from illustrations (e.g., maps, photographs) and the words in a text to demonstrate understanding of the text (e.g., where, when, why, and how key events occur).

Integration of Knowledge and Ideas
RI.3.9. Compare and contrast the most important points and key details presented in two texts on the same topic.

Craft and Structure
RI.3.5. Use text features and search tools (e.g., key words, sidebars, hyperlinks) to locate information relevant to a given topic efficiently.

Reading Foundational Skills
Phonics and Word Recognition
RF.3.3. Know and apply grade-level phonics and word analysis skills in decoding words.
• b. Decode words with common Latin suffixes.

Figure 3.6 *An example of the standards planning and documentation tool for a unit that Lynsey uses to jot her notes daily.*

(Recall other examples of this tool in use from Chapter 2.) We use these forms during each reading time as a place to capture the language and behaviors students utilize as they relate to the standards. The tool includes the main standard we are working on at that point in time, as well as other standards that are related in some way.

We also use a name grid documentation sheet [Figure 3.7] as we observe our students daily. The name grid allows us to focus on each individual child. We jot down notes as related to standards we are working on as we teach. This form allows us to ensure that each individual reader is growing. It also allows us to see patterns across our class that help us plan whole-group instruction.

We have come to view our standards as tools to cultivate critical thinkers, analyzers, questioners, experts, and most importantly students who

Liya	Damian	Naomi	Jeremiah	Kenzie
Carina	Austen	Eli	Thiago	Lily
Lexi	Carter	Lorenzo	Chole	J.P.
Amari	Shanya	Atticus	Dave	Raelyn
Summer	Brahim	Benjamin	Hana	

Figure 3.7 *An example of a name grid from Lynsey's class.*

are free. In learning from revolutionaries such as Freire, hooks, and Souto-Manning we interpret free children in the classroom setting in this way:

* Free children will claim their identities.
* Free children will affirm each other.
* Free children will know they are part of a beloved community.
* Free children feel safe and loved.
* Free children will use their cultural legacies to discuss, debate, question, celebrate, connect, predict, conjecture, and respond during whole-group reading instruction.

Our understanding of Freire's work underpins our beliefs that learning standards, targets, and goals aren't delivered through the teacher, but rather they are negotiated between teacher and student.

CHAPTER 4

Getting to Know Books

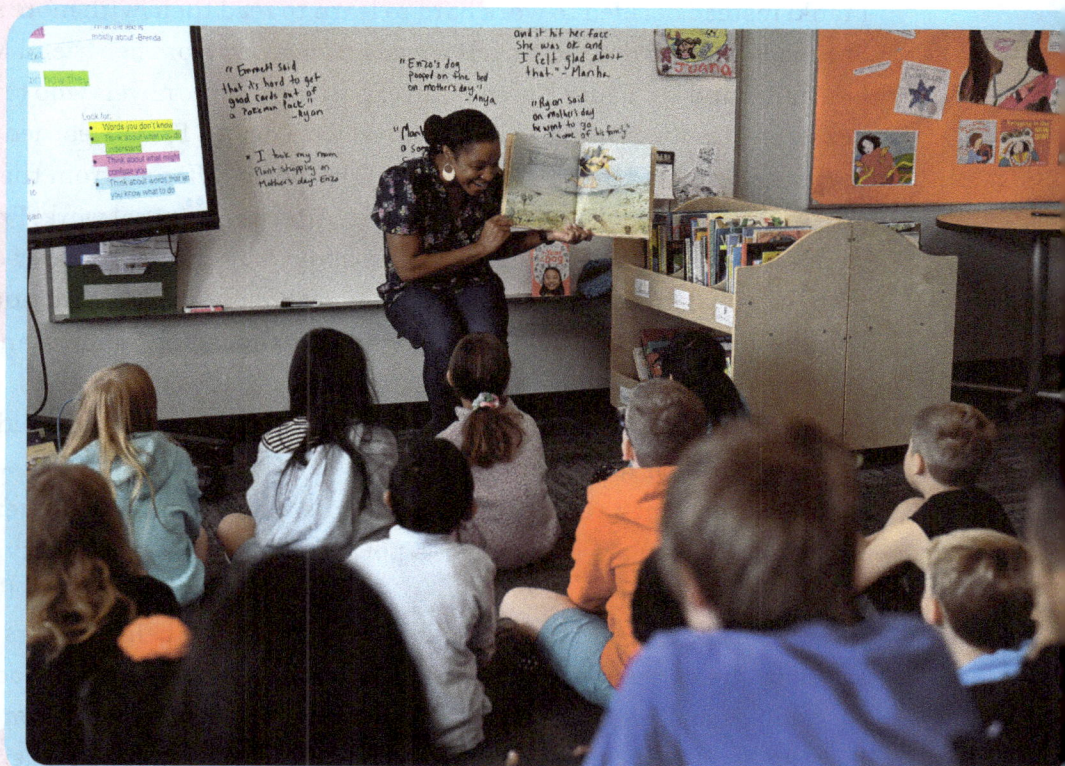

Each year, before the school year begins, Franki thinks about her identity as a reader. Although her reading history remains the same and she will always have fond memories of the Betsy books and the Nancy Drew series, each year things change about her reading preferences and practices. In 2010, Franki jotted down that "I occasionally enjoy science fiction and fantasy." But in 2021, when she was thinking about her reading, she realized *Klara and the Sun* by Kazuo Ishiguro, which she had recently read, was one of her favorite books of all time and it was science fiction. This insight changed what she was looking for in books.

Part of the power of thinking about our reading identities with students is that they can see that who we are as readers grows and changes. Not only do our tastes and preferences as readers change, but we also grow and change as readers by learning new things and setting new goals. For example, graphic novels are very difficult for Franki. She misses so much and gets easily frustrated. Years ago, rather than merely deciding, "I do not understand graphic novels, so I am not a graphic novel reader," Franki instead decided to work hard to learn to read them with more skill. She made reading graphic novels a goal and learned from her friend Mary Lee Hahn, and Dr. Laura Jiménez, an expert on graphic novels who taught her strategies for reading a graphic novel with depth. Franki learned that the way she approaches a graphic novel should be different from the way she would read a book with mostly words. After some initial work, Franki went on to read articles and learn more about ways to improve her comprehension when reading graphic novels. Although they are still not her favorite format, she is slowly getting better at reading, understanding and enjoying graphic novels and has read a few that she truly loves.

Franki shares this story with students because she wants her students to know that their reading identities grow and change over time. She wants them to know that a reader's identity is more than tastes and preferences. Knowing who you are as a reader is powerful as it gives you agency over your own reading life.

We share this story here because we believe that being readers ourselves is one of the most important parts of the job we have as teachers of reading, and we know that it takes commitment. Franki's commitment to her graphic novel goal was not made because she is a reader, but because she is a teacher of reading and being a teacher of reading requires

Figure 4.1   *The reading community reads and self-selects books based on what they know about themselves as readers.*

a commitment to reading widely for her students. We know reading for our students is critical when matching readers to books, but we also know it is essential when we are selecting books for instruction.

In *Game Changer!: Book Access for All Kids*, Donalyn Miller and Colby Sharp state, "As educators mentoring young readers, building our knowledge of books available for children and adolescents to read remains an ongoing part of our professional development" (2018, 76). And if we are serious about our students developing identities and agency as readers, then we must commit to being readers ourselves and understanding our own reader identities. When we do that, not only are we able to find the best books for our students but we include ourselves as part of the beloved reading community. The act of understanding our own identities allows teachers to be conscious of the way they facilitate learning and select books. This in and of itself is an intentional act to create an equitable beloved reading community.

When creating a beloved reading community that is centered around invitations and conversations students need a Menu of Mentors that will capture their attention. While students engage in the process of reading to learn they will need texts that reflect who they are and provide windows into worlds and communities with which they have not had experiences. Dr. Rudine Sims Bishop's transformational work on mirrors, windows, and sliding glass doors is work that we must rely on when choosing books for our classrooms (1990). Bishop teaches us that all readers need books that are mirrors into their own lived experiences. Books where readers can see themselves. Readers also need books that are windows into lived experiences and worlds they do not know. These types of books help to create empathy and a greater understanding of the world around them. Readers need windows, mirrors, and sliding glass doors to be able to learn from books and negotiate the world through literature.

Knowing Books Helps Us Be Responsive to Students

Mornings in Lynsey's classroom always begin with Talking Circles. Talking Circles are a time where students gather in small groups to talk to each other about various topics that arise in the community. One morning during Talking Circles Megha was really upset. She started saying, "They don't let us throw our colors."

She must have repeated this sentence three times until Daniel interjected, "Who won't let you throw your colors?" Megha shared that her family and other families in her apartment building were trying to celebrate Holi over the weekend and part of their celebration includes throwing colored powders up into the air. She told the circle of students that the office staff in her apartment building told the residents that they could not throw the colored powders on the community green space.

This conversation spread throughout the entire reading community as the students were really concerned about what happened to Megha and the other families. The conversation evolved to discussing this question: What holidays do you notice celebrated in the public spaces around us?

As Lynsey listened, she noticed that her students were really invested in this conversation, both as learners and as researchers. She also knew that her class was getting ready to think about the following literacy standards:

RI.3.2. Analyze informational text development. (a) Determine the main idea of a text. (b) Retell the key details and explain how they support the main idea.

RL.3.2. Analyze literary text development. (a) Determine a theme and explain how it is conveyed through key details in the text. (b) Retell stories, including fables, folktales, and myths from diverse cultures.

Knowing books helped Lynsey quickly pull together a set of texts from the classroom library to help students learn both the literacy skills in the upcoming unit and how to think critically about what is going on in the community. The texts she chose included:

* *Holi Colors* by Rina Singh
* *Holi Colors!* by Devin Jatkar
* *Crayola Holi Colors* by Robin Nelson
* *Holi Hai!* by Chitra Soundar
* *Festival of Colors* by Surishtha Sehgal
* *Let's Celebrate Holi* by Ajanta Chakraborty

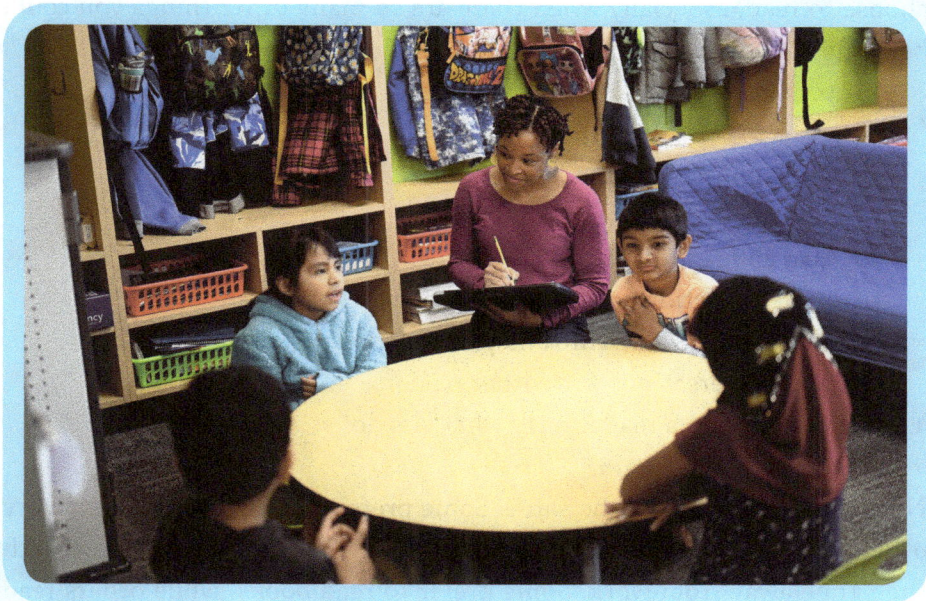

Figure 4.2 *Lynsey listens closely while students are having conversations.*

As reading teachers our specialty is knowing books and matching texts to readers and reading experiences. The books we choose to read with the whole class have the power to make reading instruction a humanizing and transformational practice.

A Personal Reading Identity

When it comes to planning and implementing whole-group instruction in which students are engaged, participating, and thinking together as readers, it is important that students see us—their teachers—as readers with our own personal reading identities. When we know our own reading history and our identity as a reader, we can teach more authentically because we know the joys and challenges that readers face. When we teach, our lessons feel like a community of readers engaged in the work they love rather than a teacher delivering a set of standards to students. When we are readers ourselves, we become a contributing member of our classroom community of readers.

As the "lead reader" in our classroom communities, one of the most important things we demonstrate to students is *why* it matters that people read. What is the value in reading? Think for a moment about *why* you choose to read, especially when there are so many other things you could be doing with your time.

If you are like most readers, you read:

* to learn about yourself,
* to learn about other people,
* to learn about the world,
* to answer questions and find out information,
* to reflect on your own life and your relationships with others,
* to have conversations with other readers,
* because you are a reader—it's what you do!

Now, not all readers are the same. Some prefer reading over almost every other activity! Some read a lot for work, but choose to do other things with their time away from work. Some prefer to read books, while others read just as voraciously but in shorter forms. Some read mostly to help them do other things they like to do—like cooking or gardening or tinkering with old cars.

The thing is, there's not just one way to be a reader, but if we want students to develop reading identities, then in addition to knowing *why* we read, it's also important to think about *who* we are as readers. Our students need us to show them what it means to have a strong reading identity, to know ourselves in that particular way.

To begin thinking about your own reading identity, consider that as readers all of us have histories, preferences, practices, and futures. Take a few moments to think about how well you know yourself in these different ways. And if you are reading this book with colleagues, you might use this exercise to help you think about how you are similar and different as readers.

Readers have histories:

* They have childhood memories of reading/storytelling, both inside and outside school.
* They know the best book they ever read, and the worst.
* They can recall texts that they thought about for years after finishing them.
* They have read enough to know their strengths as readers, and their needs.

Readers have preferences:

* for authors, genres, and topics,
* for fiction or nonfiction,
* for a strong character or a compelling plot,
* for places to read and times to read,
* for formats for reading (print, digital, audio),
* for length—books or shorter forms.

Readers have practices:

* Some reread great books.
* Some abandon boring books or articles.
* Some read with others (in book clubs).
* Some write notes in the margin.

* Some like to share what they're reading on social media.
* Some always read the book before they see the movie.

Readers have futures:

* They have books they know they want to read.
* They subscribe to newspapers and magazines.
* They read *about* books and anticipate new releases.
* They have goals.

Minding Our Gaps as Readers

Understanding who we are as readers is important for other reasons as well. In his book *Teacher and Child: A Book for Parents and Teachers*, Haim Ginott reminds us that teachers are the decisive element in the classroom—their approach shapes the learning, the environment, and the climate (1993). As teachers, then, our reading identity has the power to influence the books we choose to share with students, place in our classroom libraries, and use for instruction. We each have stories that we gravitate to and stories that we would not personally choose because they don't reflect our personal interests. But when we are selecting texts for whole-group instruction and read-aloud, we have to be mindful so that we don't merely select texts that reflect our own reading identities and personal preferences.

As teachers, we need to consider our own identities, and also the identities of other people in our community and the world when we select books for instruction: age, gender, race, religion, ethnicity, ability, language, socio-economic status, national origin, sexual orientation, marital status—basically any socio-cultural factor that might comprise a person's identity. To help us be mindful, we ask questions like these:

* Which of my own identities do I think about most often? Why? In what ways do they affect my daily life?
* What identities do I think about least often? Why?
* What identities that I hold are hard to acknowledge? Why?
* What identities do I want or need to learn more about? Why?

Now, think about how your own identities impact your teaching decisions. Take a moment to reflect on the last five texts you used for instruction or bought for your classroom library. Why did you choose those texts? What did you think about when selecting them? How much did your own identities influence the decisions you made?

≋ Classroom Story Box ≋

Lynsey

At a conference a few years ago, Lynsey came to the shocking conclusion that she was allowing her personal identities alone to guide the way she was selecting texts for whole-group instruction and read-aloud. At the conference the presenter asked each participant to complete a social identity wheel. While the purpose of this activity was not for teachers to think about the texts they select in their classrooms, Lynsey immediately made a connection to what she was learning and how it impacted her instruction as a reading teacher. As she reflected on her many personal identities, Lynsey began to understand how they were guiding many of her decisions about text selection. In her notebook Lynsey wrote:

As a Black, middle-aged mother of a girl and a boy, I have found myself buying books all about the experiences of Black children and people. I was on a relentless pursuit to make these types of stories available because these were the identities that I think about most often. But then I thought about all the other identities I was missing. Because I didn't often consider my identity as an English-speaking citizen of the United States, I didn't understand the impact it had on my students who weren't citizens or didn't use English as their first language. I experienced ability similarly. Being an able-bodied person wasn't something that I focused on as one of my identities, so my ability to search for and provide books that showed a range of ability both physically and emotionally was not always present.

Knowing Our Identities

In 2017 Lynsey attended a conference at The Ohio State University on Diversity and Race. One of the sessions led participants through assessing their own social identities. This process was powerful for Lynsey and upon reflection she began to see how this work could transform her practice. The social identity wheel exercise was created to help individuals identify and reflect on the identities they hold and how their identities intersect and shape the way they interact and are seen in the world. If Lynsey were to fill her wheel out today this is what it would look like:

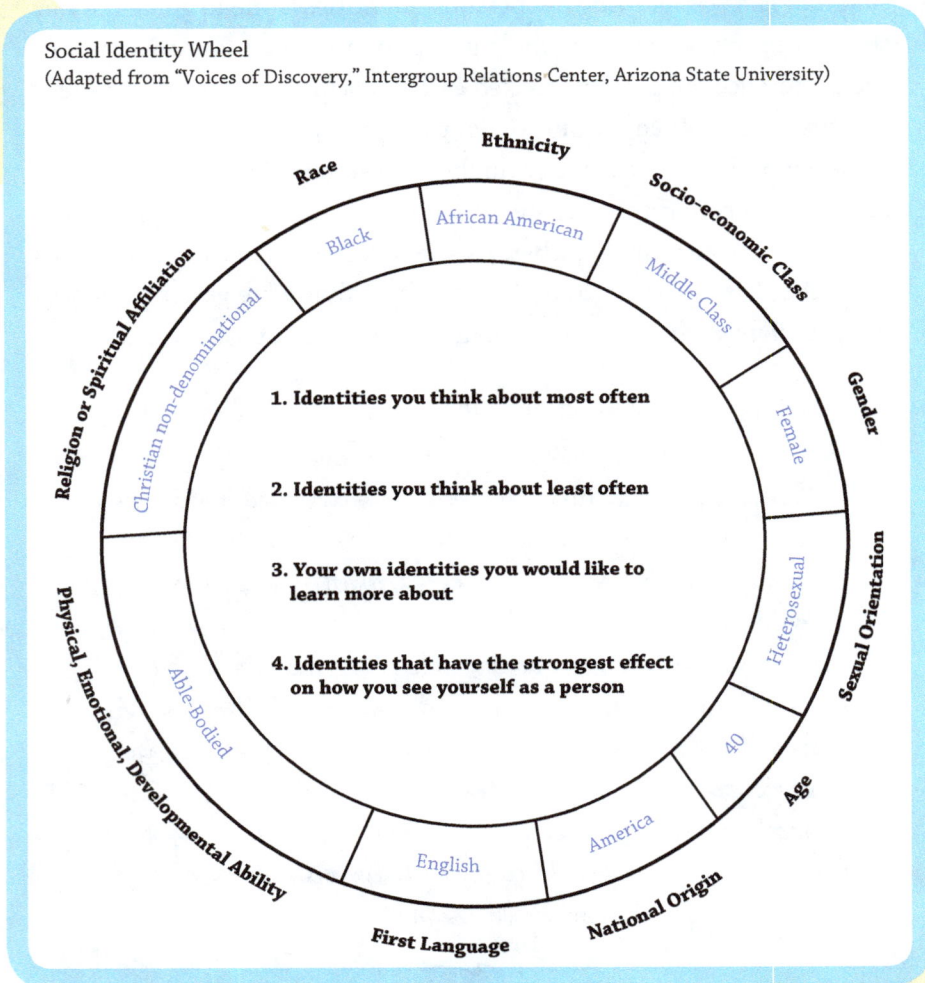

Social Identity Wheel
(Adapted from "Voices of Discovery," Intergroup Relations Center, Arizona State University)

Ethnicity
Race
Socio-economic Class
African American
Black
Middle Class
Religion or Spiritual Affiliation
Christian non-denominational
Female
Gender

1. Identities you think about most often

2. Identities you think about least often

3. Your own identities you would like to learn more about

4. Identities that have the strongest effect on how you see yourself as a person

Heterosexual
Sexual Orientation
Physical, Emotional, Developmental Ability
Able-Bodied
40
Age
English
America
First Language
National Origin

Figure 4.3 *Lynsey's identity wheel. See Appendix A for a blank copy of the identity wheel.*

As a teacher, the identities Lynsey thinks about most often are the ones she sees most in the work she does with her students. The identities she thinks about least often are the ones that she may not see in the work she does with children. For example, because Lynsey thinks often about her identity as a Black woman, she is more likely to include books that will help the reading community think about racial identities. However, as a cisgender, Christian, heterosexual woman married to a cisgender heterosexual man, Lynsey has not had to spend as much time reflecting on her own gender, sexual orientation, or religion. Living in a society that values and reinforces these identities as the norm means that Lynsey has never had to worry about not seeing families like her own or religious holidays she celebrates represented in books. As such, Lynsey needs to be much more intentional about reflecting on these parts of her identity and making sure she chooses books that represent the wide variety of identities and lived experiences in her classroom.

This reflection process keeps Lynsey looking for what she might be missing when it comes to diverse representation in the books she chooses for her class. She pays close attention when she's listening to students' stories. She thinks about the books she chooses and if they represent lived experiences and identities of the students in the reading community. The process of better understanding her own identities influences Lynsey's role in the classroom community as well as her actions in the classroom. This personal identity work is important for setting the tone for how we recognize students' lived experiences and identities in humanizing ways. Completing an identity wheel is something we both do periodically, and has been incredibly important to our work. We invite you to complete an identity wheel [Appendix A] as well and reflect on your full identity and how it impacts your reading and teaching life. Doing this work with trusted colleagues is transformational. This activity is not something we do one time, but instead we revisit this practice often.

Choosing the appropriate texts or sequence of texts for whole-group instruction has the power to engage or disengage readers. If we are guided too much by our own personal identities and reading preferences and we don't consider our students' carefully enough, then we may end up with a room full of disengaged readers who may never become passionate about their reading journey. Once we understand our own identity and our gaps, we can make more humanizing text choices that will encourage dialogue and understanding of the world in and beyond our reading community.

≋Classroom Story Box≋

Franki

One year, at the end of teaching third grade, Franki looked back at her display of read-alouds as a way to reflect on the year. Some books she had read aloud were:

Lulu and the Brontosaurus by Judith Viorst
The Meanest Birthday Girl by Josh Schneider
Leroy Ninker Saddles Up by Kate DiCamillo
Bink and Gollie by Kate DiCamillo
The Chicken Squad by Doreen Cronin
The Quirks: Welcome to Normal by Erin Soderberg
Tuesdays at the Castle by Jessica Day George
The Miraculous Journey of Edward Tulane by Kate DiCamillo
The Fenway Foul-Up by David Kelly
El Deafo by Cece Bell
The Terrible Two by Mac Barnett and Jory John
The Thing About Georgie by Lisa Graff
How to Steal a Dog by Barbara O'Connor
Rump by Liesl Shurtliff

As she looked over the list, Franki noticed some important things that worked well across the year:

* Franki began the year with several short series books that helped students learn to follow plot and also introduced them to several series they might read on their own.
* Several of the books invited quality conversations around real-world issues.
* The progression of books helped Franki's third graders learn to read with more depth.

> But Franki also noticed several gaps in the choices she had made that year:
>
> * There was little variety in the format of what she read. All were traditional chapter books (for example, Franki had read aloud only one graphic novel and no novels in verse).
> * Most of the main characters in the books Franki read aloud were female.
> * Every book was either fantasy or realistic fiction.
> * Every book was written by a white author.
> * Most of the authors of the books she read aloud were female.

Franki realized that many of the books she read aloud matched her own tastes and needs as a reader, but not necessarily her students' tastes and needs. There were gaps in her reading, and if she was committed to creating an inclusive classroom, Franki knew she needed to expand her own reading to include authors of different races, religions, ethnicities, genders, sexual orientations, national origins, languages, and abilities. Franki knew she needed to read more graphic novels, more nonfiction, more novels in verse, and more books with male main characters.

A Teacher-of-Reading Identity

Knowing ourselves as readers is important, but we are also teachers of reading, and that means we have to know our students as readers too. The lure of a ready-made book list that appears to perfectly fit the content of our next unit is real. But we don't teach books, we teach readers, and these alluring book lists are curated by someone who doesn't know our students. As teachers of reading, we spend time thinking about our students' reading identities and how their identities influence their learning. And then we have to be readers, avid *teacher* readers so we can carefully match our book selections to the needs and interests of the students in front of us.

> ## ⁝Tip Box⁝
> ## Tips for Reading Widely
>
> As teachers, fitting a lot of reading into an already busy life can be a challenge, even when we know it's the most important part of our planning. Here are some tips for reading widely based on our own experiences. Because we are teachers of reading, we:
>
> * take advantage of vacation time to read—#BookADay,
> * set aside an hour a week to read books and/or book reviews in journals and on social media,
> * listen to audiobooks on our way to and from work,
> * place books on hold at our local library the minute we hear about them,
> * make weekly trips to the local library to pick up a stack of books,
> * share books with each other,
> * read with children in our own families and our students,
> * keep books with us at all times so we can fit reading into small spaces in our day such as while waiting for appointments,
> * make reading a part of our daily life, even if we can only give it a few minutes on some days.

We have both been involved in the Build Your Stack® initiative of the National Council of Teachers of English (NCTE) since its inception. If you visit NCTE's Build Your Stack® webpage, it says:

> NCTE's members are readers—for themselves as they seek to grow their professional knowledge, and for their students as they seek to find texts that will inspire—because NCTE members know: *the right book in the right hands can transform a life.*

This is why we started Build Your Stack®, an initiative focused exclusively on helping teachers build their book knowledge and their classroom libraries.

(NCTE 2023)

We've come to rely on initiatives like Build Your Stack® and Disrupt Texts, an effort "to challenge the traditional canon in order to create a more inclusive, representative, and equitable language arts curriculum that our students deserve" started by four educators, Tricia Ebarvia, Lorena Germán, Dr. Kim Parker, and Julia Torres, to keep up with children's books (Ebarvia, Germán, Parker, and Torres, 2021). Here are some of our favorite resources and knowledgeable groups and individuals:

*   Professional reading (books and journals)
*   Blogs (Nerdy Book Club, Fuse #8)
*   Children's Book Review resources (*The Horn Book*)
*   Organizations such as We Need Diverse Books and the American Library Association
*   Individuals and groups who share on social media (@edicottonquilts @donalynbooks @booktoss_public, @dreese-nambe, #DisruptTexts, and #BuildYourStack)
*   Conversations with colleagues
*   School and local librarians

Filling Our Gaps as Readers

In order to know and recommend books to a diverse group of student readers, we often have to read outside our comfort zone. For example, even though we are not huge sports readers, both of us read Kwame Alexander's *The Crossover*, knowing it would be a book that would appeal to many of our students. (And how happy we were that we stretched ourselves because this book was about so much more than sports and we both fell in love with it.)

We reflect often on our own teacher–reader identities so that we are aware of the gaps in our reading, and then we turn to trusted sources to find out about books and help us fill those gaps. American Indians in

Children's Literature, a website founded by Dr. Debbie Reese, has been one of our most trusted sources in filling our gaps as readers (2022). We rely on the authors of this blog to support us in finding quality books written by Indigenous authors. We've also recently discovered the Hijabi Librarians, a blog that reviews children's books that feature Muslim characters and communities (2023). We are always working to find quality sources that help us discover books we may not otherwise find.

We are always aware of the gaps in our classroom library when it comes to language and accessibility. We try to keep track of whether a book we might read aloud or use in a minilesson is available in languages other than English. We also keep up with quality audio versions of books that would be worth sharing. We know that for our emerging bilingual students, having a copy of the read-aloud in their first language might be a good support. We also know audiobooks often support readers in a variety of ways. We follow awards like the Odyssey Award that help us keep up with incredible audiobooks for children.

Being Intentional About Reading Quality Books That Represent Our World

In any collection of books, whether it is a set used for whole- or small-group instruction or for our classroom libraries, readers need to experience themselves *and* others not quite like themselves in books. Dr. Rudine Sims Bishop's work has been instrumental in helping us make this a reality. She writes:

> We DO need diverse books. We need diverse books because all our children deserve to know that they have a voice in the choir that sings the song of America. When diversity is absent from the literature we share with children, those who are left out infer that they are undervalued in our society, and those whose lives are constantly reflected gain a false sense of their own importance, a sense that they are the privileged "norm."
>
> (2016, 120)

So, how do we find quality books for our read-alouds and minilessons with diverse representations that are engaging and culturally authentic? Lee

& Low Books (2019a) offers these reflective questions that help us think about book choices:

* Do you have books that are written or illustrated by a person of color or a Native/Indigenous person?
* Are there books that explore different socio-economic backgrounds?
* Can you use your books to teach about Black/African American contributions to the United States beyond the Civil Rights Movement?
* Do you have books that feature characters with different types of gender identity and gender expression?
* Are there books that are written in languages meaningful to your students' backgrounds or the community in which they live?

These five questions help us continuously reflect on the books and resources we share with our students. We would also add a few more:

* Do you have books that represent abilities and disabilities? Physical, neuro and emotional?
* Do you have books that have characters of various faiths?
* Do you have books that depict both incidental representation and issue-based representation? Check out the textbox on pages 102–103 for more on incidental diversity.

Additionally, Lee & Low Books has a great online resource for teachers called the Classroom Library Questionnaire to help you reflect and take action around these questions (2017).

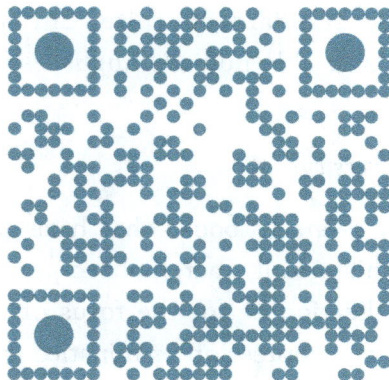

Another resource around these issues is Tricia Ebarvia's blog post "How Inclusive Is Your Literacy Classroom Really?" (2017). This blog post includes several important questions for teachers around this work.

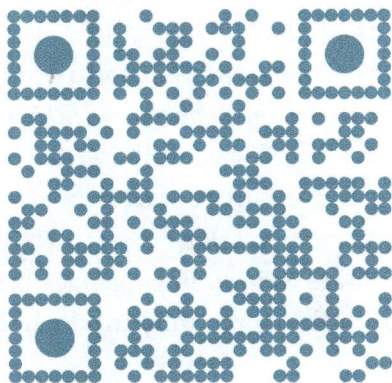

We find all of these resources helpful in ensuring we are intentional about the books we put in our classroom libraries and the books we use for whole-class instruction.

Incidental Diversity

What does diversity mean when thinking about books?

When the word diversity is used in the context of children's books, it is important to define what we mean by this term. In this context, diverse refers to any lived experience that departs from the socialized standard of white, Christian, cisgendered, straight, middle-class, able-bodied, English-speaking, American nationality.

What is incidental diversity?

Incidental diversity refers to books that have characters and storylines that depict historically marginalized people or communities but whose marginalization is not the focus of the book. The storyline is not about the oppression or injustice that the community has historically faced or currently faces. The story features Black, Indigenous, and people of color (BIPOC), linguistically diverse, religiously diverse, and/or gender non-conforming characters in their everyday life.

Why do we need books with incidental diversity?

While we do need books that teach us about injustices and histories of all people, we also need books that show communities of people experiencing the human experience of everyday life. Having both types of books prevent children from only seeing characters and people in one way. For example, if students only saw Black characters in books that deal with racism, then some students may start to form inaccurate assumptions about a group of people. Books featuring incidental diversity allow for all children to see people and communities in ways that connect across the human experience.

How do we determine if a story depicts diversity in incidental ways?

When we are reading a book, we think about:

1. Does the story feature characters from a community that has been marginalized?
2. Does the storyline acknowledge the main character's identity in some way, but the story and themes are not focused on trauma facing that community?

If we can answer yes to those questions then typically we consider the book an incidental diversity book.

When it comes to choosing books for whole-group instruction, we think about the identities of our students and of our class as a whole. Using books that represent our world has become even more critical as we strive to develop well-rounded literate students. Aspects of identity such as language, culture, ability, race, religion, and all the many types of identities we hold as humans should be present in the books we use throughout the year in both incidental and informational ways.

Reading with a Teacher's Lens

When we are reading books that we may use in our classrooms, we read with a teacher's lens. We pay attention to the topic and ideas or story, but we also are paying attention to all the ways the book could invite important conversations for our readers. We are considering how our students may experience the book as they read it, keeping track of the things that make the book both accessible and also challenging. Let's take a look at that process in action.

Reading with a Teacher Lens

Ask Yourself...	Consider...
What questions would this book raise? What connections might my students have to it?	Think about how the text builds on or connects to other books you've read or ways it might connect to the lives of your students.
What information or ideas in this book might stretch my students as readers?	Look for what might be new and challenging to your students' thinking.
How does the author, their work, and their identity impact students' reading experience?	Does the author depict the story in an authentic way from their own lived experiences?
	Is this an author who has written other books that the students have read or might want to read in the future?
Does the book include an author's note?	When authors communicate directly with readers it adds an important layer of meaning to the main text.
How is the book structured and what does it require of readers?	Is it a sequential narrative, a book told through different perspectives, a piece that includes both text and visuals, etc.?

(Continued)

Ask Yourself...	Consider...
How does this book engage readers at different places in their development?	Is there a plot or big idea that will be easy for readers to follow? Are there ways for students who are ready to read more deeply and go beyond literal comprehension and main idea?
What skills are needed to understand this book?	Consider length, stamina required, level of inferring required, background knowledge.
What features does the book include?	Are there chapter titles, a table of contents, visual contents, different text formats, etc.?

≡Classroom Story Box≡

Lynsey

Figure 4.4   *The community reads* When Langston Dances *together.*

Lynsey remembers the first time she read *When Langston Dances*, written by Kaija Langley and illustrated by Keith Mallett, to her class. The book is about a child impacted by the world's limited view of gender. Lynsey remembers reading it first through her own personal lens and the thoughts it provoked in her as a mother of two Black children, a Black woman, a friend, a wife, a teacher, a daughter, a forty-ish-year-old, and again a Black mother. Then she read it again, and started thinking about her students. What might *they* see in a book like this? Recently, Lynsey had recorded student comments on her recording sheet and the community's whiteboard as they talked around gender and tried to make sense of what they were seeing and hearing in the world around them. She used their comments to reflect on what they might see in this book in particular.

* Langley writes Langton's story in third person.
* Langley's words take readers through Langston's inner thoughts, while Langston's mother's thoughts and experiences are largely revealed through Keith Mallett's illustrations.
* Langley and Mallett rely heavily on the interplay between the words and illustrations to tell Langston's story.

During a whole-group reading minilesson Lynsey focused on the reading standard, "Ask and answer questions to demonstrate understanding of a text, referring explicitly to the text as the basis for the answers," a standard that the class had worked on a few days prior (Ohio Department of Education 2017). A conversation in Lynsey's classroom broke out around this book:

Harper: See, the kid just said, "Boys don't dance like that." Why would he say that? Can you write that down as my wonder on this page? I want us to talk about that, Mrs. Burkins!

X'Zayvier: Harper, I know why he said that. He said that because we don't see boys dance like that all the time. I mean, do you?

Lynsey: I think we have lots to think about here. How can we together co-create a larger question that helps us study this text to understand both why that character might have said those words and X'Zayvier's thinking about what we see in our world?

Lynsey knew there were so many questions her readers would want to explore and connections they might make to the story and its characters. She knew the theme of the book tied seamlessly to both the standard around engaging in thinking about how characters overcome major events and the standard around questioning. She knew based on who her students were as readers at the time that this would be the perfect whole-group instruction book.

≶Classroom Story Box≶
Franki

One summer, Franki was reading middle-grade novels searching for new possibilities for her teaching. As she read *Operation Frog Effect* by Sarah Scheerger through her reading teacher lens, she jotted down notes to help her decide whether to read this book aloud at some point during the school year. Franki noticed:

* The story is told through several perspectives, which might make keeping track of the plot and characters challenging for fifth graders. However, it ties in nicely to the standards on perspective in reading and writing.
* The story is told through journal entries which are written and drawn by a variety of characters. Each entry requires something different from the reader to build understanding.
* There are some visuals throughout the book so this would be a good way to talk about the ways readers combine information from text and visuals when reading fiction.
* The book takes on issues (friendship, homelessness, immigration) that seem appropriate and interesting for fifth graders to discuss with each other.

* The title of the book is meaningful and is mentioned a few times in the context of the book. This might invite discussion about how a title often gives readers a clue into the theme of a book.
* The problem and solution of this book are clear and easy to spot— should be easy for readers to follow.
* Characters face both internal and external conflicts.
* The book is 320 pages long, but because of the unique format, there is not always a lot of text on a page so this seems like it would be an average length read-aloud.

Keeping Track of What We Read

It is hard to keep track of all that we read (especially when it comes to books we borrow from the local library and then no longer have at our fingertips to return to) but we need a system to keep track of our teacher-as-reader reading in order to build our Menu of Mentors for instruction. Without a system that is easy to revisit, we tend to fall back on those books we've used before instead of finding the books that would work best for this class at this time.

While there are lots of different tracking options, Franki uses Goodreads both to log her reading and to make notes of things she notices with her teacher lens. In the app, she creates "shelves" that are specific to minilesson topics. For example when she read the book *Ojiichan's Gift* by Chieri Uegaki, she put it on both her "picture book" shelf and her "minilesson-theme" shelf. When she read *Her Fearless Run: Kathrine Switzer's Historic Boston Marathon* written by Kim Chaffee and illustrated by Ellen Rooney, she tagged it as nonfiction, biography, and picture book in her Goodreads account. When planning for whole-class instruction, Franki can search through her shelves on the Goodreads app in a variety of ways to help remember all of the books that might work for teaching a specific idea or skill.

Our Commitment as Teacher Readers

When we reflect on our commitment to being teachers who read, we stand on the shoulders of Dr. Rudine Sims Bishop who said:

> When children cannot find themselves reflected in the books they read, or when the images are distorted, negative, or laughable, they learn a powerful lesson about how they are devalued in the society of which they are a part. Our classrooms need to be places where all children from all the cultures that make up the salad bowl of American society can find their mirrors.
>
> (1990, ix-x)

We are committed to discovering and using books in our classrooms that reflect our community. And we are also committed to finding books that support readers as they grow and change. In planning whole-class instruction we read widely so that we can rely on books that honor our students' lived experiences while also engaging them in the important work of reading.

CHAPTER 5

Getting to Know Your Students by Listening with Love and Intention

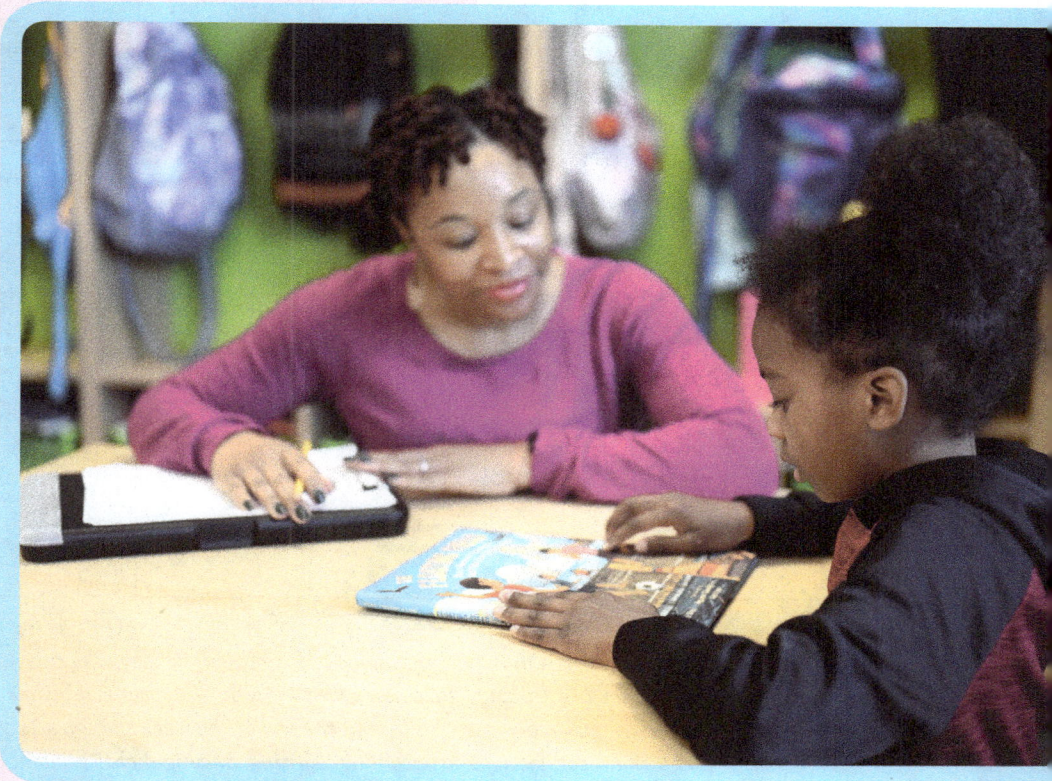

As Lynsey's third-grade students entered the classroom one morning, Carter announced to the class that it was Earth Month. "Earth Month? Is that like Earth Day?" asked Jackie. As the buzz grew with students asking questions and sharing what they knew, Lynsey suggested they use this topic for their morning Talking Circles. Carter wrote the topic on the whiteboard and the class knew exactly what to do—they settled into their Talking Circles of four or five students, spread out in areas around the room, and continued their spirited discussions about Earth Month.

As Lynsey walked around the room listening to each group, she heard Tracy say to her group, "Let me go grab my Chromebook so we can look up Earth Month." Lynsey then moved on to watch Anya and her group write questions on sticky notes about taking care of our Earth. As Lynsey continued to move about the room listening to the small-group conversations,

Week of: April 11				Unit/Area: O/Talking Circles
Student 1	Student 2 "I don't know why kids don't like video games."	Student 3	Student 4 "We found a kitten at our door last night."	Student 5 "Why did they change it to Earth Month?"
Student 6 "What do you do if you find a kitten just sitting there?"	Student 7	Student 8 "Did you guys know that it's Earth month not Earth Day?"	Student 9 "My mom's car wouldn't start this morning."	Student 10 "What books did you order this time?"
Student 11	Student 12 "How can anyone not know about plastic in our ocean?"	Student 13	Student 14 "Wait who changed it to Earth month?" "We should do something for it."	Student 15 "The second graders take the breakfast and they don't even eat it."
Student 16	Student 17	Student 18 "I can't wait to see my cousins this weekend. We are having a party."	Student 19	Student 20

Figure 5.1 *Lynsey's notes from the Earth Month conversation. Lynsey uses this tool to keep her Talking Circle notes for the week. She records multiple conversations on one sheet so that at the end of the week she can study it and look for connections to upcoming learning. She highlights student quotes that she can use with the whole class to extend learning.*

she documented their thinking on her clipboard before adding these notes to the whiteboard.

The Talking Circle routine is one way we make time and space for intentional listening in our classrooms. For Talking Circles (or any routine) to be impactful, it is important that the classroom is set up for authentic talk. You might be wondering what small-group Talking Circles have to do with whole-class reading instruction. As Lynsey took notes on these Talking Circle conversations [Figure 5.1] she was also thinking about how her students' words and ideas connected to the informational text reading standards she planned to focus on in the upcoming unit. Later Lynsey used the highlighted notes alongside these standards to plan a Menu of Mentors and whole-group reading instruction. All this planning and thinking about whole-group reading instruction was grounded in listening to and knowing students.

Creating the Conditions for Listening in a Beloved Learning Community

In her book *Teaching to Transgress: Education as the Practice of Freedom*, bell hooks writes, "To teach in a manner that respects and cares for the souls of our students is essential if we are to provide the necessary conditions where learning can most deeply and intimately begin" (1994, 13). In the classroom, one of these necessary conditions for learning is teacher listening. And in order for listening to inform our teaching, it is critical that children are free to be their authentic selves in the classroom. The community must value and support every individual as both a human being and an intellectual learner. Let's explore some of the pillars of pedagogy that can help us cultivate these necessary conditions for children to be free and for us, as teachers, to listen.

Listen in Culturally Responsive Ways

Whole-group reading instruction must be equity-minded, culturally relevant, and use anti-racist and anti-bias pedagogies. It must be anchored around listening with a lens of love. Whole-group reading instruction is a critical piece of our instruction because it brings the entire reading community together to learn. Students in our classrooms may come from different backgrounds, multiple languages, ethnicities, races, family structures, gender, socio-economic statuses, religious affiliations, and other identities that make the group diverse. Some classrooms may seem to be less diverse. In these classrooms it is just as important for our instruction to be equity-minded, culturally relevant, and use anti-racist and anti-bias pedagogies. As literacy teachers, we must help all students become literate as they read and write their world. Listening as love, a genuine care about the words and actions of each child, has the power to shift whole-group reading instruction from a teacher-centered activity to a co-created reading community to which children are able to bring their whole selves. When we model listening as love, children experience being seen and heard as their whole selves. They in turn learn that every child is an important member of the community and that every member should be free to be their whole self.

Use an Asset-Based Approach to Listening

In order to be the kind of listeners who can be responsive teachers, it is important that we listen with an asset-based lens. That means we are always listening to learn and understand all that our children *can* do and all of the brilliance they share. It is important that we honor and celebrate each reader and what they bring to the community. It is also important that each and every member of the classroom community has opportunities to grow from where they are. Our main goals as teacher listeners are to:

* Listen with a researcher stance
* Listen with genuine curiosity and wonder
* Seek to understand children's ideas based on what each child knows and brings to the community at a particular time
* Listen in order to make connections to student thinking and the curriculum
* Listen in order to amplify the thinking of students

Develop a Researcher Stance

In order to know our students, we must listen more than we speak. Deep listening depends on the teacher remaining quiet and making space for student talk. While it is impossible to completely set aside our own biases and personal motivations, we can continually grow as listeners who are curious about children's ideas and believe they are worthy of our consideration. Whole-group reading instruction is a time when we, as teachers, make our genuine love for our students apparent by listening with a curiosity void of any deficit thinking. We are listening in order to plan responsively. We do this by:

* Quieting inner thoughts that may stray to deficit thinking
* Watching students' body language as a way of understanding them
* Listening for how students are interpreting what is happening in a book and what is being discussed around them
* Recording exactly what students say, without any of our own interpretations
* Recording what you see
* Asking and recording your own teacher questions (but separating your questions from your listening data—keep them off to the side from the student data)
* Creating a system for coding who said what so you can make your note-taking a quick and efficient part of your regular practice

Creating Predictable Routines and Structures for Listening

Samantha Bennett wrote in *That Workshop Book*, "If a teacher is constantly pursuing the answers to 'How do I know?' the school day builds around what comes out of the mouths, pencils, and actions of students instead of what comes out of the mouths of teachers" (2007, 6). Building the school day around what students are saying rather than what teachers are doing requires that teachers build structures that allow them to listen to students and record the information they see and hear. Let's take a look at some of the classroom routines and structures that make space for teachers to listen with love and intention.

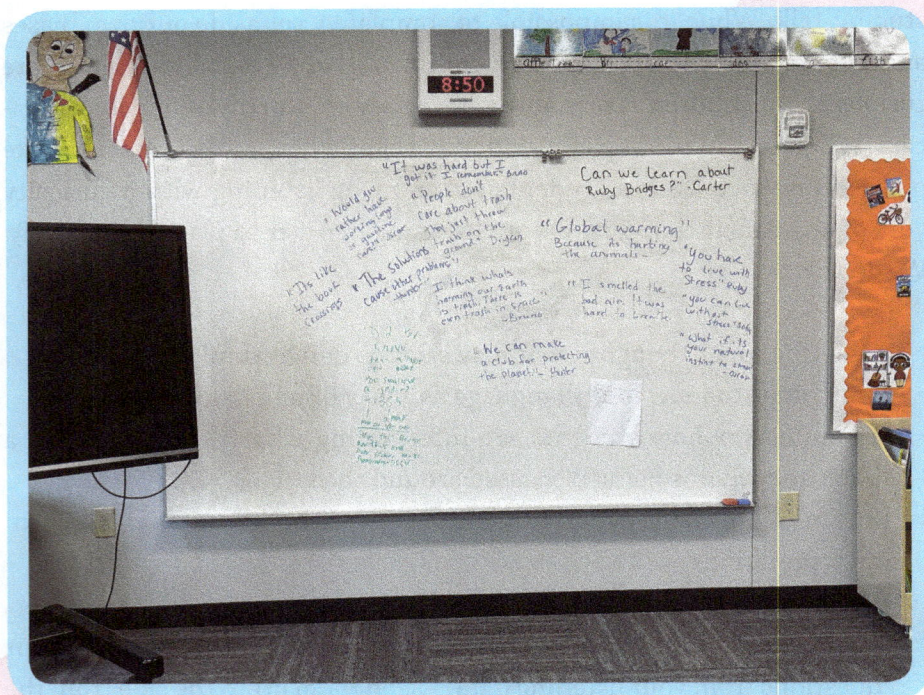

Figure 5.2 *Capturing students' thinking while they talk is a regular routine in Lynsey's classroom. She uses the whiteboard located front and center in the classroom to capture students' quotes throughout the day. This whiteboard becomes a visual anchor for their thinking, a place to return to again and again as they revisit a topic or idea. This photo captures notes from Earth Month Talking Circles.*

Talking Circles

As you read about at the beginning of this chapter, Talking Circles are a daily practice that occur at the start of each day in Lynsey's classroom. Small groups of students gather in circles around the room. Some groups sit on the floor, while others pull together chairs or other furniture to make a circle. Some days, the conversation is open to anything on the children's minds. Lynsey says, "Share what's on your heart." Other days, Lynsey invites conversation with an open-ended prompt such as asking students to respond to a quote. Lynsey often uses a quote that a student said in the class or sometimes she presents a situation that happened at school for students to discuss. Later in the year, the students themselves begin to suggest topics for Talking Circles.

> ## ≈Tip Box≈
>
> ## Questions We Ask Ourselves During Talking Circles
>
> Talking Circles is one routine that allows us to listen to students and to use what we hear to plan instruction. During Talking Circles, we ask ourselves these questions as we listen:
>
> * Is this topic something most children might experience or have experienced?
> * Do the other children ask a lot of questions about this topic?
> * Does there seem to be buzz around what the student is saying?
> * Are there ways to integrate this conversation into the learning standards?

During Talking Circles the teacher looks and listens for:

* Topics discussed among the groups
* Shifts in topic and who makes the shifts
* Physical behaviors students exhibit
* Curiosities, wonders, confusions, and passions shared
* Engagement during the conversation and what engaged/disengaged students

Turn and Talk Partners

While turn and talk is not a new practice, it remains a powerful one worthy of our focus. During whole-group reading lessons, the teacher may pause to give students the opportunity to turn and talk with a partner in order to process the learning. While teachers often use turn and talk time to listen for evidence of students' understanding, this is also a time for teachers to engage in even deeper listening. Listening for power relationships, listening for perspectives, listening for connections, listening for unintended biases that arise, listening for any information that will connect the literature, standards, and how the students are understanding the world around them.

At the beginning of a lesson cycle on synthesizing information, Franki shared a book with her class about Native American history. During the turn and talk, one group talked about how Native Americans either "lived in the woods" or "were no longer here." After the turn and talk, when the students shared this idea with the whole group, many in the class agreed. Franki listened and understood that most children in the class had a huge misconception that Native Americans were people who lived only in the past. So instead of proceeding as planned, Franki chose a new Menu of Mentors featuring contemporary stories with Native American characters as well as biographies of Native Americans such as *Mission to Space* by John Herrington. She continued her plan to focus on synthesis across texts, but realized after listening to turn and talks during that first lesson that she needed to change the books she had planned to use.

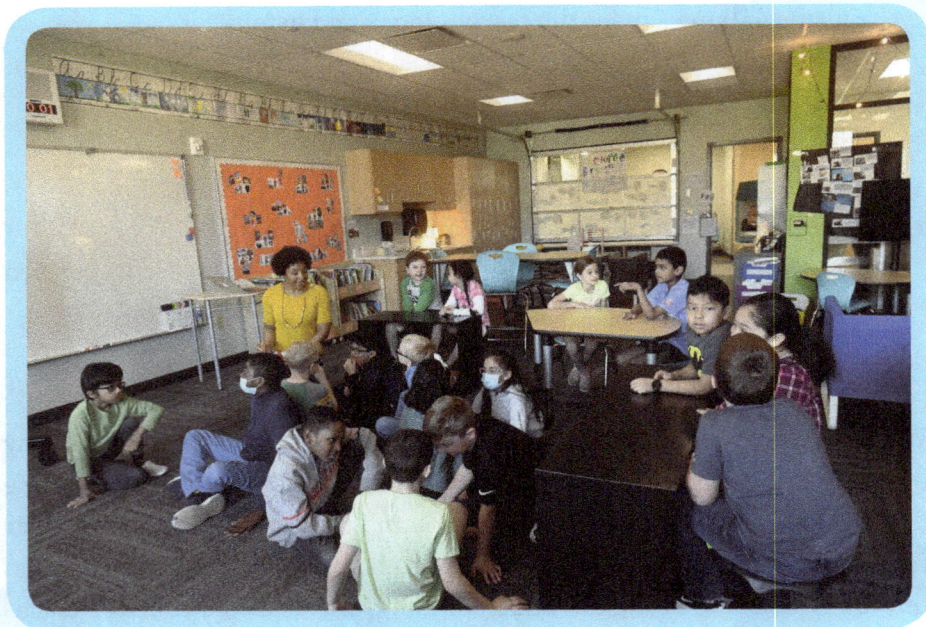

Figure 5.3 *Students turn and talk during a reading minilesson.*

Thought Partners

Thought Partners are similar in some ways to turn and talk partners in that they both consist of two students discussing reactions to content. Unlike turn and talk partners in which students talk to whomever they happen to be sitting by during a particular lesson, Thought Partners are longer term thinking relationships. When Thought Partners can think together over time, the conversation can go deeper and become more interconnected. As Thought Partners converse during whole-group instruction there is a rich opportunity for teachers to collect data. The information that teachers collect as they listen to Thought Partners will be used to guide whole-group instruction moving forward. This information will allow teachers to plan lessons and find mentor texts that recognize the interests, cultures, and identities of the students in front of them.

Thought Partners usually meet during a segment of whole-class instruction. For example, Franki often assigned Thought Partners for read-aloud so that fifth graders had one partner to talk to throughout the entire book. There are other times that we assign Thought Partners across a series of minilessons. For example, when fifth graders in Franki's class were comparing themes across several picture books on the same topic across multiple days, Thought Partners made sense. However, when thinking about how a character changed in a single picture book, turn and talk worked best. We think it's important that children have multiple people to talk to across the school year in order to expand perspectives so the Thought Partners are relatively short term.

Reading Interviews and Conferences

Making time for individual reading interviews is especially important early in the school year. In a workshop model, beginning-of-the-year reading interviews set the stage for the kind of one-on-one conversations about books and reading we will have through our reading conferences all year long. But regardless of your model for reading instruction, it is always critical to begin the school year by talking to our students about their lives as readers. Reading interviews are an opportunity to do this work. Through these reading interviews we set the stage by listening to all a child wants to share about their reading life. We begin with a set of questions but our hope is that the reading interview becomes a natural conversation between two readers, with some of these questions merely serving as a starting place.

Some questions we might ask to begin a reading interview:

* What types of books do you like?
* What types of books do you not like?
* Is there a series that you enjoy?
* Where do you read when you are at home?
* Do you have a favorite time of day to read?
* In which language do you prefer to read?
* Where do you get books that you read at home?
* Who do you talk to about books? Who recommends books to you?
* What kinds of things do the people in your family read?
* Do you have a favorite author?
* Do you prefer paper or digital books?
* Do you enjoy audiobooks?
* Do you read any blogs or websites on a regular basis? If your answer is yes, how often?

Often when we share our reading interview work, teachers suggest that a more efficient way to gather this data is to have students fill it out on a digital form. Although that would be more efficient, we find that sitting alongside a child and talking about their reading life is an experience that has so much value. Not only do we set the stage for a year of conversations but the child can see how genuinely interested we are in their thinking by our responses and nonverbals. Reading interviews also gives us one of our first opportunities to bring children's words to whole-class lessons. For example, we might bring in the words of Travis, who said he liked graphic novels. We can use his words to invite others in the class to share why they like graphic novels. This move allows us to amplify Travis's words while also helping the class as a whole think more deeply about their reading tastes and preferences. This beginning-of-the-year minilesson also helps us begin to define the format of graphic novels as a class. We think the time spent on reading interviews early in the year is well worth it!

Using Reading Interviews and Conferences as a Tool to Plan Whole-Class Reading Instruction

During reading interviews, we listen with several things in mind. We want to get to know each child as a reader—tastes, goals, challenges, and attitudes—but, more importantly, we want them to know that we value who they are as a reader at this moment. Reading interviews are also one of the first ways our students know how much we value their words. Later, when we recommend books or connect readers with similar interests, students will remember that we listened to who they are as readers and took their words seriously.

We also use reading interviews as an opportunity to listen for patterns across students. We listen for both readers' interests and misconceptions that we might use as a springboard for future minilesson work. For example, one year Franki noticed that many of her students mentioned wanting to read "fatter books." It became clear that many in this group of readers believed that books with more pages were more valuable. Franki kept that current understanding in mind as she shared books and thinking with the goal of helping students begin to expand their ideas of what makes a book worthy.

Reading interviews become the starting point for individual conversations across the year in which it is our job to listen without judgment, to value every piece of how each child sees themselves as a reader, and to bring the understandings we gain to our whole-class teaching. During these first interviews, we learn about the kinds of support different readers may need during whole-group instruction. During these interviews we often learn that some readers prefer to have a copy of the book in their hands as we read aloud or like to reread on their own after read-aloud time. We also learn the language in which our readers are most comfortable reading. These questions are a starting point for getting to know a reader but, most importantly, they open up conversations so our readers can give us insights into their needs and how we can support them during whole-group reading instruction.

We value this one-on-one time with students to talk about their reading lives. Our whole-group work is designed to help our students become strong, independent readers who are part of a reading community. Reading conferences help us see how the work we are doing in whole-class instruction is transferring to independent reading. They also give us insights into new patterns in students' reading that might help us plan upcoming minilessons and read-aloud work.

> ≋Tip Box≋
> # All Book Talk Counts!
>
> We don't only count the conferences we have during the reading work-shop. Over the years, we've noticed that many of the most important conversations we have with students about their reading happen out-side of the workshop time. Often, on our way to lunch, a child men-tions a new book they started. Or on the playground during recess a child approaches us to talk about a confusing spot in a book they are reading. Every conversation we have with a child about their reading *counts* and can inform our teaching.

Noticing and Naming as a Routine

Our language matters. We are intentional about our listening and we are just as intentional about the language we use to respond to our students' words. We are careful to use words that support our readers in a variety of ways. Here are a few examples of the intentional ways we respond to students' words:

Actions We Take as Active Listeners When Responding to Students	Words We May Use
We summarize several pieces of a conversation.	*What I hear you saying is...Did I get that right?*
We connect the words to the student who spoke them.	*I heard Carla say...*
We use content-specific vocabulary to name what children are doing/noticing as readers.	*Oh, you think the author is foreshadowing and giving us a clue about what might happen later.*

(Continued)

Actions We Take as Active Listeners When Responding to Students	Words We May Use
We connect students' words to specific vocabulary that is written in the standard.	*Wow! That is such an important detail about the character.*
We redirect or refocus the conversation when needed.	*Tomorrow, let's pay attention to the key ideas and details that will help us understand the characters better.*
We balance reading with student talk.	*I am going to read some more to see if we get an answer to the questions you've raised.*
We invite students to share places in the text that made them pause.	*I noticed you wrote something down when I read this page…Would you like to share what you wrote?*
We bring turn and talk conversations to the whole group.	*When I was sitting with Blair and Tyler, they had some new insights into the meaning of the title of our book. Blair and Tyler, would you share your thoughts with us?*
We invite children to jot down their own independent thinking.	*Take a second to capture your thinking about that in your notebook.*
We acknowledge student thinking as interesting and we let students know we are learning from them.	*It is so interesting to me…*
We stop and give the group time to think and talk about important ideas shared.	*Can I pause us for a moment and give us a minute to think specifically about what Hunter just said?*
We share our genuine noticings as a teacher with the class.	*I got a glimpse into what you are thinking.* *Or* *Here is what fascinates me about your thinking today…*

(Continued)

Actions We Take as Active Listeners When Responding to Students	Words We May Use
We connect the whole-group conversation to students' independent reading.	*Today, I invite you as a reader to look for ways the setting is important to the book you are reading on your own.*
We revisit pieces of the book that connect to the reading we are doing.	*Wow! Did anyone notice that those words were similar to the words used on the dedication page?*

Student Annotation as Routine

We rely heavily on student annotations to truly listen to students' ideas about what they are reading. We learn so much when our readers make their thinking visible. We define annotations here as the thinking readers do *while* they are reading a text. This is different from a reading response that usually happens *after* reading. Our students have learned that annotation is any written response during the reading, which *might* be writing or sketching directly on a text or it might just be making a note about the reading on a separate document.

Capturing in-the-moment thinking is one of the most important strategies readers have to build deep understanding. But annotations are not authentic or worthwhile when they are controlled by the teacher. When students are given a rigid graphic organizer, a series of questions or strict requirements for annotation, they are not free to record their true thinking. In order for the annotations to be truly authentic, students must have the power to determine the tool and the format that makes the most sense for the moment. So we are intentional about having many tools available for student annotations.

We are also intentional about using a variety of tools when annotating together as a class so that readers can see the ways different tools work and support understanding. There is no one tool that always works and we want our readers to be thoughtful about the tools they use and how they use them. Let's take a deeper look at some of the tools we invite students to use as they annotate.

Annotation Tool	Our Thoughts on Why We Use Them
Reading Notebooks	We have moved to using a blank notebook as we find that this gives children more freedom to think about the decisions they make when organizing their thinking.
Sticky Notes	Readers use sticky notes in a variety of ways. They can be placed directly on the text or they can be added to a poster or chart along with other students' thinking. Students often use sticky notes in their notebooks to gather thinking around a text.
Felt Tip Pens	We've found that felt tip pens are a great tool for writing about reading as the fine tip allows readers to write and also to use the various colors to code different kinds of thinking.
Highlighters	Readers use highlighters of various colors when they have access to text they can mark up or when they go back to their own annotations to make more sense of their own thinking around a text.
Google Slides	This digital tool allows teachers to gather student comments around an idea. Google Slides is also something available to readers both at school and at home so thinking can be added and reflected upon at any time.

(Continued)

Annotation Tool	Our Thoughts on Why We Use Them
Padlet	Padlet is another digital tool that allows readers to respond to a text and to also "listen in" on other readers' thinking by reading their words. As with Google Slides, this annotation tool is available when children are away from the classroom.
Kindle Annotation Tools	Because we want our readers to see how tools like highlighters and sticky notes can be used in digital form when reading an ebook, we often use the Kindle annotation tools during read-alouds and minilessons to make whole-class thinking visible.
Charts	We use a variety of charts as spaces to record students, thinking about texts. These may be paper or digital charts and they serve as a way to keep track of our collective thinking around a text over time.
Book Preview Posters	For each book we read aloud, we make some type of preview poster or chart. This can be digital or print and it captures the community's initial thinking about the text before we begin to read the book. This poster remains visible throughout the reading of the book as an anchor for our conversations.

(Continued)

Annotation Tool	Our Thoughts on Why We Use Them
Visual Maps	A visual map is an activity in which students build a representation of certain aspects of the text that is being read together.

Using simple classroom art tools, students create representations of characters and settings, alongside important quotes from the text.

This work helps the community create a shared meaning of the story. Students use their annotation skills to choose lines from the text to add to their creation.

Students Annotating while They Read

Offering students opportunities to write about their reading is helpful for both students and teachers. Writing gives students the opportunity to process what they have read and it gives us, as teachers, another way to "listen in" to their thinking. Students' written annotations might happen in several ways. Sometimes we might pause during a read-aloud and ask students to write in response to a question such as "What are you wondering?" Other times, students have an idea of what they want to write to capture their thinking, without the need for a teacher prompt.

As teachers read and reflect on students' responses, it is important that we not get distracted by trying to check for correctness or focus exclusively on surface-level understandings of the text. Instead, we should look at student responses as entry points into whole-group learning. We should ask ourselves questions like:

* What written assertions or questions go beyond the text?
* What written responses challenge the thinking in the text or reading community?
* What written assertions show how students are making sense of what the author is trying to communicate?
* What written assertions or responses, when shared with the rest of the class, could help bridge thinking to the standard and clear up any possible misconceptions students may have?

Using What We Learn from Student Work to Plan Whole-Class Instruction

Oftentimes students' written annotations and responses hold the keys to connecting the current learning with future learning. Finding just the right question or comment that a student wrote to share back with the rest of the class is a great start in co-constructing the learning together. Students often write down how they are processing the learning during whole-group reading instruction. Bringing students' individual processing to the larger beloved reading community shows students that the learning doesn't just happen during those whole-group lesson times, but rather continues to be developed and cultivated during individual reading times and then matured during the whole-group time. Reading students' annotations and responses plays a major role in building the intellectual pieces of the beloved reading community.

Rethinking Routines for Listening

We've had to do some shifting in our practices around how we listen to our students. We are continually reflecting and learning to be better listeners for our students. We may, for example, notice the times in which we listen more to the loudest voices in the class or respond in a traditional teacher-directed way. As we've reflected on our own listening practices, we have learned to ask ourselves questions that help support our changes in behavior. Change is often required of us if we are to truly listen as love.

Rethinking Routines for Listening

Question	If...	Then...
Who is centered in whole-class conversations?	As the teacher, you always have a spot in the front of the room	Try out sitting in a new space near different groups of students, or moving around the classroom, all with the goal of decentering yourself physically.
What are you listening for?	You find yourself listening for correct answers or understandings that were shared by students in previous years	Look over your notes after school and notice which comments from students spark your own curiosity as a member of the reading community.

(Continued)

Rethinking Routines for Listening

Question	If...	Then...
Where is student thinking recorded publicly?	You only record student thinking for your own notes or information	Introduce a variety of ways for students to record and make their own thinking visible for the community. Try creating a space on a board, a slide or some other visible places in the classroom to capture this thinking. Invite students to record in notebooks or using digital tools for their own reflection.
How do you build on student thinking in connection to the standards?	You look at the standards only when planning a unit or cycle of lessons	Look back at the standards each day during a unit and notice new connections between these standards and what students are discussing
How do you use student thinking to choose books for read-aloud and minilessons?	You choose your books based only on standards or books you've read in past years	Listen for times when the community erupts in conversation. Identify the topics, scenes, and issues that create this kind of engagement. Choose a book to read next to build on that excitement.

Developing and Utilizing Our Listening Skills as Teachers

Throughout the day teachers will hear many conversations, listen to a million stories, and even observe countless nonverbal interactions between students. Each and every one of these moments is an opportunity for the kind of research that will inform whole-group reading instruction.

When students share personal stories listen for:

* Topics and experiences that connect to the present learning or upcoming learning
* Stories with themes that have been raised by other students
* Stories that beg others to ask questions or investigate further
* Topics and experiences that lead to a discovery

When students are having conversations with each other listen for:

* Points of confusion where the speakers don't seem to understand each other
* Points of engagement where the speakers are excited about a topic, experience, or situation
* Conversations that lead to many other conversations. Conversations where the conversation started at one point but led logically to many other points and assertions
* Conversations where each speaker thinks that there is only one way of thinking about the topic, situation, or experience

When students are communicating nonverbally listen and look for:

* The proximity of the speakers to one another. Are they leaned in close or far apart?
* Moments when students' facial expressions seem to communicate one thing, but their words seem to communicate something different

Figure 5.4 *Lynsey listens closely during a reading conference.*

* Gestures with hands and arms. Do students use gestures alongside their talk or do their hands and arms show a closed or neutral stance?
* Whole-body movements. Are the speakers moving around, still in one place, or a bit of both?

When students share thinking about the text listen for:

* The assertions and arguments made by students. Are they building on previous learning?
* The use of verbal and nonverbal cues that indicate students are building on previous learning, conversations, or lived experiences
* The different ways students connect to and build off of one another's ideas
* New ideas students share that will move the conversation forward, clear up misconceptions, or help launch the class into a new deeper set of minilessons.

CHAPTER 6

A Close Look at a Minilesson Cycle

It was mid-February in Lynsey's third-grade classroom and her students were scattered around the room exploring recently published picture books. The room had a quiet hum accompanied by an infectious energy as students busied themselves reading, note-taking, and discussing books together. As Lynsey was conferring with two students around how they were capturing their thinking, she heard a voice amongst the busy hum:

Vadim:	Mrs. Burkins, we need to read this book as a class!
Lynsey:	(*Walks over to Vadim and Sanath who are both hunched over a book.*) Oh, what book did you discover?
Sanath:	It's called *Blue*!
Vadim:	(*Rushes to add.*) We have so many thoughts about it, and we really want the class to read it too!
Lynsey:	So, do you mean you want to sign up and read this for our morning book, our "Books We Should Read Together" time?
Vadim:	No, we want to read it slowly like for a reading minilesson. Like when we take time and think about it together.
Lynsey:	Now, I see. You want us all to use this book to help us learn together as readers. Why do you both think this will be a good fit for our reading community?
Sananth:	It's just so good and we had so many questions.
Vadim:	Yeah, like we just kinda want us to all think together.

Lynsey sat next to the two students and listened as they reread part of the book. She noticed that they could hardly get through a full-page spread without stopping to debate the words in the text or pointing out how an illustration made them change their thinking. Lynsey knew the boys were excited about the book. She also knew they couldn't quite verbalize why *Blue* was important to read together as a community. While Sanath and Vadim had lots of enthusiasm, they also had some confusion around the key ideas and details of the text. (Lynsey would actually argue that this confusion was productive for the two readers because it added to their desire to figure out what was going on in the book.)

What the students couldn't quite verbalize but clearly still understood was that the reading community is a place that helps them negotiate big and complex ideas together.

Lynsey continued to listen and kept this conversation and book in her mind as she considered books for the upcoming reading informational texts unit.

How Did We Get Here?

A frequent question we are often asked is how long a reading unit of study should last. Given that minilessons are only about ten to fifteen minutes long, how many days will it take for students to learn the skills we embed in the unit and transfer them to their independent reading lives? Our response is that our planning does not begin with mapping out the amount of time a unit will last. There is no magic number of days, but we find that many units span two to four weeks, depending on the standards within them.

Before we get started breaking down the minilessons in a unit of study, it is worth mentioning that every school system has their own unique way of deciding how curriculum is created and "covered." In our school system the district groups the language arts standards into four distinct units of study across the school year. The expectation is that if a standard was introduced in a previous unit then that standard should also be embedded within the subsequent unit of study. This model of unit planning allows teachers in our school system to make decisions around what texts best support students' needs and interests. However, even if you teach in a place with a required curriculum, you can still find ways of integrating minilessons that are responsive to the readers in your classroom.

Planning the Unit: Start with Standards

As we discussed in Chapter 3, we start our unit planning by taking a close look at the standards. However, starting with the standards doesn't mean we center them. The students, themselves, are always at the center. Starting with the standards, however, allows us to have a firm understanding of curriculum learning expectations so that when we craft text sets and learning experiences for the unit we are able to speak to how our book choices, text selections, and digital media all support the state's standards. This is important now more than ever with the current climate of book and media challenges, and ongoing debate about what topics students can engage with in schools.

Let's go back to the story from the beginning of the chapter and explore the steps Lynsey took after that conversation between the two students around the book *Blue*. A few days before Lynsey is ready to start the reading informational unit, she sits and thinks about the following Ohio state reading standards:

Reading Informational Text

RI.3.2 Analyze informational text development.
  a. Determine the main idea of a text.
  b. Retell the key details and explain how they support the main idea.
RI.3.5 Use text features and search tools (e.g., key words, sidebars, hyperlinks) to locate information relevant to a given topic efficiently.
RI.3.7 Use information gained from illustrations (e.g., maps, photographs) and the words in a text to demonstrate understanding of the text (e.g., where, when, why, and how key events occur).
RI.3.9 Compare and contrast the most important points and key details presented in two texts on the same topic.

She chooses a focus standard (3.2) under Key Ideas and Details within the Reading Informational Text Standards to anchor the learning around informational texts.

Focus Standard

RI.3.2 Analyze informational text development.
  a. Determine the main idea of a text.
  b. Retell the key details and explain how they support the main idea.

Next Lynsey goes through the planning work of thinking through the standards in the unit using the process we outlined in Chapter 3.

Steps for Planning with Standards in Mind	Lynsey's Thinking About This Standard
First, think of what the standard says, implies, and doesn't say.	**Says** → Understand overall text structure of the genre, in this case, informational text → Identify the main idea by going through a process of thought (exploring notices and wonders) → Use key ideas and details from the text to support the determination of the main idea **Implies** → Each student will go through a process of thought (exploring notices and wonders) that uses their background knowledge and understanding of the text to identify a main idea → There may be more than one main idea within a text, but students should be prepared to use key evidence from the text to support their assertions → Reasoning is more important than the correct answer **Doesn't say** → Students must answer end-of-text questions → The teacher must ask the questions → Whose perspective is valued when asking and answering questions → Students must answer multiple choice questions

(Continued)

Steps for Planning with Standards in Mind	Lynsey's Thinking About This Standard
Next, think of other standards that naturally align with the thinking the community will be trying to reach.	**RI.3.5** Use text features and search tools (e.g., key words, sidebars, hyperlinks) to locate information relevant to a given topic efficiently.
	RI.3.7 Use information gained from illustrations (e.g., maps, photographs) and the words in a text to demonstrate understanding of the text (e.g., where, when, why, and how key events occur).
	RI.3.9 Compare and contrast the most important points and key details presented in two texts on the same topic.
Then, think of what students already know and understand and ways these standards grouped together can push their understanding in a whole-group reading experience.	At this point in the year students are coming to these standards well versed in asking and answering questions about key ideas and details in an informational text. Students have also explored noticing words that are interesting to them either because they are unsure of their meaning or because they teach them something they are excited to remember. Annotating is also a skill that students have been working on using their reading notebooks and digital tools such as Google applications and Padlet. These are skills that will propel the next step of their learning journey as readers in community together.
Make connections to whole-class instruction	Identify reading skills and strategies that support the work of understanding main ideas of an informational text: **Engagement:** → Use the words and illustrations/photographs to authentically notice and wonder about the text.

(Continued)

138

Steps for Planning with Standards in Mind	Lynsey's Thinking About This Standard
	Working with words: → Notice new and interesting words, record them, and actively work to determine the meaning of the words. → Use the illustrations and text to help derive meaning of the words. **Summarizing:** → Identify important ideas. → Explain events, procedures, ideas and concepts that are presented in the text. **Synthesizing:** → Record new learning gained from the text. → Draw conclusions based on the text, personal input, and community thinking. **Inferring:** → Use a cause/effect structure to infer motivation and feelings of people in the text. **Critiquing:** → Whose perspective is presented in this text? Whose perspective is missing? → Who has a voice in this history? Who does not? **Analyzing:** → Notice how the author presents information in the text. → Notice how the illustrator conveys meaning. → Think about the multiple points of view within the text.

Minilesson Days 1–3: Putting the Standards in Students' Hands

As Lynsey prepares to co-create the unit with students, she is ready to move from doing the work of thinking through the standards on her own to thinking about the standard with the students. This is an important step, and it happens before even introducing the text they will study together. Analyzing the standard together allows the community to create a shared goal and focus.

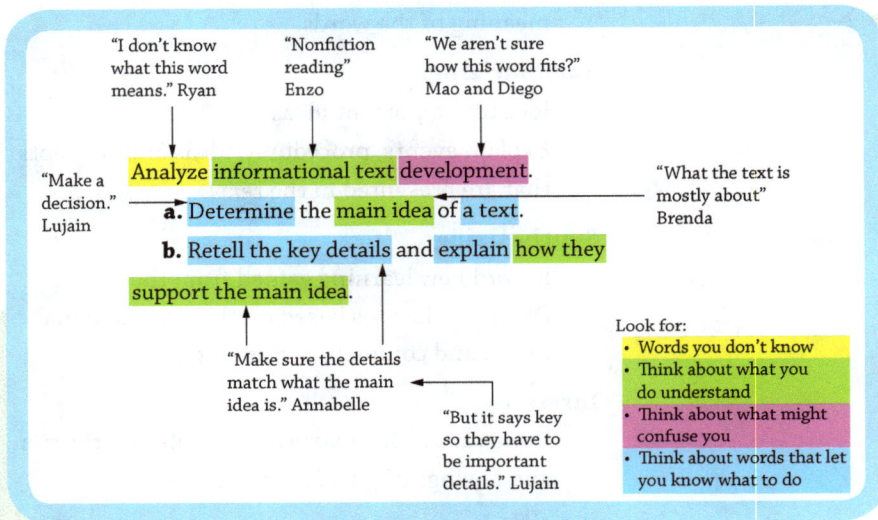

Figure 6.1 *A standard annotated by third-grade students.*

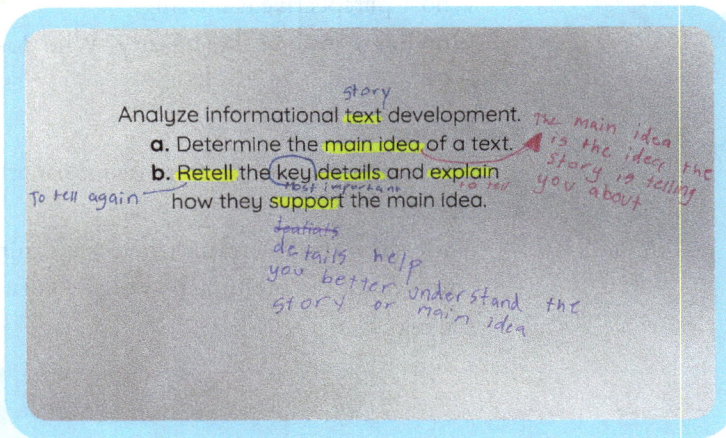

Figure 6.2 *An individual student-annotated standard in the reading notebook.*

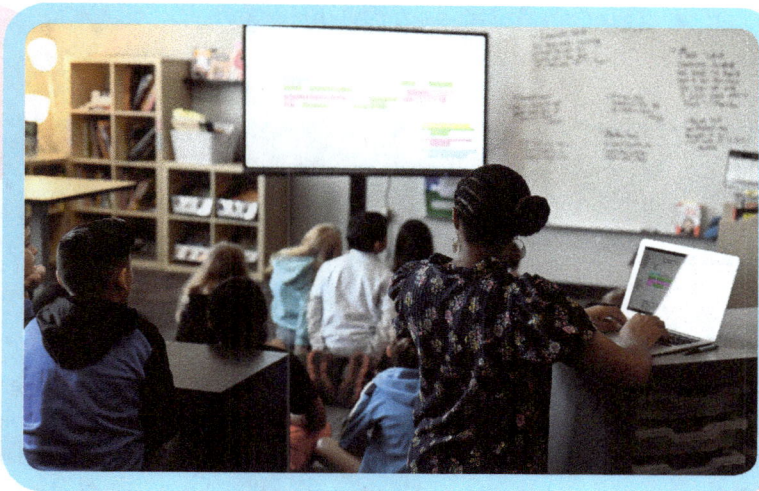

Figure 6.3 *The reading community co-creates understanding of the standards.*

Lynsey introduces the standard during a whole-group minilesson. She presents the standard on the interactive board and each student also has a copy of the standard in their own notebook. Each member of the community reads the words on their own first. Lynsey then invites them to use their notebooks to jot down their initial thoughts about the standard, knowing the community will be discussing it together as well.

After a few minutes of independent thinking time, Lynsey asks a student to read the standard out loud for the group to hear. Students are invited to turn and talk about how they are making sense of this standard. To support their talk, Lynsey prompts them to think about:

* words you don't know,
* what you do understand,
* what might confuse you,
* words that let you know what to do.

Once students have had time to think on their own and with a partner, the group comes back together to record their thoughts. Lynsey takes notes on the slide while the group has a conversation. This standards-focused conversation is the first minilesson of the unit and the process takes between ten and twelve minutes.

The minilessons over the next few days build on this first conversation. Let's take a look at what that process looked like for this unit in Lynsey's classroom.

Beginning the Unit by Studying the Standards Together

Minilesson

Day 1

Lynsey uses this day to listen for what students clearly understand about the standard and what is confusing for them. She notes this information on her documentation tool.

Focus: Students read and analyze the standard for the first time.

Students are invited to the meeting area with their reading notebooks and writing tools of their choice. The un-annotated standard is projected on the whiteboard. Students are invited to read it to themselves as the community settles in.

Each student gets a copy of the standard to glue into their reading notebook. Supplies are close by and students are familiar with the routine of grabbing a glue stick to glue the standard into their notebook and then moving on to annotating.

Students annotate in their notebooks. After a few minutes, students turn and talk with a partner about what they notice.

Students share their ideas in the whole group and Lynsey records their thinking on the slide for the community to see.

Students are then invited to start independent reading time.

Day 2

Lynsey uses the information she gathered from the previous day to help guide the conversation toward clearing up misconceptions and confirming accurate interpretations. This second day of analyzing the standard helps the community build confidence and be vulnerable in sharing what they don't understand.

Focus: Students analyze the standard for the second time and use the color-coded "Look For" checklist [Figure 6.1].

Students gather in the meeting area for the reading minilesson. The standard is projected on the whiteboard with their comments from Day 1. Students are invited to reread the thinking from the previous day while the community is settling in.

(Continued)

Beginning the Unit by Studying the Standards Together	Minilesson

Students are invited to revise and add to the thinking. They are also encouraged to make sure they have thought about: words they don't know, what they do understand, what might be confusing, and what they think they are being asked to do as readers.

Lynsey records revisions and additions. Students read the revised annotated standard and then are invited to start independent reading time.

Day 3

Lynsey is listening for and reflecting on this question: do students have an understanding of the learning standard that will support their work throughout this unit?

Focus: Students set goals around the standard.

Students gather in the meeting area for the reading minilesson. Lynsey projects the annotated standard slide as well as the title "Our Goals" next to it. Students read over the slide while the community settles in.

Lynsey spends a moment recapping their thinking from the last two days. Together, the community rereads the notes from the previous two days. Lynsey then invites the group to think about some goals they could create that would help them move toward accomplishing the work of the standard. Lynsey asks the community, "Now that we have some shared understanding of what this standard means, what are some goals we might create for ourselves that will help us be able to do the work of this standard in our reading lives?"

(Continued)

Beginning the Unit by Studying the Standards Together	Minilesson

Students turn and work in groups of three or four in the meeting area to think about this question together. After a few minutes, Lynsey invites groups to share their thoughts. She records the thinking on a blank slide. This thinking will be used to create goals as a class.

After all the groups have had a chance to share, the community uses their collective thinking to craft a couple goals connected to how they are going to accomplish the work of the standard.

Students are then invited to begin independent reading.

After the third day of work with the standard, our slide looked like this [Figure 6.4].

This work of exploring a standard is always done before introducing any books because Lynsey wants her students to know that this thinking

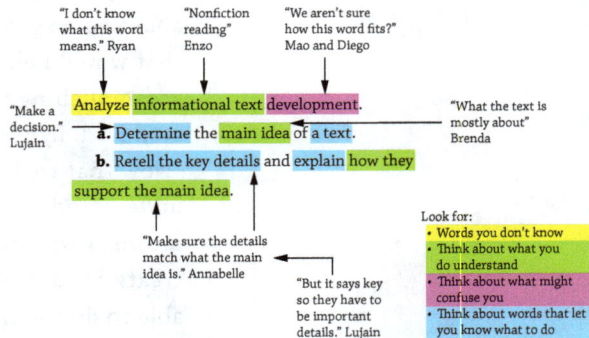

Figure 6.4 *An annotated standard slide co-created by Lynsey's third graders.*

isn't about a single book. She wants them to think about their role as a reader before they begin to practice new skills. It is important that students see the standard as a way readers think about all texts, not just the ones we will read together.

Once students have analyzed the standards, Lynsey knows it is time to think about a possible Menu of Mentors that could support student thinking through this unit. In this particular situation Lynsey knows she will be using the text, *Blue,* to begin the unit because of the experience she had with Vadim and Sanath. However, it isn't always the case that Lynsey knows right away what book would work best for an upcoming unit. When Lynsey doesn't have a concrete idea for a book in mind she goes back to her Menu of Mentors ideas that she has collected throughout the summer and school year to see if there is a good fit. In the section below, we explore what this process of text selection looks like when Lynsey doesn't already have a chosen text for the unit.

Back to Planning: Text Sets as a Menu of Mentors

Before the school year began and throughout the school year thus far Lynsey has worked to build a Menu of Mentors that could anchor a unit of study around this informational text standard. Including both print and digital resources are key when thinking about a text set as a menu of resources. Figure 6.5 is an example of the menu of print resources Lynsey collected for the reading informational standards around the main idea. When Lynsey collected these books, she was looking for informational texts that included pictures and words that would engage readers. She was looking for topics that are relevant and engaging for third graders. She was also looking for a collection of texts that had a variety of nonfiction text features, such as headings, diagrams, author's notes, cutaways, sidebars, and font changes.

As she looked at the books in the text set, Lynsey recalled the recent conversation she had with her students, Vadim and Sanath, earlier. She

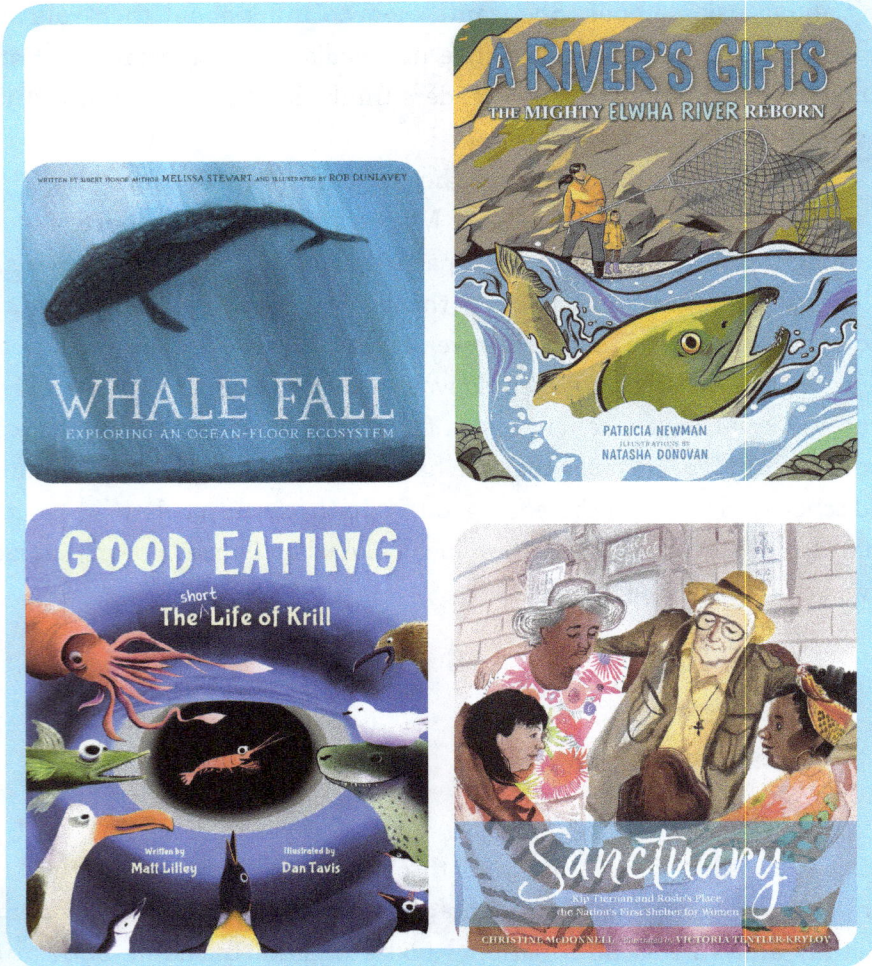

Figure 6.5 *Some books from Lynsey's Menu of Mentors.*

remembered that as they handed her the book *Blue: A History of the Color as Deep as the Sea and as Wide as the Sky* they said, "We need to read this together," "We need to read it slowly," "Read it for a minilesson." But it was one of their questions about the book that stood out most to Lynsey: "Why did people trick poor farmers to make blue and have enslaved people make blue for money? We don't get it."

Lynsey knew that her students' question was a perfect opportunity to analyze text development (determining main ideas and how they are supported by key details) and that *Blue* would be a great addition to the text set she had already curated for this unit.

Choosing a Book

Blue was not originally on Lynsey's menu of resources but the excitement from her students led her to quickly add it to her unit study plan. *Blue* is a nonfiction picture book. The text is linear as the author and illustrator take readers through a history of how the color blue has been positioned across the world and the power it has held. Before Lynsey made the decision to read *Blue* to the class she studied the book herself. She noted the key elements that would make this book a rich text to study and learn from:

* Engagement
  → What tells me students will connect with this text?
  → What have I heard or learned from students that makes me think this?
* Book Elements
  → *Peritext*: Lynsey examines the peritext, the "extra" pieces of text and images that come before or after the main text, especially in nonfiction picture books. She considers how the peritext will add to students' understanding of the book. Peritext often includes back matter. Lynsey is looking for opportunities in the back matter to extend learning and understanding of the text. Oftentimes students find answers to their questions or clear up misconceptions by what they read in the back matter.
    - Author/Illustrator Notes
    - Additional Resources
    - Author/Illustrator Blurb
* Ability to Build Resources Around a Topic
  → Could this text be one of several you read on a similar topic?
  → Does this author/illustrator have other books you might connect to?
  → Can you create a text set with a balance of print and digital resources around this topic?

So when Lynsey studied the book *Blue*, here's what her thinking around these key elements looked like:

Key Elements	Lynsey's Thinking
What tells me students will connect with this text?	*Blue*'s timeline format and the way in which the text explores many different cultures is intriguing. The visual elements tell a story alongside the facts.
What have I heard or learned from students that makes me think this?	Lynsey's two students Vadim and Sanath have already brought this book to Lynsey's attention as one they are intrigued by and want to share with the community.
Peritext element: Author/Illustrator Blurb	The author blurb for Nana Ekua Brew-Hammond shares that she enjoys digging up histories and truths and directs readers to her website. This encourages readers to do some digging of their own about the author. The illustrator blurb helps give context to readers about the kind of work the illustrator does and allows readers to think about how the illustrations help create meaning beyond the text.
Peritext element: Dedication	The dedications for this book are names of people. No other words. This is different from other books we have read together. This may open up conversations and questions as to how authors and illustrators utilize the dedication feature in their books.

(Continued)

Key Elements	Lynsey's Thinking
Peritext element: Front Matter	The endpapers include a full illustration that students can study and around which they can consider noticings and wonderings together. The title includes a subtitle. On the title page students can use the title, subtitle, and illustration to think about what the book might be about.
Peritext element: Back Matter	The back matter is usually an exciting element for students. In this case the author provides a "Want to Know More?" section. It includes more facts about the color blue.
Peritext element: Author's Note	The author's note speaks to historical connections that go beyond what is in the main text. The author gives personal connections to the history as well.
Selected Sources Section	The author includes a "Selected Sources" section. Lynsey uses this section as a teaching point to help her readers understand that the author does research in many different places in order to create this informational book. This ties really well with the research writing unit students do.

Let's now take a look at the collection of resources Lynsey curated around *Blue* as she prepared to use this book in her unit. It was important that Lynsey selected some possible mentors to support the community's thinking while reading and analyzing this text. The texts she chose are below:

Blue: *A History of the Color as Deep as the Sea and as Wide as the Sky*, written by Nana Ekua Brew-Hammond and illustrated by Daniel Minter: This book was our anchor text for the unit.

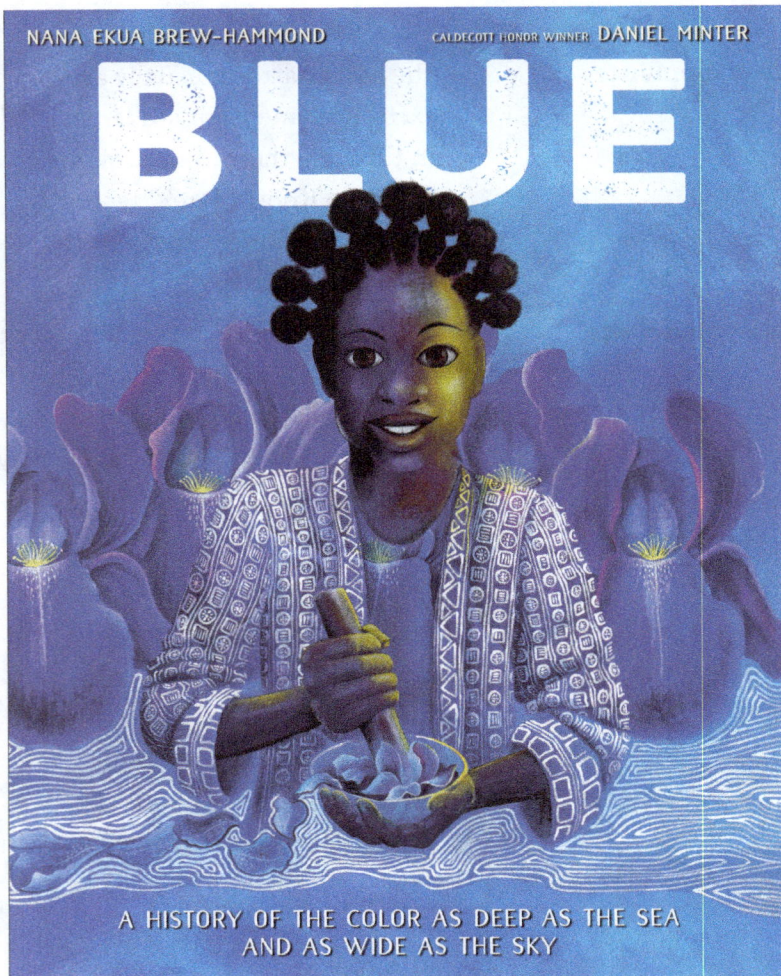

An author chat recording: This video, featuring *Blue*'s author, Nana Ekua Brew-Hammond, gives students additional context and history to support their understanding of the book.

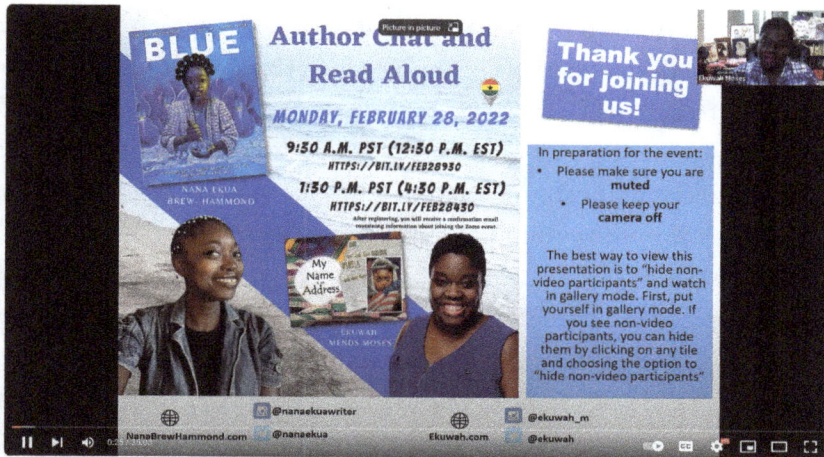

A text pair: Lynsey selected the book *Muddy: The Story of Blues Legend Muddy Waters*, written by Michael Mahin and illustrated by Evan Turk, to pair with the class's study of *Blue*. *Blue* mentions blues music and *Muddy*, a biography of a blues musician, allows students to more deeply understand the references in *Blue*.

Continuing the Unit of Study with Minilessons Days 4–6: Read the Text and Listen, Listen, Listen

The community gathered together in the meeting space in Lynsey's room. Vadim and Sanath stood in front of the class with grins as they held a copy of the book *Blue: A History of the Color as Deep as the Sea and as Wide as the Sky*. The pair did a quick book talk, flipping through the pages to point out illustrations and ideas to their classmates. They asked, "Should we read this book together?" The class was quick to respond with a collective, "YES!"

Lynsey chimed in with, "I was hoping you all would say yes because Vadim and Sanath convinced me too!" Then she linked the previous days' work of co-constructing an understanding of the standard with the book they were about to read. "We have been doing some thinking about what it means to determine a main idea and analyze text development. We said we needed to understand some of the words in the standard better. We can use this text to help us."

Lynsey knew her role over the next few days was largely to listen without judgment and capture student thinking so that she could see patterns and look for entry points to supporting her students as readers. She projected the Kindle version of *Blue* on the interactive board and invited students to record their thinking using a Padlet. We often choose to project the books on a large screen so that the community can better see and study the text and the visuals as the book is read aloud. And then she began to read the book aloud.

This day's minilesson was about fifteen minutes. It included these parts:

* Vadim and Sanath sharing *Blue* with the class and hooking their interest in the book they would study together.
* Creating the sections of the Padlet [Figure 6.6] that students would use to record their ideas as they listened to the book. Lynsey presented students with a blank Padlet and said, "Tomorrow we will start reading the first part of the book. What types of thinking should we keep track of?" Students initially named "notices" and "wonders" as Padlet sections for their notetaking, while other categories were suggested and added to the Padlet on subsequent days.
* Over the following two days Lynsey read aloud *Blue: A History of the Color as Deep as the Sea and as Wide as the Sky*. During these minilessons Lynsey read from the back of the room with the text projected on the interactive board and students recorded their thinking digitally. Verbal conversations were not happening during the reading, but rather digitally through back and forths on the Padlet.

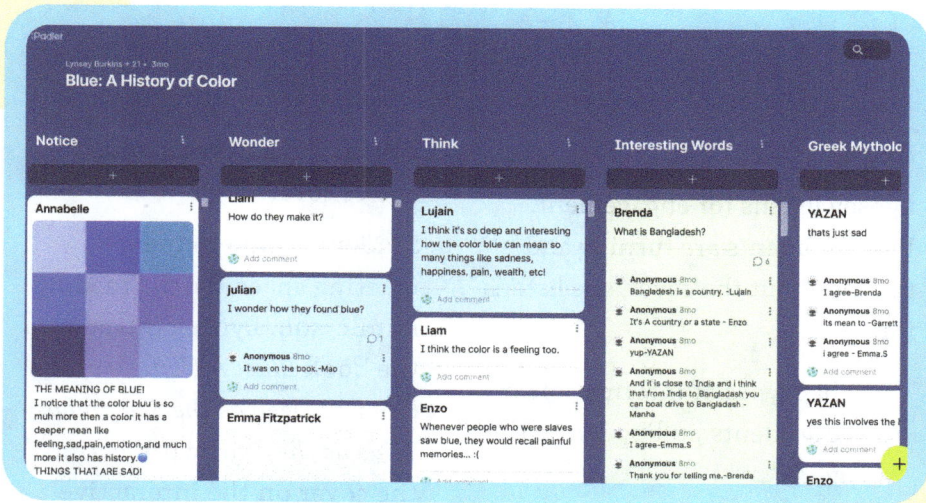

Figure 6.6 *A Padlet of students' thinking around* Blue.

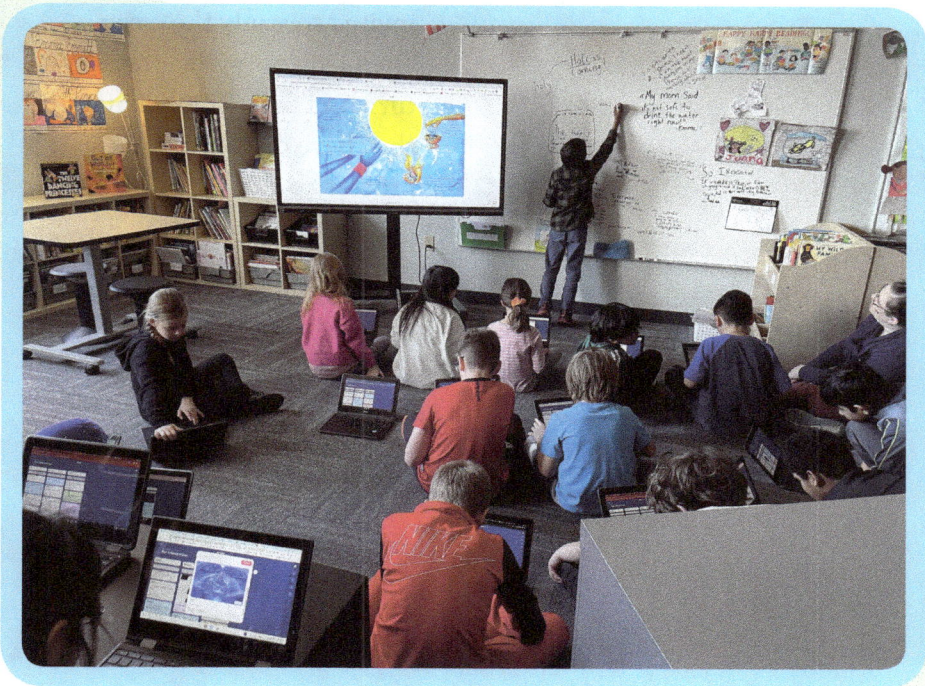

Figure 6.7 *The reading community reads and records their thinking on a Padlet and the whiteboard during the minilesson.*

Continuing the Unit by Reading the Text	Minilesson

Day 4

Lynsey listens for engagement. While students are turning and talking about the cover, she listens for:

1. What types of information are the students pulling out of the cover?
2. Are students focused on a certain part of the cover?
3. What types of questions are they asking?

Focus: Students study the book's cover.

Students come to the meeting space for the reading minilesson. Lynsey introduces the book *Blue: A History of the Color as Deep as the Sea and as Wide as the Sky* by projecting the cover on the interactive whiteboard.

While the reading community is getting settled in the meeting space, students are invited to study the cover. Then Lynsey invites them to turn and talk about what they have discovered in this process.

Lynsey allows for some time to talk and then reconvenes the group as she lets them know that this will be the book they are going to study together as they analyze its text development.

Lynsey captures the students' thinking about the cover on the whiteboard and students move to the independent reading time of the workshop.

(Continued)

Continuing the Unit by Reading the Text	Minilesson

Day 5

Lynsey focuses on reading the book. Students are listening to the book and commenting on the Padlet while Lynsey reads.

Lynsey also spends time after the minilesson reading students' Padlet comments before the next day's lesson in order to see the types of information students are capturing. This is another form of listening.

As she reads students' Padlet comments, Lynsey "listens" for:

1. Are students capturing key ideas and details?
2. Are students asking questions that are based on what is happening in the text?
3. Are students showing evidence of understanding?

Day 6

After reading her students' Padlet responses from Day 5, Lynsey continues reading aloud the second half of *Blue*.

Focus: Lynsey reads aloud half of *Blue* and students capture their thinking via Padlet.

Students come to the meeting area with their Chromebooks for the reading minilesson.

Students initially respond that they want to keep track of notices, wonders, and thoughts. Lynsey creates those sections on the Padlet as students access the Padlet on their Chromebooks.

Lynsey begins reading the first part of the book while students listen and record their thinking. Lynsey's reading pace is fairly slow, and she pauses before moving to the next page to give students time to look at the pictures and the words while they record their thinking.

Focus: Lynsey finishes reading aloud *Blue* and students record new thinking on the Padlet.

(Continued)

Continuing the Unit by Reading the Text	Minilesson
	Students come to the meeting area with their Padlets for the reading minilesson. Students are invited to read over the thinking on the Padlet from the day prior as everyone settles in.
	Lynsey begins the minilesson with, "Did anyone notice anything from our Padlet notes they think we should talk about?"
	The class discusses. Then Lynsey asks the class, "Before we continue reading the book, are there any other sections you think we should add to the Padlet that will help us analyze the text better?"
	One student suggests adding a section for interesting words and another student suggests adding one for connections to Greek mythology. Lynsey adds these sections and continues reading aloud, finishing the book.
	Lynsey then invites students to read/add/comment on the Padlet during independent reading time if they choose.

> ## ≳Tip Box≳
> ## Using Padlet
>
> Lynsey chose to use Padlet as the tool for this learning experience because of its simple structure for recording in real time. Students don't have to spend a lot of time figuring out how to use the tool, they just record their thinking under the tab they feel it belongs. Additionally, Padlet allows students to see their peers' thinking in real time and encourages quick short responses. Students also can't accidentally erase other students' thinking as sometimes happens with other digital tools.
>
> Other useful Padlet features include being able to comment on other people's posts, turning posts different colors as a highlighting tool, and being able to add quick video.

Ongoing: Record Student Thinking

After reading aloud *Blue* over two days, Lynsey took time to revisit the Padlet to read her students' thinking and chart some of the things they wrote on her standards planning and documentation sheet [Figure 6.8]. Lynsey read the Padlet with a lens of listening for ways she could connect students' thinking to the way the standard progresses. Jotting down students' comments next to the standards helps her consider how she might help students grow toward a full understanding of these standards. This information also helps Lynsey choose a focus and plan for the minilessons that follow.

Tools like the standards planning and documentation sheet help to keep the learning focused on what students are saying and doing with the standards. Using this tool in purposeful ways illuminates what learning the community might need next.

Reading Theme: Real Life Reading

"All these cultures wanted blue for different reasons." Ryan

Reading Informational Text
Key Ideas and Details
RI.3.2. Analyze informational text development.
- a. Determine the <u>main idea</u> of a text.
- b. Retell the key details and explain how they support the main idea.

"Why was it ok to hurt people for the color blue?" Enzo

"Why did everyone want blue?" Julian

"Why was blue so important?" Lujain

Integration of Knowledge and Ideas
RI.3.7. Use information gained from illustrations (e.g., maps, photographs) and the words in a text to demonstrate understanding of the text (e.g., where, when, why, and how key events occur).

"I think the picture with the woman singing is showing us that it was wrong to trade people just to get the color blue." Sanath

"Can we go back to the page with the hands and the kids flying, what does this illustration mean?" Manha

Craft and Structure
RI.3.5. Use text features and search tools (e.g., key words, sidebars, hyperlinks) to locate information relevant to a given topic efficiently.

"What does iris mean?" Brianna

"Lapis lazuli is in Roblox." Garrett

Integration of Knowledge and Ideas
RI.3.9. Compare and contrast the most important points and key details presented in two texts on the same topic.

Reading Literature
Craft and Structure
RL.3.4. Determine the meaning of words and phrases as they are used in a text, distinguishing <u>literal</u> from <u>nonliteral</u> language.

"What does luxury mean?" Emma

Reading Foundational Skills
Phonics and Word Recognition
RF.3.3. Know and apply grade-level phonics and word analysis skills in decoding words.
- b. Decode words with common Latin suffixes.

Figure 6.8 *Lynsey uses the standards planning and documentation tool to take note of student comments related to the learning goals of the unit.*

Oftentimes Lynsey uses the student quotes she records on the standards planning and documentation sheet to engage students at the start of a minilesson and also confirm to them that their initial thinking is strong and supports the class's understanding of the text and learning standards. Starting minilessons with students' words also lets them know that their words and thinking are critical to the community's learning. For example, Lynsey wrote down that Ryan said, "All these cultures wanted blue for different reasons." Lynsey thought that sharing Ryan's quote would be a great way to get readers exploring how going back to text to gather supporting details helps them think more deeply about the main idea.

Ongoing: Study Student Thinking

As the unit unfolds, Lynsey frequently returns to the goals students created as they studied the learning standards. Lynsey studies what she hears and sees from the students with these goals in mind. When she meets with students for reading conferences during the independent reading time, Lynsey may ask them to open the notes they took during the minilesson and have a conversation about their thinking. During this independent reading time, she may also pull together a small group of students who need more support during the minilesson and do another minilesson with them to bridge the whole-group learning to their own learning. Even though this studying of student thinking happens all throughout the hour reading workshop, Lynsey still records what she is learning from the students on the documentation tool so that all the thinking is together to help her move forward in response.

Move Forward in Response with Minilesson Days 7—10

As we move forward in the unit, we continue to use knowledge we gain from listening to and recording student thinking to facilitate and co-construct the learning alongside students.

Moving Forward in Response	Minilesson
Day 7 Before Day 7's minilesson, Lynsey spends time studying the content of the Padlet. She notices that students had many questions. Most questions were related to the key ideas and details of the text, but some were not. For example Julian asked, "I wonder what the big plants are called in the book?" That question is a valid wonder, but even if he found the answer, it would not necessarily connect with the key ideas of the text. On the other hand, Manha wrote, "I wonder if this is taking place in Egypt?" This question relates to setting and finding the answer to this question may connect to a deeper understanding of where the color blue was most valued, a key idea of the text.	**Focus:** Students summarize the text, looking for important ideas within it. Students come to the meeting area with their Chromebooks for the reading minilesson. They are invited to read over the contents of the Padlet as they wait for the community to settle in. Once they have had a chance to read over the Padlet, Lynsey directs the community to look at the interactive whiteboard. Students close their Chromebook screens and look toward the board. On the screen Lynsey projects a slide that has the cover of the book *Blue* on it and next this question, "What are some important ideas and details from this text?"

(Continued)

Moving Forward in Response

Lynsey also saw that the noticings students recorded on the Padlet were not exactly connected to the important ideas of the text. For example, one student wrote, "I notice that there are kids in the air."

There were, however, a few noticings that *were* related to important ideas in the text and Lynsey wrote those down to use as examples as she supports students' continued learning in upcoming minilessons. Notices such as:

- "I notice that we're getting into how blue was used for slavery."—Vadim
- "I noticed how there were different ways to get the color blue."—Emma
- "I noticed that blue might be the segregation of the rich and not rich."—Yazan

As she prepares for Day 8's minilesson Lynsey decides to focus on supporting students in identifying important ideas within a text. She wants to move slowly and develop these ideas over several days' minilessons, so that the community has time to create a process for how to look for important ideas together.

During today's minilesson Lynsey listens for evidence that students are beginning to distinguish between an idea and an important idea as related to the author's intended message.

Day 8

In the previous day's minilesson, students thought about how to determine if an idea or detail in a text is important. Students worked together to create criteria that would help them determine what is important in a text.

Lynsey decides to start today's minilesson with the students' Padlet work from the previous lesson. She wants to emphasize the strengths in the previous day's work and use them to propel students forward to today's work.

Lynsey also wants to see if students could apply the criteria they created by selecting a post on the Padlet that they feel represents an important idea from the text and explaining why. Lynsey knows that she will be able to see if they are ready to move on by what happens with this activity.

Minilesson

Students start discussing the question, going straight to examples from the text. "I noticed that blue is much more than a color; it has a deeper meaning," Annabelle shared. Typically one person says something and then other students start to chime in.

"Yeah, like when the author wrote about blue also being a feeling," Kylin added. As the conversation continues, sometimes they raise their hands and sometimes they don't.

Lynsey adds a second question mid-conversation, "How do you determine if something is an *important* idea in a text?" She quickly adds that question to another slide. Students turn and talk to think about this question before sharing their thoughts. As they share, Lynsey captures their thoughts on the slide.

Students are then invited to continue thinking about these questions as they move to independent reading time.

Focus: Students summarize the text, naming important ideas within it.

Students come to the meeting area with their Chromebooks. On the interactive whiteboard Lynsey has already projected the slide with their thinking from the previous day around the question, "How do you determine if something is an *important* idea in a text?" Students are invited to read over the slide and quietly discuss amongst themselves while everyone gets settled in.

Once students are settled and quietly discussing, Lynsey recaps their thinking from the previous day as a way to set the stage for today's learning. Lynsey is also mindful to add new thinking that she heard when students were preparing to start the minilesson.

(Continued)

Moving Forward in Response

Lynsey listens for:

1. Can students locate an important idea in the text?
2. Can students explain how they know an idea in the text is important?

Day 9

When Lynsey reviewed her notes from the previous day and looked over the Padlet she found many examples where students selected important ideas from the text. Lynsey purposefully chose three examples to highlight, one from the beginning, one from the middle, and one from the ending.

Minilesson

Lynsey then invites students to think about the criteria they created to determine which ideas are most important in a text and look back at their Padlet of notes on the text.

The criteria the reading community came up with to determine which ideas and details are most important to the text:

1. *Does the detail share something new?*
2. *Does the detail explain something that is happening?*
3. *Does the detail tell us about the setting or place?*

Lynsey asks students to take a minute to review the Padlet and each find two posts that they feel show important ideas. She asks them to mark the posts they choose in Padlet by turning them the color blue (Padlet allows users to change the background color of posts and this was a familiar routine Lynsey had previously taught her students).

Once students locate two posts each, Lynsey asks them to explain why they chose these posts.

After a few minutes, Lynsey brings the group back together, and closes with a slide that shows *Blue*'s cover and the question, "What are some important ideas in *Blue*?"

Lynsey invites students to think about this question and what they highlighted on the Padlet in order to prepare for tomorrow's minilesson. Students then move to independent reading.

Focus: Students work on synthesizing by drawing conclusions based on text, personal input, and community thinking.

Students come to the meeting area for the reading minilesson without their chromebooks. Lynsey has the slide projected with the cover of the text and the question, "What are some important ideas from *Blue*?" Today she has added three posts from the Padlet that students identified as important parts.

(Continued)

Moving Forward in Response

She did this to prepare students to be able to think across the entire text, rather than just a part of the text in a future minilesson.

Today Lynsey will listen for:

1. How are students using each other's thinking to think about their chosen important idea and finding where that happens in the text?

2. Do students automatically get physical tools to record and support their thinking or do they just use talk as their tool?

3. Is there a group that has a strategy that works that other students could benefit from?

Minilesson

> **I notice that all the pages have blue in it**
> Julian
>
> 🗨 1
>
> 👤 Anonymous 8mo
> Kind of true.
>
> 💬 Add comment

> **Anabelle**
> I notice that there is all these ways to get the color.
>
> 💬 Add comment

> **Vadim**
> I noticed were geting into how blue was used for slavery
>
> 🗨 1
>
> 👤 Anonymous 8mo
> SAME -Manha
>
> 💬 Add comment

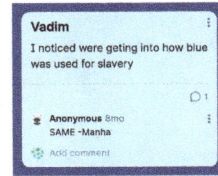

As students settle in they are invited to study the slide. To convene the group Lynsey asks, "What do you notice and wonder about this slide?" The community begins to discuss.

Lynsey captures their thinking on the slide. Lynsey then says, "Readers I bet you noticed I set multiple copies of the book *Blue* underneath our interactive board. These copies are for us to use as we investigate. Today I want you to think together in groups of three. Your group will take one of the posts that are on the slide and find where that part is in the text. Then I want your group to think about what happened *before* and right *after* that part. Finally, think about how the text ended. I want you to use all of this thinking to see if the post you chose is an important idea that helps us understand the text better and can lead us toward the main idea."

Lynsey gives the group about ten minutes to get this thinking started. She then asks students to pause their conversations and invites them to use sticky notes or their reading notebook to capture the thinking of the group quickly so that tomorrow they can pick up where they left off.

Students then move to independent reading time.

(Continued)

Moving Forward in Response	Minilesson
Day 10	**Focus:** Students continue to work on synthesizing by drawing conclusions based on text, personal input, and community thinking.
Lynsey noted from the previous day that students were paying special attention to the parts of *Blue* that occurred just before and after their chosen important idea. This helped Lynsey know students were ready to move forward and deepen their thinking.	Students come to the meeting area for the reading minilesson with writing tools (pencils, flare pens, highlighters) ready to continue their thinking. Lynsey gives students about five minutes to pick up where they left off from the previous day. Lynsey listens in as groups work together, adding pertinent information to her documentation tool.
During the previous day's minilesson, Lynsey watched a group use sticky notes to mark the parts of the book that happened before and after their chosen important part.	While students are still sitting in their groups of three in the meeting area Lynsey pulls the community back together.
Lynsey decided to model that strategy herself during today's lesson in order to stretch students' thinking toward looking across the entire book. She kept in mind her ultimate goal of students being able to identify a main idea.	Lynsey uses her notes to recap the learning that was taking place in the groups. She makes sure to capture how the groups determined important ideas and details and what those ideas and details were.
In today's minilesson Lynsey listens for which important parts from the beginning, middle, and end of the text student groups mark.	Lynsey then poses a new question, "If your group had to determine a couple of important ideas and details from the beginning, middle, and end of the book, what would they be?"
Do these parts form a thread? Are they all somewhat important but not really related? This information will inform her next instructional steps.	Lynsey gives the students a few minutes to use sticky notes to mark the parts from the beginning, middle, and end that they feel are important ideas or details the author wanted readers to know.
	Students are then invited to move into independent reading.

Although this chapter shows just one glimpse into how minilessons unfold across a unit, our hope is that you get a sense of how the process works. There is no set number of days that unit cycles must be. For this unit, Lynsey wanted to make sure students created a process to analyze a text and determine a main idea with text support. Once the reading community created this process together they moved on to another text to practice, moving more quickly this time since the stage was already set.

CHAPTER 7

A Close Look at a Read-Aloud

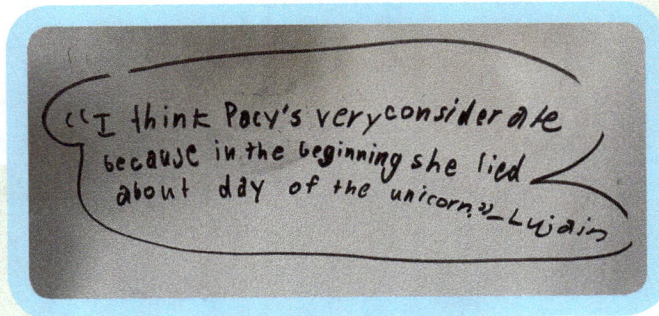

Figure 7.1 *During a read-aloud of* The Year of the Dog, *third grader Lujain writes, "I think Pacy's very considerate because in the beginning she lied about the day of the unicorn."*

In March, Lynsey read aloud *The Year of the Dog* by Grace Lin, a middle-grade realistic fiction novel, to her third graders. She read chapters of the book aloud (while also projecting the pages of the Kindle version of the book on the whiteboard) over the course of a unit of about three to four weeks. One day, when they were about halfway through the book, Yazan stopped Lynsey as she was reading aloud to the class. "Wait, can you stop reading for a little bit so we can talk about what Lujain just wrote on the whiteboard?" The class nodded in agreement.

Read-aloud is an active time in Lynsey's classroom. Students often record in their reading notebooks. At times they might signal to Lynsey to stop reading for a moment in order to highlight something in the text. Individual students might also walk up to the whiteboard and write something while Lynsey is reading, or ask to pause the book so the class can have a longer discussion. None of these things are planned; they happen naturally as the students are co-constructing the meaning of the text together.

On this particular day Lynsey had just finished the part in *The Year of the Dog* in which the main character Grace (also referred to as Pacy in the book) and her friend Becky meet new girl Melody in school who, like Grace, is also Chinese. The three characters have an exchange that reveals Grace

THE YEAR OF THE DOG (A PACY LIN NOVEL BOOK 1)

Melody nodded. "Except it's with a 'G.' L-I-N-G."

We found out that Melody and I had a lot of things that were almost the same. While I had an older sister and a younger sister, she had an older brother and a younger brother. We both had long black hair, but she had bangs and I didn't. We both played the violin, but I was in Suzuki Book 3 and she was in Suzuki Book 2. We both couldn't write in Chinese, but she could speak it and I couldn't. My birthday was May 17 and Melody's birthday was July 17.

"You're almost twins!" Becky said. "Lucky!"

"My mom must have forgotten to tell me about you," I said. "Probably because it's Chinese New Year."

"Yeah," Becky said, "it's the Year of the Dog! Grace is going to tell me when it's the Day of the Unicorn so we can celebrate that."

"Day of the Unicorn?" Melody said. "There's no Day of the Unicorn."

"Yes, there is," Becky said. "It's during a leap year, and there's a parade and we hang pictures. Grace said so."

Melody looked at me and I felt myself turning red.

"I must have made a mistake," I mumbled.

"Oooh," Melody said, "that Day of the Unicorn. I forgot. My family doesn't celebrate it, so I didn't remember. But, you're right, it's a big festival."

Melody grinned at me and I smiled back. I knew we were going to be good friends.

Figure 7.2 *A page from* The Year of the Dog *by Grace Lin*

(Pacy) lied to Becky about a holiday she named the Day of the Unicorn [Figure 7.2].

After listening to this part of the book, Lujain asked Lynsey to highlight a section of the text using the Kindle highlighting tool. Then Lujain said, "This is why I wrote: I *think Pacy's very considerate because in the beginning she lied about the day of the unicorn.* Because maybe Pacy didn't want Becky to feel left out of the holiday and also wanted a friend to celebrate it with."

Once Lujain was finished explaining her thinking, Yazan eagerly began the conversation. "I don't think it's good that she lied!"

"Why do you think she lied about there being a Day of the Unicorn?" Emmett responded. Lynsey sat in the back of the room and captured their conversation on her note-taking tool.

Anya joined in, "Maybe she wanted to fit in?"

"Maybe she wasn't trying to lie, maybe she just didn't know what to say," Enzo added.

Brianna waved her hands back and forth. "But why didn't she just say, 'No, there is no Day of the Unicorn?'"

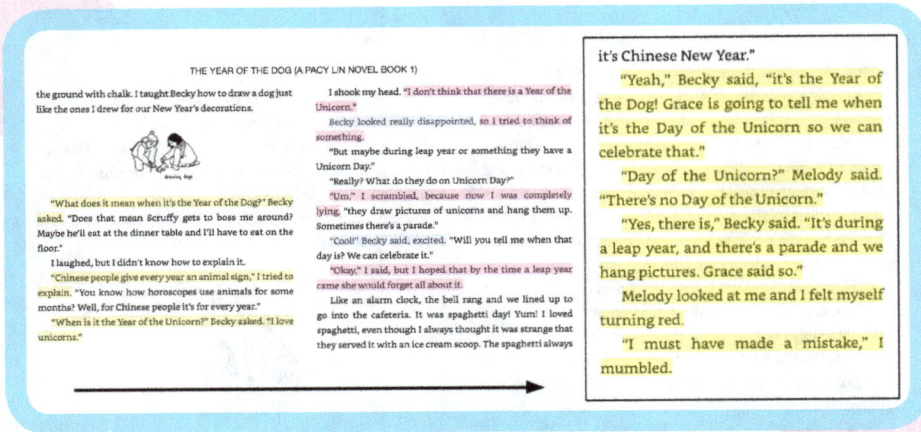

Figure 7.3 *Students study annotated pages from* The Year of the Dog *during a conversation to help understand why Lujain felt Grace (Pacy) was considerate.*

Lynsey moved from the back of the room to the side of the meeting space and said, "Hmm, I'm wondering if it's a good time to go back to the beginning of the book where Pacy first lied about the Day of the Unicorn and reread it with this new part in mind?" Lynsey quickly took screenshots of both sections of the book and uploaded them to a Google Slide so that the reading community could have this conversation. The community went back to the previous part and began to study both events side by side projected on the whiteboard before they turned and talked about what they noticed.

When the group came back together to talk, it was Emma who suggested they highlight parts of the text that might help them understand why Grace (Pacy) lied. As the group began to talk and figure out what parts should be highlighted and what colors they should use, Lynsey was already thinking about how she might use the group's thinking to plan a series of minilessons focused on character traits and motivations. While the class had previously studied this standard using shorter texts, Lynsey realized, after listening to her students, that they were now ready to revisit this standard within longer, more complex texts. In this chapter, we zoom in on one kind of read-aloud experience in Lysney's classroom, a novel study of Grace Lin's *The Year of the Dog*.

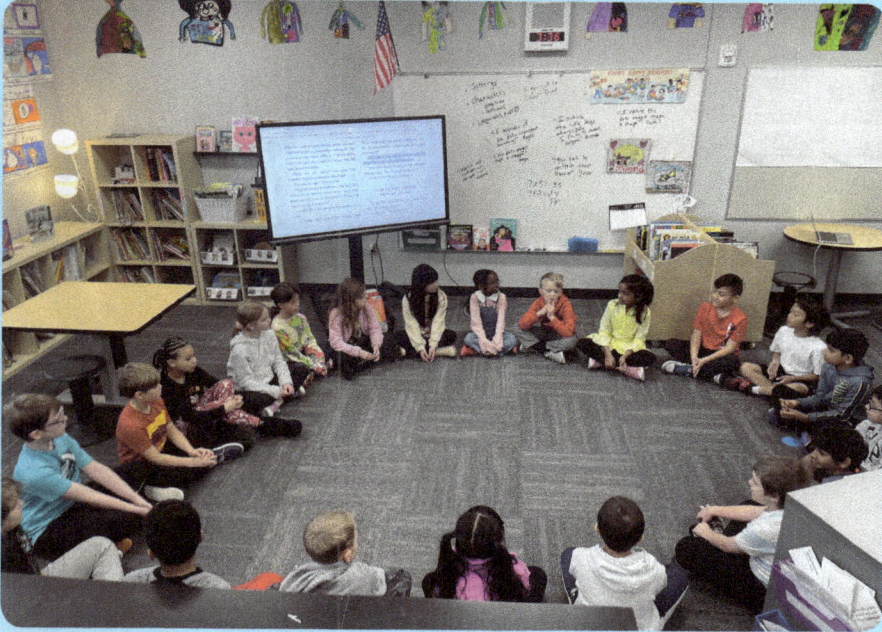

Figure 7.4   *The reading community gathers in a circle to have a conversation about* The Year of the Dog.

How Did We Get Here?

In Lynsey and Franki's classrooms, twenty-five to thirty minutes every day is dedicated to read-aloud. During this time, the beloved reading community convenes in the whole-group meeting space. Meeting in this space is important because it signals to the community that this is a time in which we gather closer together in order to co-construct meaning. In our classrooms students bring tools to this space to support their individual thinking during the read-aloud and, if they choose, to also record the thinking of their peers. *The Year of the Dog* conversation described at the beginning of this chapter transpired in the way it did because the reading community had practiced, since the very start of the year, how to think and learn together in community. The students aren't distracted by the movement of charting thinking on the whiteboard or the signals to stop and highlight,

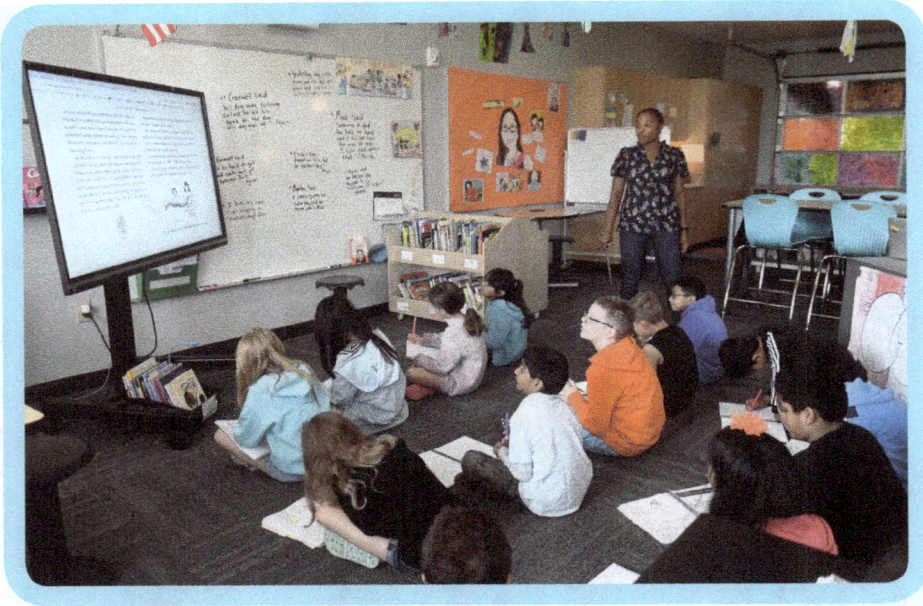

Figure 7.5 *Whole-group meeting space with novel projected.*

nor are they disrupted by the cadence of reading, discussing, reading, discussing. This read-aloud process is one that is built by the group over time, as the teacher studies and facilitates the needs of the community.

bell hooks wrote:

> I think that a feeling of community creates a sense that there is a shared commitment and common good that binds us. What we all ideally share is a desire to learn—to receive active knowledge that enhances our intellectual development and our capacity to live more fully in the world.
>
> (1994, 40)

We have come to learn that the read-aloud time of day requires community and commitment. Our goal for this time is deep learning amongst a community of readers. Some of the commitments to build this kind of community during read-aloud are:

* A central meeting space where students are in proximity to each other
* An engaging relevant text that students can see and listen to during the read-aloud experience

* Access to recording and note-taking tools (in Lynsey's classroom, these tools include reading notebooks, a variety of writing tools, Chromebooks, sticky notes, and highlighter tape)
* Access to multiple physical copies of the read-aloud book (students might follow along in the moment in the physical book or refer back to parts within it later)
* A centrally located whiteboard to capture class thinking (both the teacher and students may write on it at different moments)
* Student agency to suggest stopping points to talk about the text
* Student agency to highlight parts of the text that they feel represent key ideas and details

These necessary conditions weren't all in place on day one in our classrooms. And teachers and students didn't magically learn to use all of these tools on the first day they were introduced. Rather, the conditions, tools and strategies we use during read-aloud time are scaffolded and developed throughout the course of the year. *The Year of the Dog* read-aloud experience from the opening vignette occurred in March and was the result of intentional work to build these conditions of the beloved reading community.

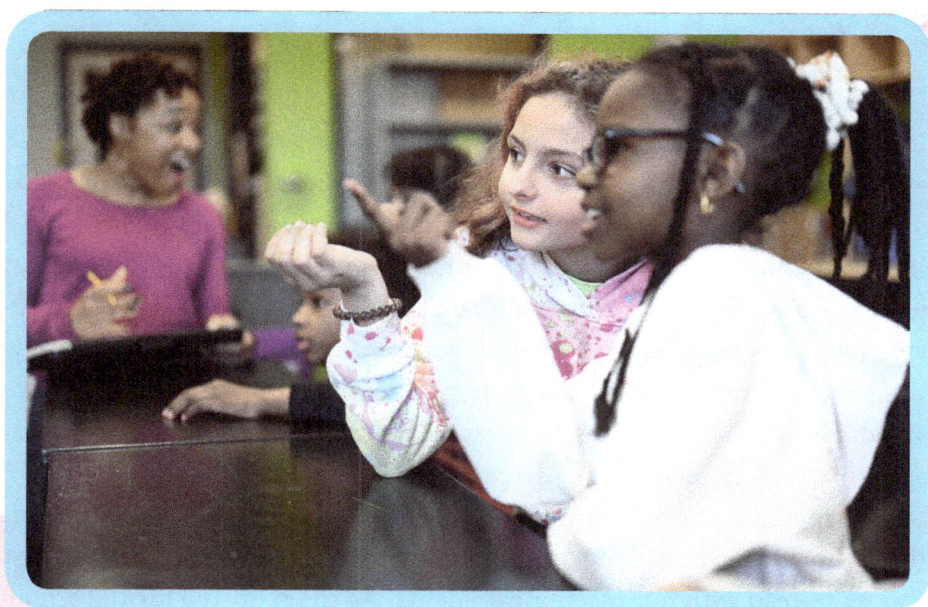

Figure 7.6   *The reading community has a vibrant conversation during read-aloud time.*

Throughout the rest of this chapter, we will take you through how this unit started, some key parts along the way, and how it ended. In our classrooms, it typically takes four to six weeks to read a novel together with all the conversations, minilessons, and ongoing learning that happens throughout each lesson. The goal in the next sections of this chapter is not to outline every detail of each day of the unit. Instead, the hope is to highlight the gist of how the unit went and provide an overall sense of how the beloved reading community comes together during the read-aloud time to co-construct learning.

The Planning Process

Planning for a novel read-aloud is much like planning for minilessons in that neither process is linear. The read-aloud of a novel is considered the unit of study for the read-aloud time of day. The grouping of standards and supporting minilessons are all centered around what the readers need in order to understand the central themes and messages from the novel. To plan we prepare by knowing novels, knowing the standards, making a novel choice, and creating a recording sheet to support assessment along the way.

Planning: Knowing Books and Knowing the Standards

In Chapter 4 we explained the process for how we get to know books. Here we'll take a look at that process in the context of planning for a novel study during read-aloud. Before the school year begins we always like to spend time rereading and thinking about our literacy standards. We think about what the literacy standards say and don't say, we think about how our previous students engaged with these standards, and we think about what new thinking we bring to our understanding of the standards. Engaging with the standards in this way ensures we always stay grounded in what the standards suggest students need.

Prepared with the knowledge of our literacy standards, we read a ton throughout the summer and create a menu of read-aloud texts that we might choose to read with our incoming students. As she prepared for the school year, Lynsey created this menu of possible read-alouds for her third graders.

A Menu of Possible Read-Alouds for Third Grade

Possible Read-Aloud/ Novel Study	Reason It Might Be a Good Choice
Mayra Khan and the Incredible Henna Party written by Saadia Faruqi and illustrated by Ani Bushry	→ Highly illustrated text format. Lots to study on one page → Main character-focused so it allows kids to really dig into the character's traits and feelings over time → Linear plot structure
Odder by Katherine Applegate	→ Novel in verse format told in two parts → The author's use of flashbacks can support readers in reading longer chapter books in which they encounter this literary feature → Strong character development and setting that plays a major role in the story events. Visuals support this as well
The Phoenix on Barkley Street (City Kids series, Book One) by Zetta Elliott	→ Opportunity to introduce students to elements of science fiction → Well-developed characters with distinct personalities that will support engagement with character traits and motivations → Story plot begs readers to ask questions and make inferences based on the events of the story.

(Continued)

Possible Read-Aloud/ Novel Study	Reason It Might Be a Good Choice
Leon the Extraordinary by Jamar Nicholas	• Graphic novel format gives an opportunity to support students in how to read and make meaning in this kind of book • The plot involves superheroes, phone apps, and zombies. Chance of engagement for third graders is high • Opportunity to focus on the reading literature standards that relate to character traits and motivations
The Year of the Dog by Grace Lin	• Sophisticated story structure with flashbacks • Grace Lin has multiple picture books that (like *The Year of the Dog*) feature members of Lin's own family, that can help readers get to know the characters even deeper • Picture support in this book is strong

As the new school year begins and we meet our students, the planning we did over the summer reflecting on standards and creating a Menu of Mentors is now paired with our knowledge of our students and the classroom community that is forming. We go back to our Menu of Mentors and think about:

* What is interesting to this group of readers?
* What do we know about their current reading habits?
* What do we know about how they talk about texts during independent reading time?
* What kinds of books are students reading on their own?
* What would hook this group of readers right now during this point in the school year?

Once we have selected a text from our menu of choices we go back to the literacy standards once again and select the standards we know students can access in this text. We want to use the novel and standards to grow students' capacity as independent readers.

After selecting *The Year of the Dog* Lynsey thought about all the book elements that would make this text the right fit for her students at this point in the school year.

* **Visual:** This book is highly visual and students have related to visual books in past readings. This particular group of students likes to study the illustrations and pair what they see with what the text says. Lynsey knew that this group of learners would engage in this feature of the book as a way to find deeper meanings.
* **Author's Note:** This book has an author's note at the end. Lynsey's students have gotten in the habit of checking for author's notes in every book they read together and in their independent reading. This year her students can be heard saying, "Don't forget the author's note!".
* **Interview:** Not only did this book have an author's note, it also had a bonus written interview with author Grace Lin at the end of the book. Lynsey knew this feature would support students in answering some of the questions they would have while reading the book. The interview was a feature that Lynsey knew she didn't have to wait until the end of the book to use; rather she could introduce it as questions unfolded across the read-aloud.
* **Novel format:** Reading widely across books with a variety of formats during read-aloud is important as young and mature readers develop. This particular book has a novel format with visual elements. The format of the book also had short stories woven into a larger story. Lynsey knew that this structure would be new and engaging for many of her students.

Lynsey's class read *The Year of the Dog* beginning in March, as their final read-aloud of the school year. This particular book has been on Lynsey's Menu of Mentors list for a couple of years and Lynsey knew that this book was going to enhance the conversations and learning that had taken place all year long.

Planning: Pairing the Book with the Standards

After rereading *The Year of the Dog* with this year's students in mind, Lynsey went back to the literacy standards and created a pairing of standards that would support the students' understanding of the text. Figure 7.7 shows the standards Lynsey grouped together specifically for *The Year of the Dog*. Because this read-aloud came toward the latter part of the school year, each of these standards had already been explored and co-constructed during previous whole-group reading minilessons with shorter texts. Now, while reading *The Year of the Dog*, students built on their prior understandings, this time throughout a full-length novel.

Read Aloud: *The Year of the Dog* by Grace Lin

SL.3.1 Engage effectively in a range of collaborative discussions (one-on-one, in groups, and teacher-led) with diverse partners on grade 3 topics and texts, building on others' ideas and expressing their own clearly.
 a. Come to discussions prepared, having read or studied required material; explicitly draw on that preparation and other information known about the topic to explore ideas under discussion.
 b. Follow agreed-upon rules for discussions (e.g., gaining the floor in respectful ways, listening to others with care, speaking one at a time about the topics and texts under discussion).
 c. Ask questions to check understanding of information presented, stay on topic, and link their comments to the remarks of others.

RL.3.3 Describe characters in a story (e.g., their traits, motivations, or feelings) and explain how their actions contribute to the sequence of events.

RL.3.1 Ask and answer questions to demonstrate understanding of a text, referring explicitly to the text as the basis for the answers.

RL.3.9 Compare and contrast the themes, settings, and plots of stories written by the same author about the same or similar characters (e.g., in books from a series).

RL.3.6 Describe the difference between points of view in texts, particularly first- and third-person narration.

Figure 7.7 *Lynsey creates a recording sheet that includes the focus standards of the unit and space to record students' words and ideas as they read* The Year of the Dog. *Lynsey will print out new copies of this sheet as necessary as she needs more space for notes.*

Planning: Creating a Recording Sheet

Lynsey chose a book that was a good match for her students. She considered which literacy standards pair best with the teaching of this book, and now she is ready to begin her teaching! But before she begins, she makes sure to get a new recording sheet ready to capture students' thinking as they begin a new book and a deeper dive into the skills of the focus standards of this unit. This form [Figure 7.7] is her last planning step before the read-aloud begins.

Teaching with *The Year of the Dog* Read-Aloud

Just as in the planning phase, we find naming the major components of the teaching phase to be helpful. When we are in the teaching phase of the read-aloud unit we are listening, recording student thinking, studying, and moving forward in response to what we see and hear from the students. We call these components previewing the book; listen, listen, listen; recording student thinking; studying student responses; and moving forward in response.

Previewing the Book

Previewing is always our first step when starting a new read-aloud. For *The Year of the Dog*, Lynsey asked her students to record their thinking around the preview in their own notebooks. They were invited to organize their thinking in a way that made sense for them as they looked at the cover, title page, first page, back cover, and author website.

Lynsey launched the novel study by inviting her students to preview *The Year of the Dog*'s cover and title page. "What are you noticing? What are you wondering?" Lynsey asked as her students glued copies of these parts of the text in their reading notebooks and began to annotate. Every read-aloud unit follows a similar structure of inviting students to notice and wonder and keep track of their thinking in their reading notebooks while the text is being read aloud. This structure allows students the space to process their thinking throughout a longer text and allows teachers the opportunity to better understand students' thinking and plan responsive instruction.

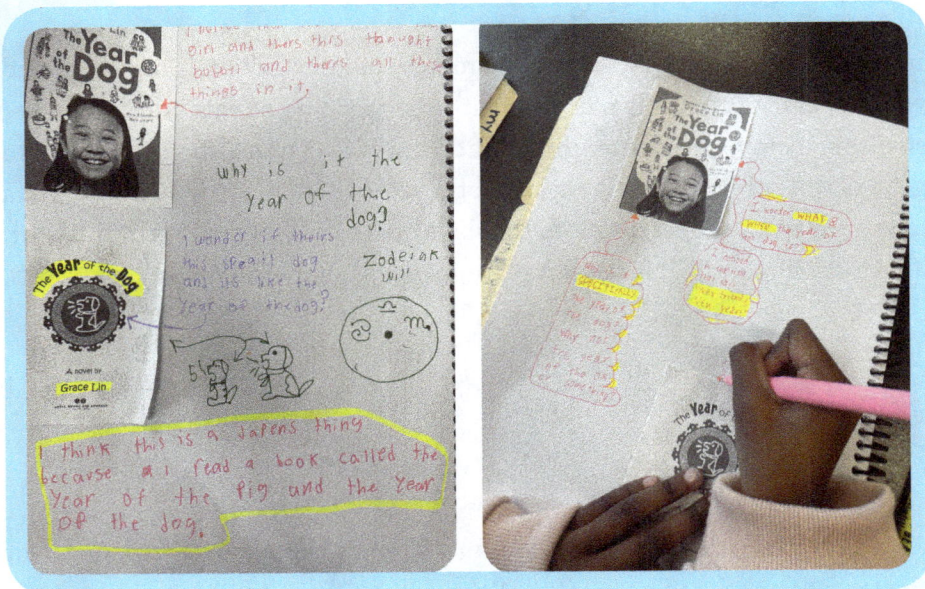

Figure 7.8   *Before beginning to read, students preview the book's cover and title page, making annotations in their reading notebooks.*

Listen, Listen, Listen

Listening to what we hear from students is at the core of our decision making. When we are highly in tune with what our students are saying and understanding as they experience the read-aloud, we can facilitate learning experiences that are tailored to their needs as readers. We view listening expansively here and it includes both listening to students' conversations and "listening in" on thoughts they record in writing.

During *The Year of the Dog* read-aloud Lynsey used the following methods of listening in order to understand how students were engaging with the text and consider what specific instruction would benefit the community.

Highlighting of Text

Lynsey uses her web-based Kindle app to have students collectively highlight parts of the text they felt the community should keep track of. This highlighting happens on the whiteboard and students collectively choose what to mark on that single copy that is projected. As we saw in the opening vignette, as Lynsey's class read *The Year of the Dog*, students often choose to highlight key ideas and details as well as parts that resonate emotionally for them. To facilitate the balance of read-aloud and stopping to highlight, students decided on a hand signal to use when they wanted Lynsey to pause reading so that they could highlight something.

Student Annotations

After a student highlights a section of text from the digital book projected on the whiteboard, they provide a quick statement to explain why they chose to highlight this part. We also use the tools within the Kindle app to capture this explanation in writing. This digital highlighting and note taking helps the group keep track of and return to key parts in the book.

Whole-Group Discussions

Whole-group discussions occur regularly during read-aloud time. As Lynsey's class read *The Year of the Dog*, whole-group discussions were particularly useful as students processed questions such as:

* How do we read a book that has stories within stories embedded in it? (*The Year of the Dog* toggles between stories of the past and stories from what is happening in the present.)
* What would it feel like to be the only person (or a few) of your race, religion, or culture at school (as the character Grace is at her school)?
* What does it mean to "find yourself"?
* What does it mean to be an American?
* Why would Grace lie about the Day of the Unicorn?
* What are the illustrations throughout the book teaching us so far?

Turn and Talk

During the reading of *The Year of the Dog*, Lynsey's students turned and talked multiple times during each read-aloud session. The group decided that it was helpful to talk with a partner every few pages. Lynsey would read and then find a natural stopping point every few pages unless a student asked to stop before.

Whiteboard Annotations

As you read about in the opening story of this chapter, Lynsey and her students often use a large whiteboard in their classroom to record quotes from the community's thinking that they want to hold onto. At times this looks like a student walking up and writing down their own quote or that of another student during a discussion. At other times this looks like Lynsey writing down a quote from a student or summary of thinking from the community. Recording on the whiteboard is a routine that has developed, over time, into a critical part of the culture of read-aloud time in Lynsey's classroom. It is a cherished part of the community experience and neither the students nor Lynsey seem to get off track when someone gets up to jot a quote on the whiteboard. At the end of the week Lynsey takes a picture of the board from that week and wipes it clean for the next week. There are times where Lynsey uses a picture from a prior week to start conversation around the book.

Reading Notebooks

Each student has a reading notebook they are invited to use during read-aloud time. Students often use these notebooks to jot down noticings and wonderings, track events in a book, or develop theories about characters. In Chapter 8 we share more details and tips for getting started with reading notebooks.

Recording Student Thinking

Just as with minilessons, it is important for teachers to have a note-taking system to keep track of student thinking during the read-aloud. Lynsey uses the standards recording sheet [Figure 7.9] to write down the ideas she hears from students or sees in their written work. But Lynsey doesn't write down *everything* she hears or sees. She carefully listens for:

* Key ideas from the text that support comprehension
* Concepts about which students seem confused
* Information about characters that reflect traits and/or motivations

Studying Student Responses

Studying students' responses to text is a critical part of teaching through read-aloud. Lynsey studies the notes she takes on her recording sheet and

Read Aloud: *The Year of the Dog* by Grace Lin

SL.3.1 Engage effectively in a range of collaborative discussions (one-on-one, in groups, and teacher-led) with diverse partners on grade 3 topics and texts, building on others' ideas and expressing their own clearly.
   a. Come to discussions prepared, having read or studied required material; explicitly draw on that preparation and other information known about the topic to explore ideas under discussion.
   b. Follow agreed-upon rules for discussions (e.g., gaining the floor in respectful ways, listening to others with care, speaking one at a time about the topics and texts under discussion).
   c. Ask questions to check understanding of information presented, stay on topic, and link their comments to the remarks of others.

"I think Pacy's very considerate because in the beginning she lied about the day of the unicorn."

RL.3.3 Describe characters in a story (e.g., their traits, motivations, or feelings) and explain how their actions contribute to the sequence of events.

"Pacy loves her culture."

"Grace is interested in learning about her parents past and about her religion."

"Pacy is a good friend because she does everything with Melody now."

"I wonder what it feels like to be the only person of your culture in the school?"

RL.3.1 Ask and answer questions to demonstrate understanding of a text, referring explicitly to the text as the basis for the answers.

"Why did Becky say that Grace couldn't be Dorothy because Dorothy is not Chinese?"

"Why did the lunch lady not know it wasn't Grace who went through the lunch line?"

RL.3.9 Compare and contrast the themes, settings, and plots of stories written by the same author about the same or similar characters (e.g., in books from a series).

"When Grace said, 'If we planted flowers instead of Chinese vegetables,' was it connected to her story *The Ugly Vegetables*?"

RL.3.6 Describe the difference between points of view in texts, particularly first- and third-person narration.

Figure 7.9 *Lynsey notes students' words and ideas on her standards recording sheet as she reads* The Year of the Dog *by Grace Lin.*

considers this question: what explicit reading instruction might support the community's understanding of this text (and other texts they will encounter in future reading)? Based on her answer to this question, Lynsey designs a minilesson that is responsive and supportive to her students' needs as readers. While these minilessons won't happen every day, when they do, Lynsey uses the first fifteen minutes of read-aloud time to engage the community in this learning experience. It is important that the reading of the text still continues that day, so Lynsey makes sure to save fifteen minutes after the minilesson for diving back into the story and continuing the read-aloud journey.

Let's take a look now at an example of this work as Lynsey considers students' responses to *The Year of the Dog* read-aloud and plans minilessons that will support her readers' learning.

Student Response During Read-Aloud	Lynsey's Plans for Follow-Up Minilessons
"Why did the lunch lady not know it wasn't Grace who went through the lunch line?"	**Focus Standard: RL.3.1** Ask and answer questions to demonstrate understanding of a text, referring explicitly to the text as the basis for the answers. **Lynsey's Plan:** Short explicit instruction on how readers use the text to support the basis of their answer. Allow students time to use their notes and copies of the text to locate places that support their conjectures around the question.
"Pacy is a good friend because she does everything with Melody now."	**Focus Standard: RL.3.3** Describe characters in a story (e.g., their traits, motivations, or feelings) and explain how their actions contribute to the sequence of events. **Lynsey's Plan:** *Day 1:* Use the student statement, "Pacy is a good friend because she does everything with Melody now," to think about if being a "good friend" is one of Pacy's character traits. Allow students time to locate two places in the text that show Pacy being a "good friend." As a whole group, chart the places in the text that were located by the students on a shared Google Document. *Day 2:* Each student gets a printed copy of the Google Document they created on Day 1. Students use this document to have a whole-group conversation around the questions: "What are you thinking now about if Pacy is a good friend? How do you know?"

(Continued)

Student Response During Read-Aloud	Lynsey's Plans for Follow-Up Minilessons
"Why did Becky say that Grace couldn't be Dorothy because Dorothy is not Chinese?"	**Focus Standard: RL.3.1** Ask and answer questions to demonstrate understanding of a text, referring explicitly to the text as the basis for the answers.
	Lynsey's Plan:
	Day 1: Each student gets a copy of the page where this part of the story occurred. They glue the page in their reading notebook and quietly annotate their thinking around the event on their own. Together in the whole community a student rereads this section of the story aloud to the group. Students are invited to share their annotations under the document camera.
	Day 2: On Day 1, many students recorded responses such as "That's not fair" and "This makes me sad" in response to the part in the text when Becky tells Grace that she can't be Dorothy because she's Chinese. Using these student annotations as starting points, the whole group discusses this part of the story while Lynsey facilitates by noticing and naming the students' conjectures and charting them on a Google Slide.
"When Grace (the character) said, 'If we planted flowers instead of Chinese vegetables,' was it connected to her other story *The Ugly Vegetables*?"	**Focus Standard: RL.3.9** Compare and contrast the themes, settings, and plots of stories written by the same author about the same or similar characters (e.g., in books from a series).

(Continued)

Student Response During Read-Aloud	Lynsey's Plans for Follow-Up Minilessons
	Lynsey's Plan: Use a read-aloud block to study the book *The Ugly Vegetables*, a picture book also by Grace Lin. Make multiple copies of the book available to the class. Ask students to work together to make comparisons between what they know about the book *The Year of the Dog* and *The Ugly Vegetables*. Ask students to consider characters, settings, problems, and themes as they compare and contrast.

The Read-Aloud at a Glance

Let's take a look now at how this read-aloud progressed over the course of the unit.

Day of the Unit	Read-Aloud Focus
Day 1 *Lynsey listens for students' notices and wonders as they engage in the book preview.*	**Focus: Book preview** The focus for the first experience with *The Year of the Dog* by Grace Lin is a book preview. Lynsey made copies of the front cover, back cover, title page, and table of contents for students to glue into the Read-Aloud section of their reading notebooks. (For more on setting up reading notebooks, see Chapter 8.) Lynsey invites the reading community to gather in the meeting area for read-aloud. Students know it is time for a new text but did not know what it would be. Preview day is always a big day for the reading community because the unveiling of the new book is exciting.

(Continued)

Day of the Unit	Read-Aloud Focus

As students gather they see the cover of the book projected on the interactive board and three paper copies of the book in a book bin underneath the interactive board. Lynsey hears chatter right away about what they notice about the cover.

It is a regular part of the book preview routine for students to grab the small photocopies of the book pieces (front cover, back cover, etc.) as they get to their space in the meeting area and begin gluing them in their notebooks. Students also know that they can talk to the reader next to them about what they are thinking as they glue the parts. Once they finish gluing, students begin annotating.

Readers record their notices, wonders, and thoughts and they move through the different parts of the book to preview [Figure 7.10].

Lynsey allows about twenty minutes for this process and the last ten minutes of this time is for the reading community to share what they found with one another. While the community is sharing, Lynsey records the students' ideas on a Google Slide.

After the share is over students clean up and transition to the next part of the day.

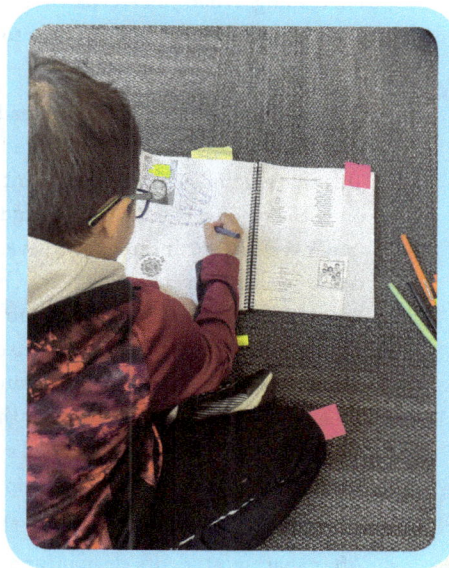

Figure 7.10 *A reader engages in a book preview of* The Year of the Dog.

(Continued)

Day of the Unit	Read-Aloud Focus

Days 2–7

Lynsey listens for how students keep track of what characters are in the book and information about these characters.

Focus: Read chapters and discuss

The reading community gathers in the meeting area for read-aloud time. Students know to bring their reading notebooks and any tools they want to use to keep track of their thinking.

During the reading of a chapter, Lynsey invites students to signal if they want a part highlighted or if they want to stop to talk as a community. Stopping to talk has a rhythm to it. It took the class a novel or two in the beginning of the year to figure it out. They know if they stop too much it's hard to keep track of what is going on in the book and if they stop too little they won't get the rich thinking of the collective group to support their own interpretations of what is happening.

Lynsey reads the first chapters stopping as the students indicate. Lynsey used to have planned stopping points when reading but she realized students naturally wanted to share their thinking in places she hadn't preplanned. Before Lynsey reads, she invites her students to stop her by saying, "Everyone, I know you will be thinking while I'm reading. When you feel like it is a good time to share what's on your mind, signal for me to stop and we will listen."

She saves the last ten minutes of read-aloud time for students to share what they captured in their notebooks. This sharing time is a very important step, especially early on in the reading of a new book. Students love to share under the document camera but, even more importantly, doing so allows them to get ideas of how their classmates are organizing their thinking in their notebooks as they begin a new book. For students who do not quite know how they might capture their thinking, this sharing time gives them a place to start for the next day. For students who feel they have a good system for organizing their thinking, the sharing time helps them find ways to enhance their process.

After sharing, students clean up and transition to the next part of the day.

(Continued)

Day of the Unit	Read-Aloud Focus
Days 8–13 *Lynsey listens for evidence of comprehension.*	**Focus: Read chapters and make sure all students have a way of keeping track of what they are learning about the central characters, settings, and key story events** By Day 8ish, the reading community has had time to read multiple chapters of the novel. They have also had time to have short discussions around key events and what they have learned about the characters and settings. This is the point at which Lynsey starts incorporating intentional minilessons that are embedded throughout the days. Lynsey utilizes her notes from the standards recording sheet to help craft minilessons.
Days 13–20 *Lynsey listens for evidence of synthesizing information and making inferences based on individual students' thinking and thinking of the reading community as a whole.*	**Focus: Synthesizing information and co-constructing visible learning journeys** During a novel study there usually comes a point in time at which students' individual thinking and the community's group thinking begins to merge into co-constructed visible learning. This co-constructed visible learning looks different depending on the novel the reading community is studying and based on the types of thinking the community has engaged in. **A few things that are always present in this co-construction are:** • Some type of artistic expression. • An explanation of art created using text evidence and quotes from students. • The visible representation is created over time from about the middle of the read-aloud to the end. For the visible learning journey representation for *The Year of the Dog* novel study the learning community focused on the standard: *RL.3.9 Compare and contrast the themes, settings, and plots of stories written by the same author about the same or similar characters (e.g., in books from a series).*

(Continued)

Lynsey requested all of Grace Lin's picture books from the local library. The class knew from reading an author interview with Grace Lin that she often writes about her family in her books. The class used Grace Lin's picture books to build knowledge around the characters and settings we read about in her novel *The Year of the Dog* by using a compare and contrast strategy.

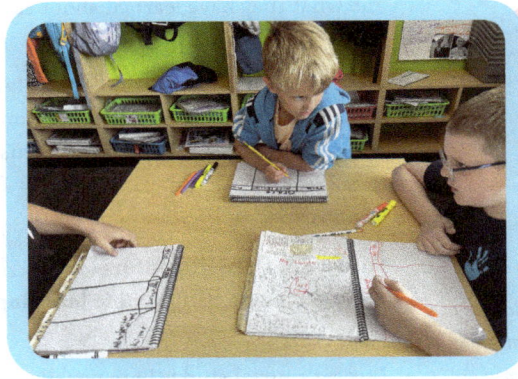

Figure 7.11 *Students work to synthesize information they learned from the texts we read together in order to think about the author's messages. This information will be included on the visual representation board.*

Figure 7.12 *Students create a visual representation using information from the novel study of* The Year of the Dog *and the picture book study of Grace Lin's other books.*

Figure 7.13 *The reading community works together during the read-aloud time of day.*

It is during read-aloud time that our readers transfer all that they learned in minilessons to a longer text, one that they read over time. We have found that the read-aloud time allows the community to read with depth and build understanding as a community. The combination of intentional planning and responsive teaching is key.

CHAPTER 8

Planning Intentionally for the First Eight Weeks of School

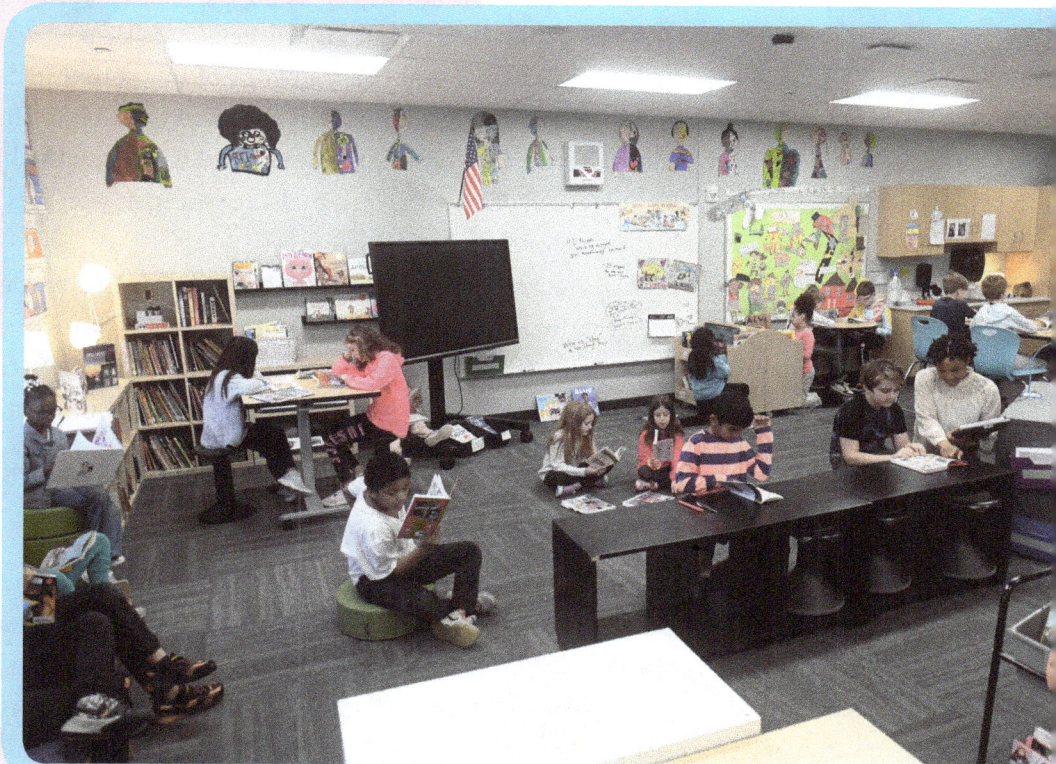

bell hooks taught us, "Seeing the classroom always as a communal place enhances the likelihood of collective effort in creating and sustaining a learning community" (1994, 8). We are always reminding ourselves of the communal nature of our classrooms as we think about what it means to plan intentionally at the start of the school year. The journey to centering students as we create an intellectual reading community starts long before the first day of school. The work begins before school starts and the set up continues during the first eight weeks or so of the school year. These first weeks are extremely important.

Preparing for the New School Year: Our Goals for the First Eight Weeks

We have very big and intentional goals for the first eight weeks of every school year. In order for the community to build trust in each other and themselves, taking things slowly the first eight weeks is critical.

We keep the big goals we have at the forefront of our thinking during the full eight weeks. We have learned over and over and over again that we can't rush what happens during these early weeks and if we take the beginning of the year slowly and stick with our goals, learning accelerates once we move past those first weeks.

In these first few weeks our main goal is to get to know this new group of children, both individually and as a community. Much of our work during this time is designed to allow us to listen and learn so that we can be teachers who are responsive to their interests and who can build on their strengths. We have several strategies for working toward this goal:

* ***Invitations***

    As we think about literacy and student agency, it is critical that we use the first weeks of school to shift the power dynamics that students may be used to in school. In order to do this, our focus is on providing students with invitations and conversations. By this, we mean that almost everything we ask children to do is an invitation. We offer students invitations into reading and community and watch how they take them up (or don't). This careful listening helps us plan responsively. We use language like, "Readers you are invited to try this in your reading to see if you find it helpful." Or, "Readers, I invite you to try out using sticky notes or a digital tool to keep track of your thoughts while reading to see what works best for you as a reader."

* ### Intellectual Conversations

Creating the conditions for authentic, intellectual talk takes time. The conversations that you've read about in this book so far are not typical of the first few weeks of school, so don't worry if your first conversations don't go exactly as you imagined. During these weeks, our students are often trying to determine what it is we want from their talk so it takes a while for them to trust that we are hoping for each person to bring their whole selves to each conversation. It also takes time for them to begin to see the power in collective thinking and how community conversations can support deeper understandings.

For example, Lynsey recalls a conversation with one of her third graders early in the school year. Liya approached her one morning and clearly had something to share with her. "Mrs. Burkins!" Liya said excitedly. "I just finished *Critter Club!*"

"You did!" replied Lynsey. "I can tell you are very excited, tell me about it!"

Liya looked up at Lynsey and said, "It was so good. I loved it!" Lynsey could tell Liya was excited, and Lynsey also knew that something Liya and the rest of the class needed was minilessons on how we can talk about what we are reading with others using details and sharing key ideas from the book. Lynsey made herself a note to plan minilessons around intellectual conversations in the next week to support reading conversations early on.

* ### Valuing Thinking Over the Right Answer

One thing that we've really had to practice is saying very little during these first eight weeks. As teachers, it is sometimes in our nature to correct errors or to respond to student thinking. But much of our work during this first part of the school year is making space for children to navigate conversations and get comfortable articulating their thinking to the group. So we might say things like, "Oh, I hadn't thought of it that way. Can you share what makes you think that?" We want them to

Figure 8.1 *Lynsey listens and records as students share their thinking at the beginning of the year.*

value their own thinking as well as the thinking of others so we often say things like, "Does anyone else have thinking that is similar to or different from that?" This type of talk is critical to deeper comprehension and being able to share one's in-process thinking is an important step toward comprehension.

Lifting and Naming

We use the first eight weeks of school to notice and name all that children are doing. We want every child to feel a valued member of the classroom community so we are always looking for student actions to notice and name aloud. During these weeks, it could be as simple as, "Wow! I noticed that Trevor listened to what Jolene said and her words inspired new thinking for Trevor." Or "I noticed that some of you used words in your notebooks today and some of you sketched your ideas. Both are great ways to record thinking. Does anyone want to share what they did?"

Amplifying Student Words

It is during the first several weeks of school that we build in routines to amplify student words. For our students to trust that their words are more important than the teachers' words, they need to see and hear

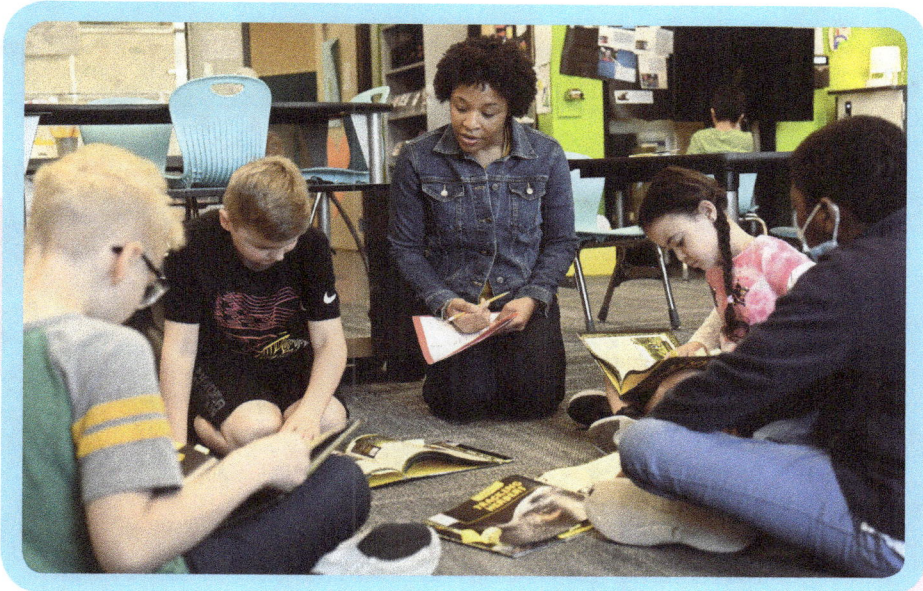

Figure 8.2 *Lynsey pulls a smaller group of readers together to intentionally notice and name what readers are doing.*

that message often. We say things like, "What you said was so inter-esting. Will you write that on the board so we can think about it?" and "Can you repeat what you just said? I want to write it down and think about it." These seemingly small practices help children trust that their words will matter in this classroom. They also give everyone in the classroom some helpful sentence stems that they might begin to use on their own when talking to classmates.

Listen, Listen, Listen

For us, so much of the work of the first eight weeks is to listen, listen, listen. We are careful not to overplan or to fall back on expecting this year's new students to do and say things in the way last year's group did. Instead we listen and record as a way to get to know each student individually and the class as a whole. We choose books and lessons that have little teacher talk and focus instead on eliciting student talk so that we can observe and listen to ways they approach various things. We ask big broad questions like, "What are you thinking now?" and "What are you noticing and wondering?" as we read aloud to students, making lots of space for the students to talk and for us to listen.

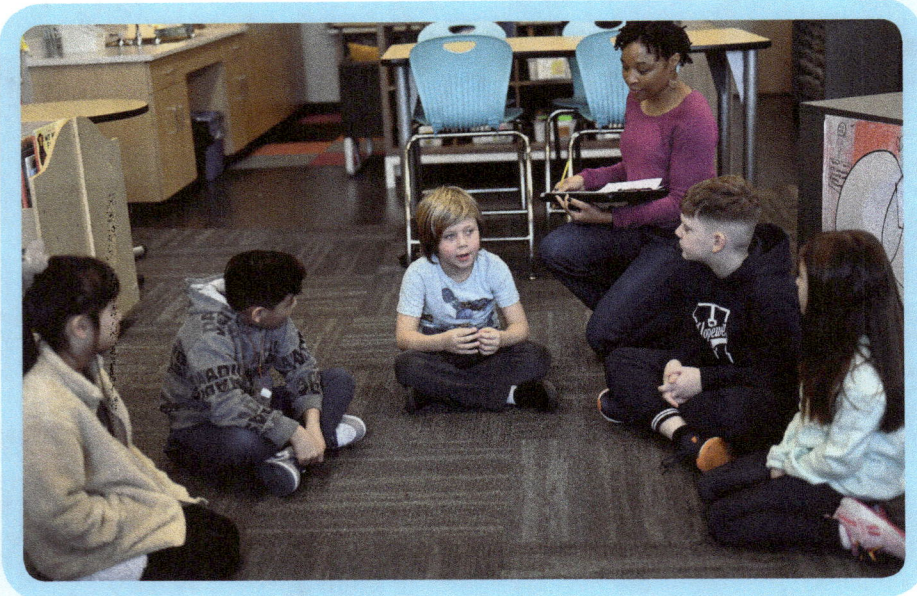

Figure 8.3 *Lynsey practices amplifying students' words early in the year in smaller groups so students can learn how this practice sounds in a more intimate setting.*

≥ Tip Box ≤

Ways to Listen Responsively No Matter What Curriculum Your School Follows:

1. If your school system assigns specific texts to use for reading instruction then you may try to start with recording student quotes and thinking from the text on a whiteboard, piece of chart paper, or on sticky notes. This process will allow both students and teachers to see patterns in the collective thinking and use them to enhance comprehension.

2. If your system provides daily lesson plans for you to follow, try spending some time together as a class annotating the standard that connects to that lesson. This process will give you opportunities to formatively assess how students are accessing the standard and where they may need support. This will also

give students the opportunity to be part of the learning as they create goals for themselves and their reading community.

3. If your school system has a planned curriculum you may try looking for ways to embed more student talk. You can do this by flipping some of the teacher talk in the plan to student conversation and by posing the content of the teacher talk as questions rather than completely following the script. This will free you, as the teacher, to listen to what the students are saying and doing during this talk and embed the strengths of the conversation and places of confusion throughout future lessons.

Preparing for the New School Year: Designing a Classroom Space for Intellectual Learning Community

Setting up a physical environment that supports an intellectual learning community is one of the most important things we do. We know we need to create a space that offers many opportunities for collaboration and conversation. Here are some of the spaces we create even before the school year begins.

Whole-Group Meeting Space

Before we set up anything else in our classroom, our first priority is to create a space where the entire community can gather to have conversations. We need a space where students can see the screen we use to project ebooks and student thinking, where they can turn and talk, and where we can, when needed, form a circle. Often we create a space with two levels of seating (floor and chairs/benches). This two-level design helps students have enough space to see and hear each other well. We also create a meeting space that does not center the teacher so we are intentional in thinking through various options for where the teacher might place themself during whole-group meetings—in

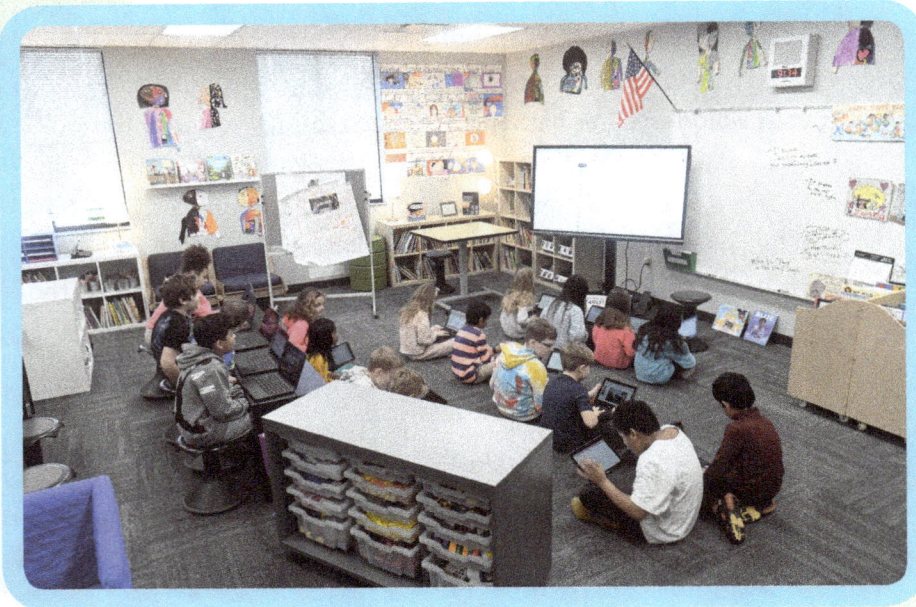

Figure 8.4 *A view of Lynsey's whole-group meeting space.*

Figure 8.5 *Students gather in different spots around the room.*

the back, to the side, or on the floor with children. From the very first day, we want students to see that they are centered, not the teacher. We have written extensively about the ways in which we design our classroom in our book *Classroom Design for Student Agency* (Burkins and Sibberson, 2023).

Various Spaces for Conversation Around the Room

After we create a whole-group meeting space, we make sure that there are a variety of spaces around the room for small groups to gather. We want varied seating options for students so we create some spaces at tables, some spaces at low tables, and some carpet areas. We also want spaces that invite different group sizes (partner talk, Talking Circles, etc.) so we keep that in mind too.

Wall Space

Much of the wall space in our classrooms is left blank before school begins. We want to co-create this space with students. We think through the wall/board spaces where we will make student thinking visible, and post work that invites conversations and collaborations.

Figure 8.6 *The wall space in Lynsey's classroom at the beginning of the year is mostly empty.*

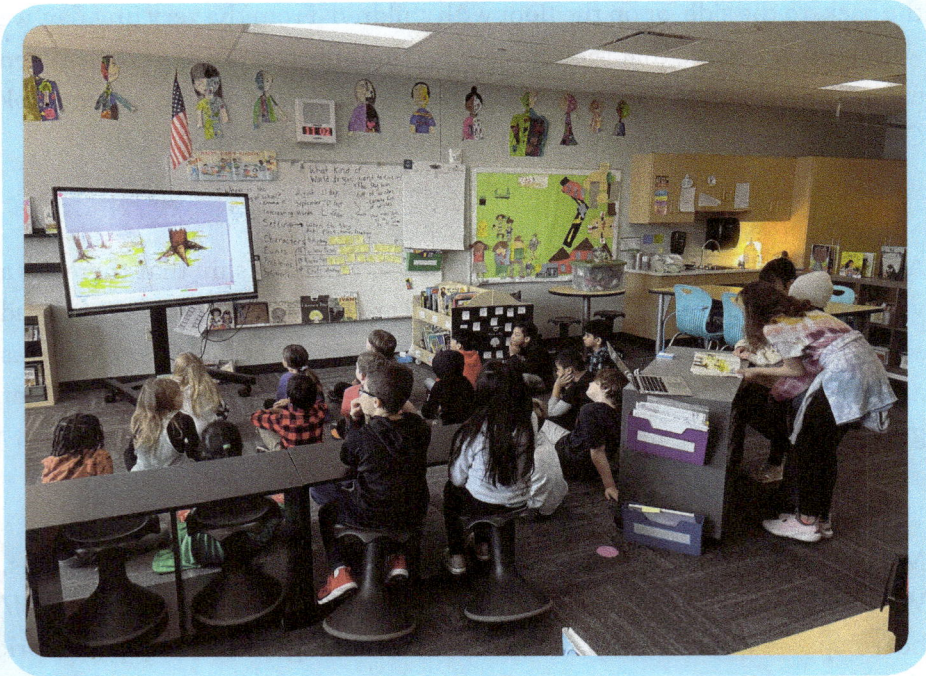

Figure 8.7 *The wall space in Lynsey's classroom after the first twelve weeks or so of school.*

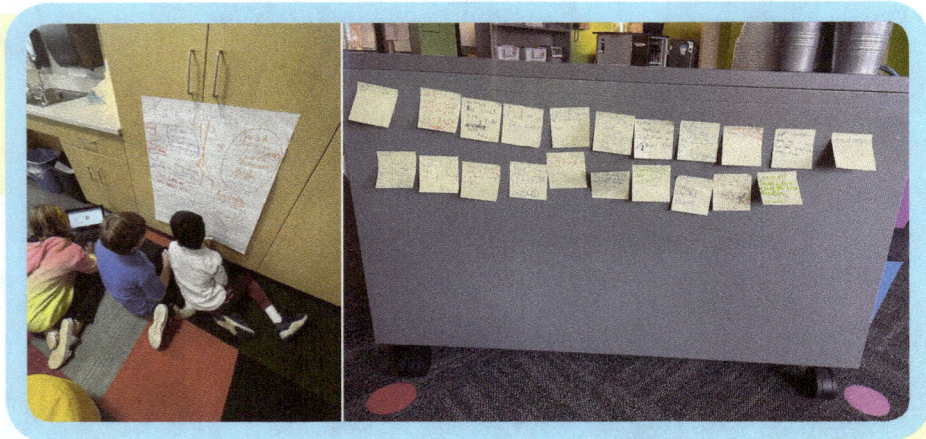

Figure 8.8 *Where space is tight, we get creative by using spaces like the fronts of cabinets as wall spaces.*

The Classroom Library

The classroom library is the fabric that weaves all the other classroom space together. When students are extremely familiar with the books in the classroom library and know how to look for books within the classroom library it opens up opportunities for co-construction of learning within whole-group instruction. Students start suggesting books to one another and creating text sets that help continue the learning. To cultivate the practice of collective curation we take the time in the first few weeks to:

* Allow students long periods of time to explore books that are in the classroom library.
* Allow students time to talk together about the books they are reading from the classroom library.
* Create minilessons that focus on students sharing books they found in the classroom library.
* Early on in the school year, leave empty book bins on bookshelves for students to place books they liked and think others should read from that particular section of the library.

Freire's ideas of co-construction has led us to the understanding that the classroom library should be co-curated between students and teachers (2000).

You might try grouping together series with similar characteristics and themes. Try chunking your library in sections around your classroom. Possible sections might be:

* Fiction
* Informational
* Poetry
* Series books
* Collections by certain authors or illustrators
* Novels
* Digging Deeper (book bins that contain text sets that explore a particular message or topic—these bins often have multiple genres and text structures within the set)

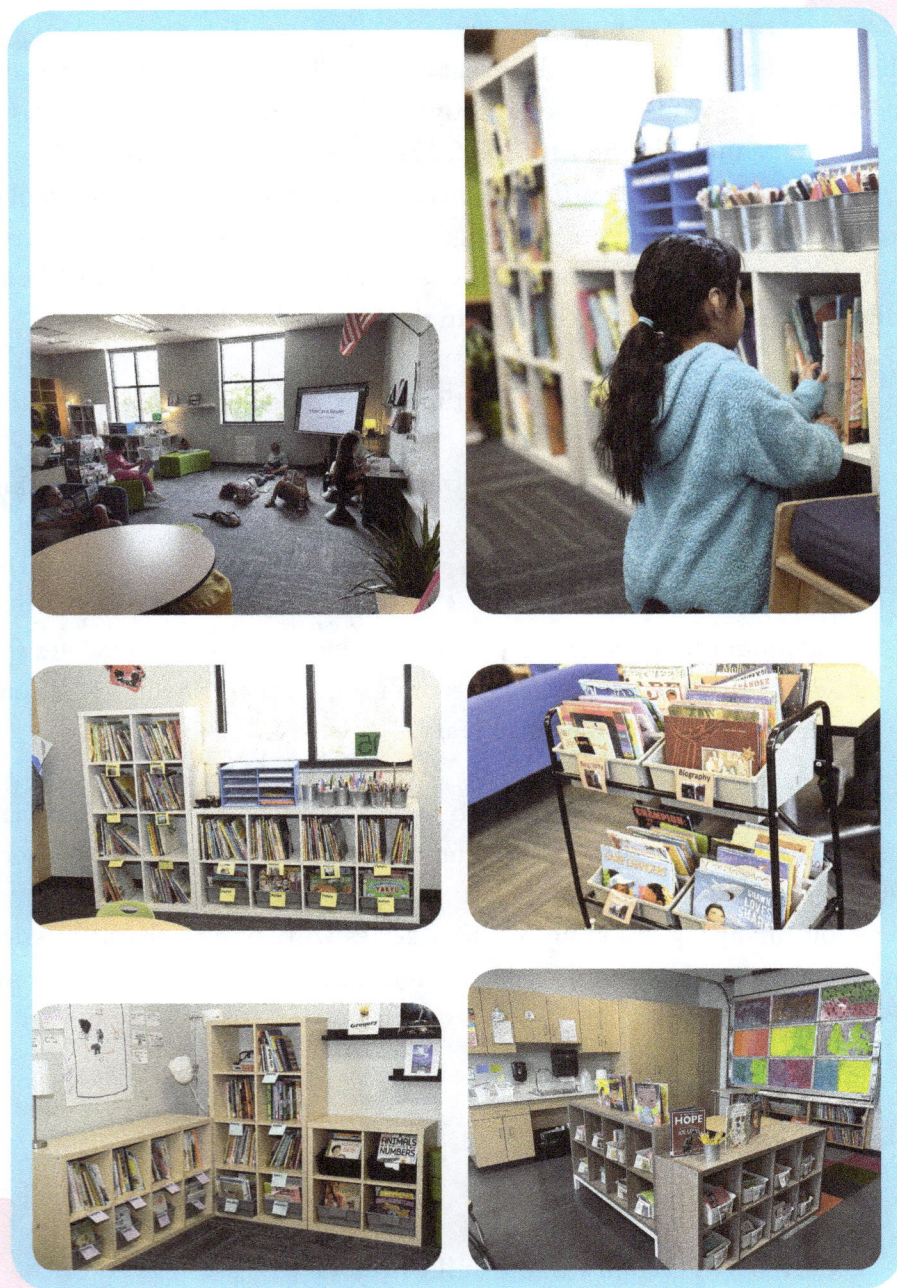

Figure 8.9 *The classroom library is spread out around the room.*

If you like **Goofballs...**

You might also like:
- Cam Jansen
- Jack gets a Clue
- Museum Mysteries
- The Haunted Library
- A to Z Mysteries
- Jaden Toussaint, the Greatest

Figure 8.10 *In Lynsey's third-grade classroom many kids were reading Goofballs and other series books. The reading community worked together to think about books that are similar to this favorite series and place them in the same basket, and create a label for the basket to help other readers in the class find new books to love.*

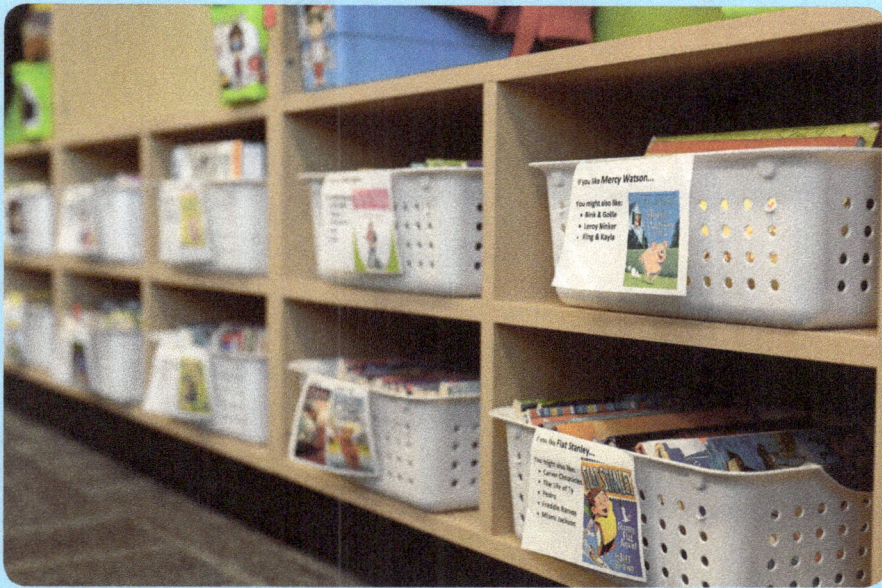

Figure 8.11 *Creating a series book section in your classroom library is one way to get students in the habit of browsing books.*

Intentional Book Displays Around the Classroom

Curating book displays around the classroom that center students' ideas and interests is an important part of our classroom design. Creating engaging book displays often prompts conversations between students both within reading time and beyond it. Book displays also support students' independence and agency as they decide if they want to learn more about certain topics raised in class or discover new topics they are interested in.

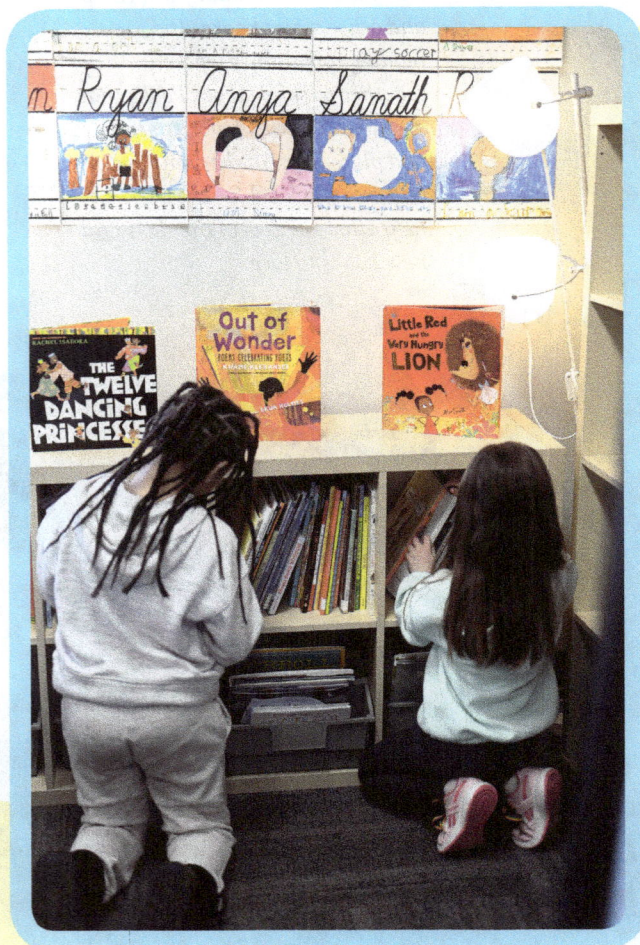

Figure 8.12   *Two of Lynsey's students browse the classroom library.*

Figure 8.13 *Students gather at a table, surrounded by the classroom library.*

Providing physical spaces for students to browse and talk together about books is a special kind of invitation. This routine also gets students familiar with the books in the classroom library. We want students to know the books and feel comfortable making book suggestions to one another. Additionally, many of these books are used, at some point in the year, for whole-group reading instruction and we want to offer students the chance to revisit titles they have experienced in the whole-class community.

Launching the Year with Tools That Support Student Agency

Creating an environment that supports whole-class reading and independence means that students have access to all of the tools they need at all times. We are intentional about having supplies throughout the room so that students can easily access what they need. We know that students will overuse these tools during the first several weeks. (Who among us doesn't like to try out fresh new sticky notes and pens?!) We know we will go through a lot of sticky notes as students play and learn how to use these tools and discover the power in choosing tools to match their purpose.

We set up the classroom so that students have access to supplies and choice in the supplies they use. Felt tip pens, sticky notes, and other tools are placed in spots where children can access them at any time.

Materials We Make Accessible to Children at All Times

Figure 8.14 *Tools and materials are at the ready for readers and writers.*

* Sticky notes of various sizes and shapes
* Felt tip pens
* Colored pencils
* Pens
* Pencils
* Variety of paper
* Highlighters
* Markers
* Crayons
* Paint and paintbrushes
* Chart paper
* Laptops
* Dry erase board
* Clipboards

Reading Notebooks

While students have many purposeful tools to choose from in the classroom, one common tool they all have is a blank, unlined notebook that we use as a reading notebook. Beginning with these blank notebooks, we set up the reading notebooks together as a class in the first weeks of school.

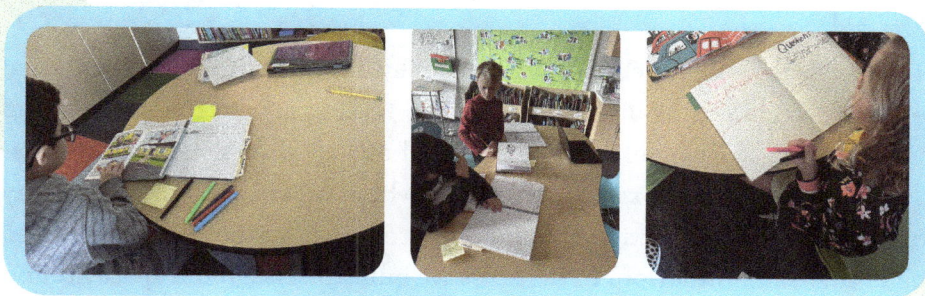

Figure 8.15 *Students engage with their reading notebooks.*

Our reading notebooks have three sections: My Spot, Group Thinking, and Read-Aloud. The My Spot section is a space for students to use during their independent reading time. They use this part of their notebook to think about their reading lives by keeping track of books they read, recording their thinking around texts they are reading, and making plans for future reading. Students themselves are really in charge of how this My Spot looks and many times students get ideas from other students on how they use this section of their reading notebooks. The Group Thinking section of the reading notebook is a space for student-selected book club thinking, or small-group instruction with Lynsey. Anytime students are engaged with thinking that involves other readers this is just the spot to record what happens. Finally, the Read-Aloud spot is where students keep track of the chapter book or novel we are studying together during the read-aloud part of the day. Students are invited to do the following in this section during the read-aloud:

* Book preview
* Keep sketch notes while they are listening to the read-aloud
* Make sections to keep track of parts of the story they feel are important such as:
  → Characters
  → Settings
  → Problems/solutions
  → Questions they have while listening
  → Answers they have discovered
  → Important events or ideas
  → Quotes from the story

Digital Tools

The digital tools in our classroom are equally important to more traditional ones. We value setting up our interactive whiteboard near the whole-group meeting area so that text can be centered during read-aloud and minilessons. We have been in many classrooms where we did not have autonomy over where the interactive board was placed in the room. You might also be in that same situation. In that case we built the classroom space around where the interactive board was placed and made sure there was enough room for the reading community to gather in front of it.

We know that we'll read several digital books over the course of the school year and that we'll use digital tools to make students' thinking visible. Having a space for displaying a digital text that is visible from the whole-group setting as well as accessible throughout the day is important. We also want our students to know that digital annotations are always an option for their individual notetaking so we make sure laptops are also available to students at all times. We have been in different school contexts in which students

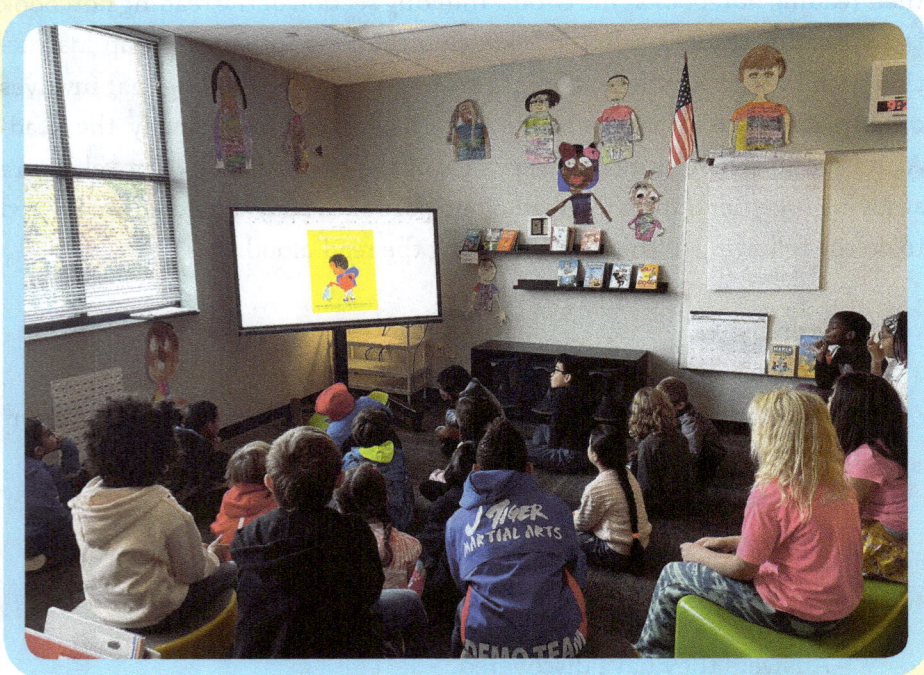

Figure 8.16 *In Lynsey's classroom, the whole-group meeting area is located near the whiteboard for access to digital texts.*

brought their own devices to school, where the school has provided ten to twelve devices for the class to use, or where the school has provided one-to-one devices. Having experienced all these situations has made us think very intentionally about what digital tools to introduce during the first week of school so that all students, no matter what the device situation is, can access them. At this moment in time we have found that Google applications and Google Classroom have allowed us the greatest success with teaching students how to annotate digitally and the sharing capability and accessibility.

The first eight weeks we "play" a lot with functions of the digital tools. We know if we can introduce these six skills over the course of the first eight weeks of school and students explore them during this time we will be able to use these functions in dynamic ways later:

1. Taking a picture
2. Taking a screenshot
3. Importing a picture from a device to a shared folder or into a doc and slide
4. Creating a video
5. Sharing a video to a shared folder or stream
6. Creating a text box on a slide

What this might look like early on is students taking a picture of a book they found in the classroom library and posting it to the Google Classroom stream. After a few weeks of exploring this skill, students may be ready to take a screenshot of a page they connected with while reading a book on Epic (an ebook digital library). Students might then learn to import that screenshot to a Google Slide where they can use text boxes and arrows to tell about what in the text they connected with. They can even add their voice! Learning how to use just these six basic skills during the first eight weeks of school allows students to use digital tools in authentic and meaningful ways. Learning this skill set also prepares students to learn other online tools important to our classroom culture such as Padlet. Our goal for these tools is that they become so intuitive that students are no longer thinking about the technology itself but rather are focused on the learning at hand. We want them to experience these digital tools and their functions as fully as possible during these early weeks so that we can use them throughout the year to share ideas and create community.

Preparing for the New School Year: Setting Up Teacher Tools for Planning and Assessment

We set up a variety of blank assessment tools once we have our class lists at the beginning of the school year. The variety of tools is important as different forms are used for different purposes. Having these forms set up with multiple copies at the ready and on our clipboards is key to our role these first eight weeks. Above all, these forms help us to really focus on the listening we are doing early in the school year. Below are some examples of forms we create which you can also find in the appendices:

* Name Grid [Appendix B]

Figure 8.17   *As teachers, we always have a clipboard handy so we can jot down all of the brilliance we hear. This note-taking practice helps us plan responsively.*

* Standards planning and documentation sheet [Appendix C]

Unit: _____	Week of: _____
Focus Standard:	Focus Standard:
Focus Standard:	Focus Standard:

Document Recording Sheet

We also set up digital spaces for collecting and sharing photos, student thinking and artifacts, including:

* A digital folder or other tool for collecting photos
* A slide template for collecting student thinking
* An online learning management system (we use Google Classroom) with intentional spaces for students to access tools, minilesson slides, read-aloud annotations, etc.

Preparing for the New School Year: Reading to Create a Menu of Book Titles

As we wrote about in Chapter 4, we spend time over the summer reading in order to create a Menu of Mentors we may use with our new group. We read as many new books as we can and we also revisit some of the older books that we think might be good fits for the coming school year. We know we have far more books on our list than we'll ever use with our new class but we also know that if we are going to be responsive to children, we will need options. That is why we call it a menu! We'll pick and choose from this menu and add titles as the year goes on based on what we learn from our students.

Inviting Conversation Around Books in the First Weeks of School

During the first eight weeks of school, intentional book choice for minilesson work offers invitations to conversations that will allow us, as teachers, to gain information about the readers in the community and their identities. This also allows time for the reading community to learn to have conversations together and to learn to build thinking and create new ideas as a community.

As we create this menu of books, we consider all that we want to know about this new group of students. We read, thinking about all the conversation that a book might naturally invite. We read to find new books. We know that the lived experiences of the students in our rooms will be vast, complex, and intersectional. As such, we want to share books by authors from communities that have been marginalized. We want to share books that show joy. We want to share books that represent the global community. We want to share books that elicit joyful reactions and also books that beg students to wonder and think.

While we read many longer texts over the course of the school year, we find that reading picture books with students early in the school year allows us to share a variety of texts and provides accessible entry points for all kinds of readers in our classroom. Let's take a look at a few types of picture books we often read early in the school year.

Types of Picture Books We Share with Students in the First Eight Weeks	An Example of This Type of Text
Humor We want to know what this new class finds to be funny and what they respond to. Creating joyful classrooms with lots of laughter is a goal of the first few weeks of school and all year long.	*Bathe the Cat*, written by Alice B. McGinty and illustrated by David Roberts A family needs to clean the house to get ready for Grandma's visit, but the cat has other silly plans!
Identity and Community We want to invite our students to talk about themselves as both individuals and community members. We look for books that share about the different identities we hold in ways that draw students into the conversation and allow for reflection. Often these books naturally invite conversations around character.	*What I Am*, by Divya Srinivasan As the character in this book reflects on her identity she considers all the parts of herself that make her who she is.

(Continued)

Types of Picture Books We Share with Students in the First Eight Weeks	An Example of This Type of Text
These conversations are key when thinking about supporting the literacy journeys of the class and connecting to the standards around understanding characters.	

Informational Books

Sharing informational books about engaging topics invites talk about various facts and issues in our world. These books allow us to listen for what interests and excites students and also helps us understand how students navigate informational texts and topics.

Butt or Face, by Kari Lavelle

Jam packed with information, this playful and interactive text invites readers to join in the fun while learning about animals.

Families

Books focusing on families give children the opportunity to talk about their own families.

We look for books that depict many different kinds of families. We want to listen for how students see their own families and other families in the school and community. These early-in-the-year conversations are crucial to building ideas and understandings in other texts that will unfold throughout the school year.

Powwow Day, written by Traci Sorell and illustrated by Madelyn Goodnight

Following an illness, River is hesitant to join in one of her favorite community celebrations. But with the support and love of her family, she is able to join in her community's powwow day.

Memories

Books that focus on memories give students an accessible way to begin having collaborative conversations and to learn about one another. Following a narrative is often part of these texts so listening and watching for how children make sense of plot gives us, as teachers, a great deal of information.

River of Mariposas, by Mirelle Ortega

Recalling happy memories from her past, a young girl seeks to recreate and restore what was lost during her immigration journey to the United States, and in doing so, discovers so much more!

(Continued)

Types of Picture Books We Share with Students in the First Eight Weeks	An Example of This Type of Text
Wordless Books Wordless books always invite so much conversation. These books support readers at all levels to talk about the story without being concerned with text. They also invite a variety of interpretations and prompt lively conversations with students as they learn to go back to parts of the book to support their thinking.	*Forever Home*, by Henry Cole Follow a boy as he falls in love with an abandoned dog and this new companion finds his home.
Communities Right from the first day of school, we want students to begin to think about what it means to be part of a classroom community, as well as give space for students to talk about the communities of which they are already a part. Community-focused books help with creating norms for our beloved reading community and help us imagine how we want to grow with each other. Many of these books have very accessible themes to which students will make connections.	*The Year We Learned to Fly*, written by Jacqueline Woodson and illustrated by Rafael López We learn to fly when we seek community to support us. Follow the children in this story as they learn how community and relationships can get you through the hardest of times.
Books That Show Caring for One Another We can use this kind of book to study the ways characters care for one another. These books serve an important purpose early in the school year as students study a text as both readers and community members considering how they will care for one another in the classroom community.	*I Can Help*, written by Reem Faruqi and illustrated by Mikela Prevost The simple words "I can help" can change the culture of a classroom. Follow these students as they discover the power of community and the ways we can care for one another.

(Continued)

Types of Picture Books We Share with Students in the First Eight Weeks	An Example of This Type of Text
School Stories and Stories About Learning These books invite conversations that help teachers gain more understanding of their students' emotions around how they see themselves in school and as learners. These books also encourage conversations about books that have similar settings (i.e., school) but different themes, characters, etc.	*Raj's Rule (For the Bathroom at School)*, written by Lana Button and illustrated by Hatem Aly Raj has many rules about going to the bathroom at school. How can Raj navigate not going to the bathroom at school all day?

Inviting Conversations About Books Beyond the First Weeks

When it comes to read-aloud, we try to create a mental list for ourselves of books that might be a good fit at some point during the school year. We know that readers change and grow across the year, so we are really just building a menu of possibilities. We look for quality books that are engaging to the age of child we are teaching. We look for accessible themes, strong characters, and issues that we know children will want to discuss. Across the year, we know that we want to read aloud a variety of books so we are looking for diversity across characters, genre, and format.

Over the summer, we read widely. We read new middle-grade novels in order to add to our possible read-aloud books for the upcoming year. We rarely read aloud a book we've read with another class. We've found that when we do that, we go in with expectations of the other class's conversations and thinking. We've learned that in order not to fall back on books we've shared in the past, our summertime is well spent reading with our eye toward new read-alouds. As we are reading over the summer, we are looking for books that will invite authentic conversations around a variety of issues as well as books that highlight various features that add to the text complexity. We are looking for a variety of genres, knowing that read-aloud may be the first time children engage with a specific genre, such as historical fiction or fantasy. We know that read-aloud time will change as our readers change. Let's take a look at a list of possible read-aloud books beyond the first weeks of school for a fifth-grade class.

New Books We Might Add to a Menu of Mentors for Fifth-Grade Read-Aloud	Notes About Why It Might Make a Good Read-Aloud for Fifth Grade
Operation Frog Effect by Sarah Scheerger	→ Told from various perspectives → Takes place in a school → Visual elements that go along with text → Invitation to discuss character → Realistic fiction → A title worth thinking about
Harbor Me by Jacqueline Woodson	→ Various perspectives → Character development → Title as metaphor → Themes of collective impact/knowing others → Realistic fiction
Dragons in a Bag by Zetta Elliott	→ First in a series that children might read independently → Early fantasy for readers new to this genre → Variety of characters to study → Variety of settings (time and place)

(Continued)

New Books We Might Add to a Menu of Mentors for Fifth-Grade Read-Aloud	Notes About Why It Might Make a Good Read-Aloud for Fifth Grade
Rez Dogs by Joseph Bruchac	→ Novel in verse → Set in current times during the pandemic → Set on a Wabanaki reservation → Strong main character to study
Solimar by Pam Muñoz Ryan	→ Fantasy → Traditions and stories embedded within the main story → Map at the beginning of the book (setting) → Character overcoming a challenge → Character changes over course of book → Short text with depth
The Last Cuentista by Donna Barba Higuera	→ More complex fantasy → Introduction to dystopia subgenre → John Newbery and Pura Belpré Award winner (great introduction to these awards) → Longer book so opportunities to model strategies for comprehension and stamina
Yusef Azeem Is Not a Hero by Saadia Faruqi	→ Historical fiction → Character dealing with prejudice → Author whose other books students may go on to read independently after being introduced to her work through this title → Themes of activism/standing up for what is right

(Continued)

New Books We Might Add to a Menu of Mentors for Fifth-Grade Read-Aloud	Notes About Why It Might Make a Good Read-Aloud for Fifth Grade
Maizy Chen's Last Chance by Lisa Yee	→ Realistic fiction → Historical time period → Immigration → Humor throughout → Strong character development → National Book Award finalist → Asian/Pacific American Award for Youth Literature
Stuntboy, in the Meantime written by Jason Reynolds, illustrated by Raúl the Third	→ Realistic fiction → Opportunity to study how visuals and text work together → Story within a story → Character dealing with anxiety → Illustrated novel format → Great audiobook option
The List of Things That Will Not Change by Rebecca Stead	→ Realistic fiction → Character's internal conflict → Child dealing with divorce → Short book with depth → Character with internal conflict
A Rover's Story by Jasmine Warga	→ Science fiction → First-person narration → Possible connection to nonfiction books about the Mars Rover → Accessible themes of identity, friendship, and courage → Nonhuman main character who changes over time

This list is only an initial menu because once we read aloud the first book of the school year, our listening to students will guide us in choosing which book to read aloud next. We may choose a book on this list or we may not, but the list helps us think about possibilities for read-aloud and how it might grow over the course of the year.

Sometimes, we do not start a chapter book read-aloud right away. Instead we spend the time sharing picture books and building conversation. Other years we begin the school year with a short chapter book read-aloud. Regardless of when we do the first longer read-aloud of the year, we always want to choose the book carefully. We know the first book we choose will set the stage for the kind of conversation and collective thinking we will do all year long. We also know that we'll learn a great deal about our readers during the first read-aloud. In fifth grade, we typically choose a shorter chapter book to launch the year to allow us to learn read-aloud routines and get to know our students better before choosing a longer book.

Figure 8.18   *Readers engaged in a read-aloud at the beginning of the school year.*

Go back to the list you created over the summer. One important component of this menu is realizing that what we choose to read aloud is what children often see is valued in the classroom. So it's important that we read books that are a variety of lengths, making sure to model for students that longer books don't mean better or harder—we purposely choose several shorter books to read throughout the year. We also keep in mind the variety of authors we are choosing because we know these are authors students will get to know and may read more on their own.

Preparing Book Talks

As we prepare for the new school year, we consider how we might use book talks to introduce readers to series, authors, and topics. During a book talk we may hold up a book and talk about it informally or we may read aloud a bit from the back cover and the first few pages. Book talking early and frequently at the beginning of the year supports students in their independent reading, helping orient them to genres and formats as well as digging into the types of books that most interest our students.

We find book talks around series books to be particularly engaging at the beginning of the year, and we know these series books are often what hook middle-grade readers. Here are a few series that we might book talk at the beginning of the year.

Early Series Books That We Might Book Talk in Third Grade

Bad Guys
Goosebumps
Desmond Cole, Ghost Patrol
Tales of Bunjitsu Bunny
King and Kayla
Dog Man

Series Books That We Might Book Talk in Fifth Grade

The Baby-sitters Club graphic novel series
The Wild Robot
JoJo Makoons
Maybe Marisol Rainey
The Truth About Your Favorite Animals
Percy Jackson
The Quirks
Whatever After
Julian and Lucas
Ryan Hart series
Jason Reynolds' *Track* series
Frazzled
Rip and Red

The First Eight Weeks: Building Routines

So much of the first eight weeks of school is setting up routines, but it is really our mindset around setting up these routines that is most important. It is easy to get caught up in modeling routines for children and then expecting them to follow our lead. However, if we are serious about supporting student agency, we must instead build and grow routines alongside our students based on their strengths. Instead of us teachers deciding each and every step of what kids need to learn to do in each routine, we can co-construct these routines by watching, listening, and building on what students bring to our classrooms. We build routines to discover brilliance, support independent as well as collective thinking, and value student agency. So what does this routine building look like in practice? Let's take a look.

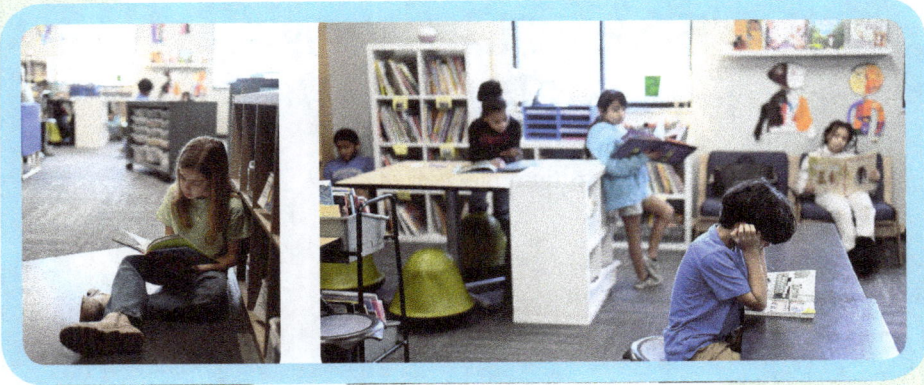

Figure 8.19 *Students build the routine of independent reading.*

The Routine of Sharing Student Thinking and Work

Early in the year, we have several opportunities throughout the day for students to share their work. These invitations to share can be as easy as saying, "Who can share a strategy they used in their notebook today?" or "Who has a notebook entry that they'd like to put under the document camera for us to study?" Instead of a lot of step-by-step modeling early in the year, we are instead focused on amplifying all of the things children are already doing and highlighting possibilities for others.

The Routine of Students Recording Their Thinking

Student thinking can be captured in many ways. We want students to experience using as many annotation tools as they can during the first eight weeks so they can begin to see what works for them in different situations. This early exploration of recording tools allows students to make intentional choices of the tools that work for them.

We use these tool-exploration invitations as a way to engage children with various digital tools as well. We may open a Padlet and invite everyone to add their thinking and then ask a few people to share. We may pass out sticky notes and then invite students to share which part in the text made them want to write something on the sticky note. We offer invitations and then celebrate all of the ways children participate.

The Routine of Centering Student Thinking Visibly

We want students to know from the first day of school that their words matter and that we are listening to all they have to say. We also want to build routines that allow students to listen to and learn from one another. Making student thinking visible provides a scaffold for this listening as students have a visual of one another's words at all times.

Sometimes, as you've read about in previous chapters, we capture students' thinking on a big shared whiteboard. Other times students use sticky notes or digital tools to hold very important thinking. These artifacts, whether print or digital, big or small, hold crucial information that can be used to advance conversations during read-aloud or minilessons.

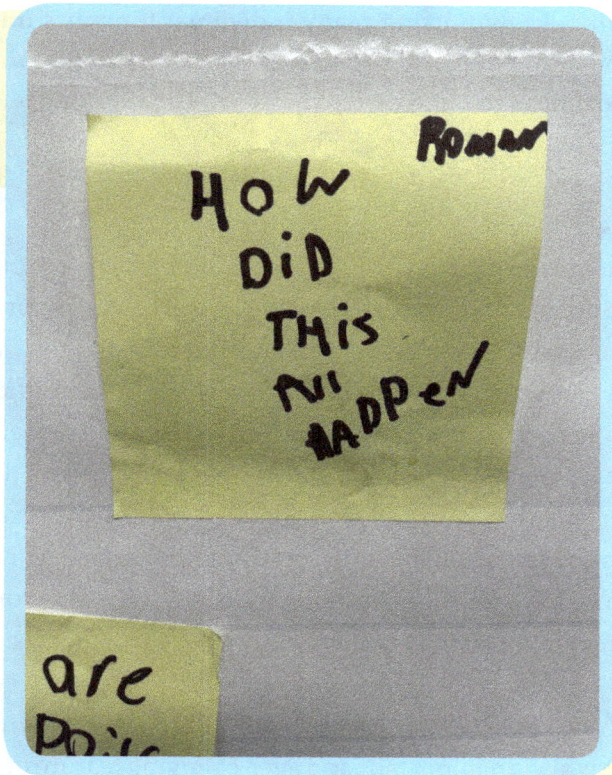

Figure 8.20 *Sticky notes are a form of note taking that holds students' important thinking and can be shared with the class to spark conversation.*

It is important during these first few weeks that we make sure to value all types of recording. Children who are working on developing their writing skills or who are learning English may be most comfortable sketching their thinking or writing in another language they know. What is important during these first weeks is that we value and lift up all thinking and all of the ways that students record their thinking.

Charts as a Way to Center Student Thinking

We often use charts to track the class's collective thinking. Charts allow us to collect many ideas from students in one place and then look across the ideas for emerging patterns. For example, we might use charts when we preview a book, when we think about the ways a character has changed in a book or when we stop and think deeply about a line or phrase that is repeated in a book. By putting many individual thoughts on a chart, we can look at them together and come to new, deeper understandings. These charts invite children to build on and question the thinking of others while learning the power of collective thinking.

Board Space as a Way to Center Student Thinking

We use our walls as a space to hold student thinking by recording their direct quotes. We've done this in several ways. We've used chart paper, sticky notes on posters, an easel, and a whiteboard that is mounted to the wall.

Lynsey's class uses the whiteboard as a space to hold students' thinking by recording their direct quotes. Both students and teachers are invited to share quotes. Lynsey begins using this board on the first day of school, listening for gems to add to the wall. There is no right or wrong quote to put on the board. Lynsey listens for anything that feels like it might start a good conversation and engage others. It doesn't take long for students to begin recording quotes (their own words or those of others) on the board.

Classroom Wall Space as a Way to Center Student Thinking

The wall space is also an important and ever-changing feature of whole-group reading instruction. We use our wall space as a way to make our learning visible during reading units. We archive thinking at the end of each unit and create new space for the next cycle. Charts, maps, sketches of characters, and sticky notes all fill the walls at various times during the year. We want

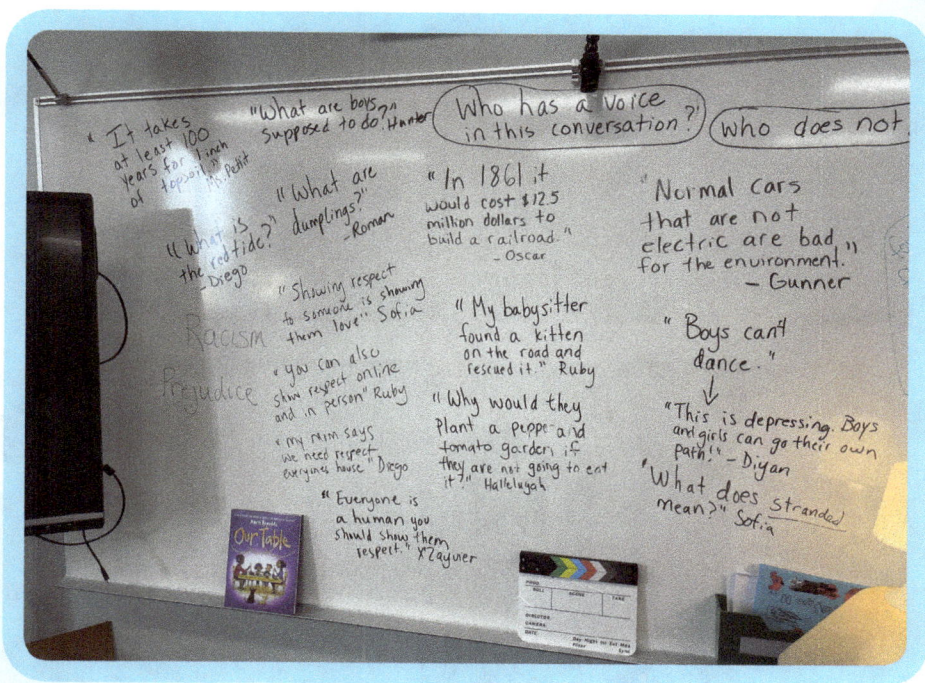

Figure 8.21   *The whiteboard in Lynsey's room is covered in student quotes. It grows from a blank wall to an incredible recording of student thinking across each week.*

students to use various ways of making sense of text and we want that thinking to be available as we work through a read-aloud or minilesson cycle.

Noticing and Naming as a Way to Center Student Thinking

We don't jump right into teaching minilessons on how to talk and write about text on the first day of school. Instead, we use the first eight weeks to build on and capture what children already do in their talk and writing. We informally notice and name what we see. Often, after a few weeks of school, we begin to create charts [like the ones in Figure 8.22] to make visible the strategies and ways of thinking about text that we've discovered informally as a class. We do not have these charts or their contents created before the school year begins, but rather we co-create them with students after a few weeks of reading, talking, and reflecting together. These charts are not finalized and can be added to as we discover new strategies. As we create these charts together, students begin to notice strategies they already use and they also begin to pick up on the strategies of others.

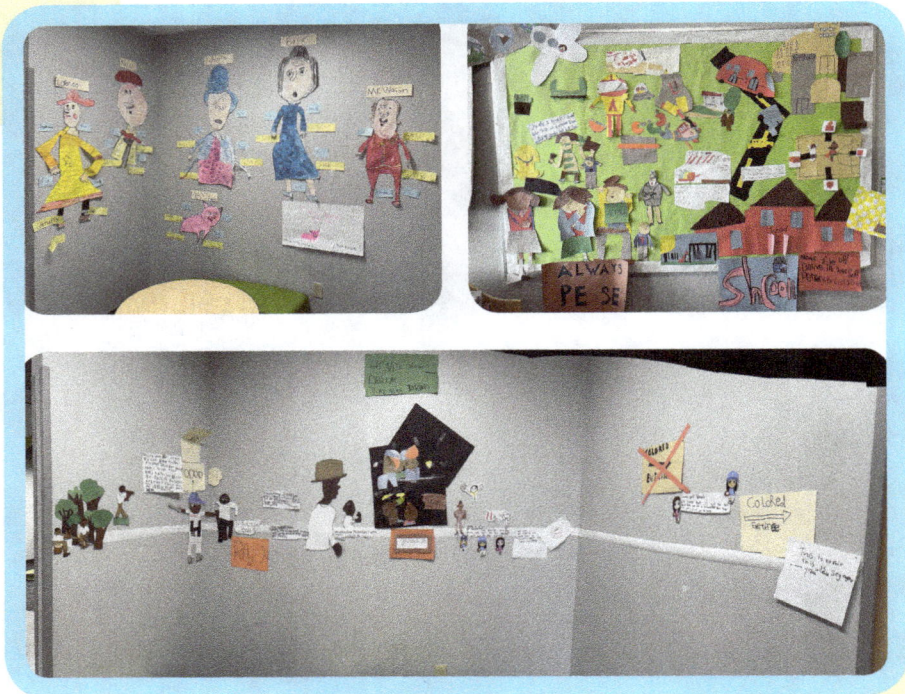

Figure 8.22 *Wall space is used by students as they co-create meaning around longer texts over time.*

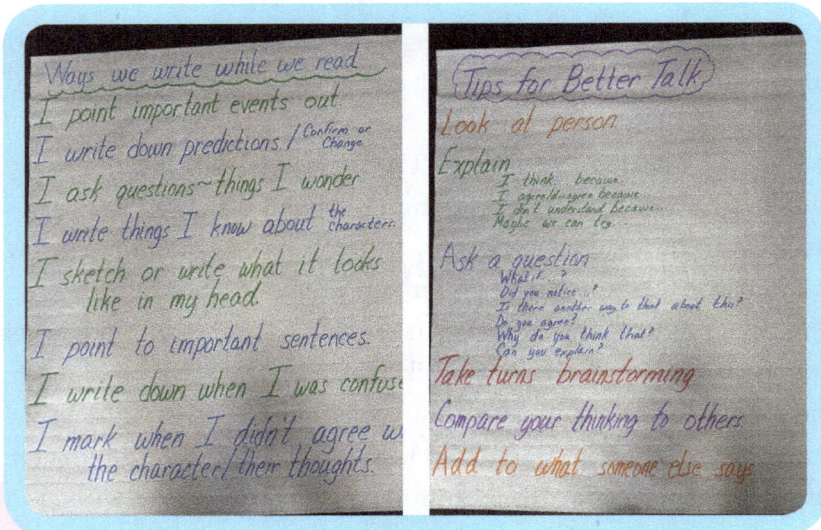

Figure 8.23 *Two charts that we created with a fifth-grade class during the first month of school. One chart (left) captures strategies for having good conversations in small and whole-group settings, while the other (right) is a list of ways students can annotate as they read.*

Reading Notebooks as a Way to Center Student Thinking

We set up reading notebooks during the first week of school. Our reading notebooks have evolved over time but the more we have learned to watch and listen to our students, the less we have dictated when it comes to how students set up and use their reading notebooks. The goal is for the reading notebook to become a place that is useful to the individual reader. We have used a blank sketchbook or notebook for years—a spiral-bound notebook without lines. We've found that this type of notebook gives students the freedom to determine how to organize their thinking. It invites them to write or draw or both. It allows them to write on one page or the full two-page spread. It is incredible to see what young readers do when they have this freedom without graphic organizers, lines, or page parameters. They find powerful ways to record their authentic thinking as they build understanding. We don't model during the first eight weeks of school. Instead, we invite children to record their thinking while reading and then notice and name all that we see. Because we want to build on student thinking, it is important that students have choice in how they write and collect their thinking. Instead of assigning a way to write in their notebooks, we listen and watch and then use whole-class sharing sessions to raise up the different ways students are using their notebooks. In this way, we can open up possibilities for annotation and thinking while also showing children early in the year that it is their thinking that is centered.

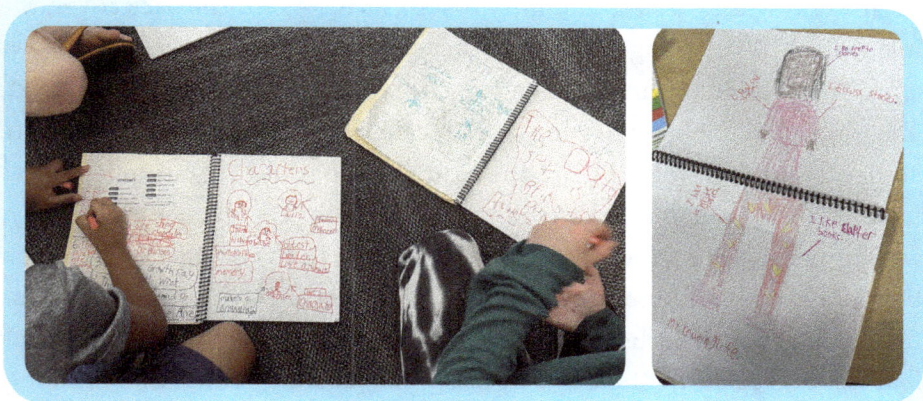

Figure 8.24 *Students in Lynsey's classroom record in their reading notebook early in the school year.*

One of our goals is for students to know that they have power in our classroom and for them to use their voice and contribute to the intellectual learning community. In our classrooms you will often see students writing their thoughts on the whiteboard, emailing the class their thinking, and contributing to classroom conversations during whole-group learning times. Making sure students' voices are shared is a goal that everyone works on throughout the school year but is practiced often during the first eight weeks of school. Here are a few tips for that work early in the year.

1. Make a conversation map of who is talking during one of your whole-group reading times. Take a look at it with students and make plans to incorporate everyone's voice.
2. Try to cultivate a conversational style of talk rather than always raising hands during the whole-group time.
3. Explicitly teach and make visible student conversation stems that help them add on to the group thinking and link their thinking with that of other students. As you are listening to groups, capture the stems they are using and name those aloud as you add them to a chart.

Book Previews as a Way to Center Student Thinking

During read-aloud, previewing is a key routine for every new book we begin. Taking time as a community to look at the cover, the back cover, the inside flap, the first page, and any other special features of the book allows us to think together and set the stage for talk around the common text. The routine of book previewing gives teachers the opportunity to listen to students' thinking even before the read-aloud has begun and collect ideas to return to throughout the reading of the book. We change up the ways we do previews but the goal of preview is always to think together as a class before we read and to capture that early thinking to return to later. For the first preview of the school year, we usually make copies of all of the book features and examine them one by one while recording the class's thinking. What do we notice and wonder when we look at the cover? What do we

Figure 8.25   *Students in Lynsey's room begin Talking Circles on the first day of school.*

notice and wonder when we read the back cover? What do we notice and wonder when we read the table of contents?

Talking Circles as a Way to Center Student Thinking

Lynsey starts Talking Circles on the very first day of school. Think about how hectic it is on that first day! Students rushing in with a ton of supplies, questions, smiles, and more questions. Even on this busiest of days, Lynsey always makes it a point to start Talking Circles.

On the first day of school the Talking Circles happen at the end of the day. This is an intentional move so that students remember this new routine when they come in for the second day of school. On that second day, Talking Circles happen in the morning before the first minilesson of the day.

But on the first day Lynsey introduces Talking Circles to her new group of students by gathering students in the meeting area. She says something like, "What a wonderful day we had today. Do you all feel that same way? Anyone want to share something wonderful from today?"

As students share, Lynsey writes their quotes on the whiteboard. When there is a lull in this conversation, Lynsey continues:

> I'm really excited to share something we will do every day. I want you to see how it goes today so we can continue it tomorrow. We will practice the art of conversation by having Talking Circles each morning. This will be a time to share whatever is on your heart, mind, soul. Some days I may give you all a prompt to talk about and other days you will decide in your circle what to talk about. There are five places in the classroom where we will have the circles. Let me show them to you. At each of these spaces there will be four or five of you having a conversation. Today we will practice what it will look and feel like to have a Talking Circle.

Lynsey spends about thirty minutes having the students try Talking Circles with different people in different spots. She lets them talk for a bit then switches them to a new group and space. Her goal is to watch groupings and see how the conversations flow between different kids. On day two Lynsey will select the groups and the place they will have their Talking Circle. They usually keep in the same circle groups and space for four weeks and then switch.

The first full week of Talking Circles looks more like a share out. Lynsey will have a prompt on the board that says something like this, "Share what is on your mind today." While this prompt is the initial scaffold, it is common for some groups to be unsure of how to get started or for some students to not know what to say. Lynsey walks around and supports groups by getting the other kids involved. "It looks like Kevin is stuck, can someone ask him a question like, 'What did you do last night?'"

After a couple of weeks of more casual Talking Circles, Lynsey uses the speaking and listening standard for third grade as a guide to coach students as they grow their conversational skills. Topics start to arise as Lynsey supports students by asking prompts around things that are going on in the first weeks of school. While Lynsey continues to keep the conversation prompt broad ("Share what is on your mind today") students are often eager to discuss popular topics such as lunch, recess, and video games.

Ohio Speaking and Listening Standard SL.3.1

Engage effectively in a range of collaborative discussions (one-on-one, in groups, and teacher-led) with diverse partners on grade 3 topics and texts, building on others' ideas and expressing their own clearly.

a. Come to discussions prepared, having read or studied required material; explicitly draw on that preparation and other information known about the topic to explore ideas under discussion.

b. Follow agreed-upon rules for discussions (e.g., gaining the floor in respectful ways, listening to others with care, speaking one at a time about the topics and texts under discussion).

c. Ask questions to check understanding of information presented, stay on topic, and link their comments to the remarks of others.

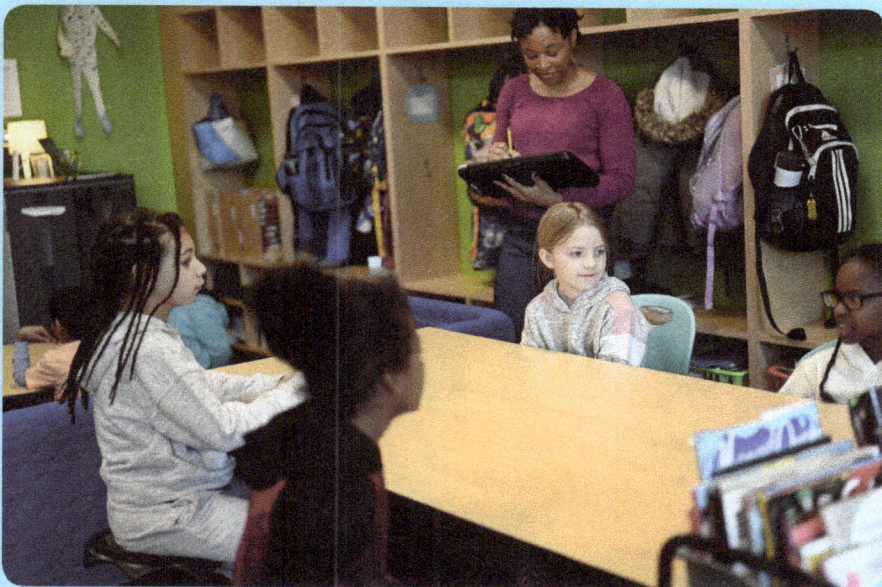

Figure 8.26 *Students gather in their morning Talking Circles. We view Talking Circles very fluidly in the beginning of the school year. We switch groups often and allow extra time for students to share what is on their minds.*

Active Engagement During the First Eight Weeks of Whole-Group Instruction

At the beginning of the school year, we don't only want to create routines for whole-group instruction but also create routines for active engagement during whole-class instruction. We work to use the whole-class space in a

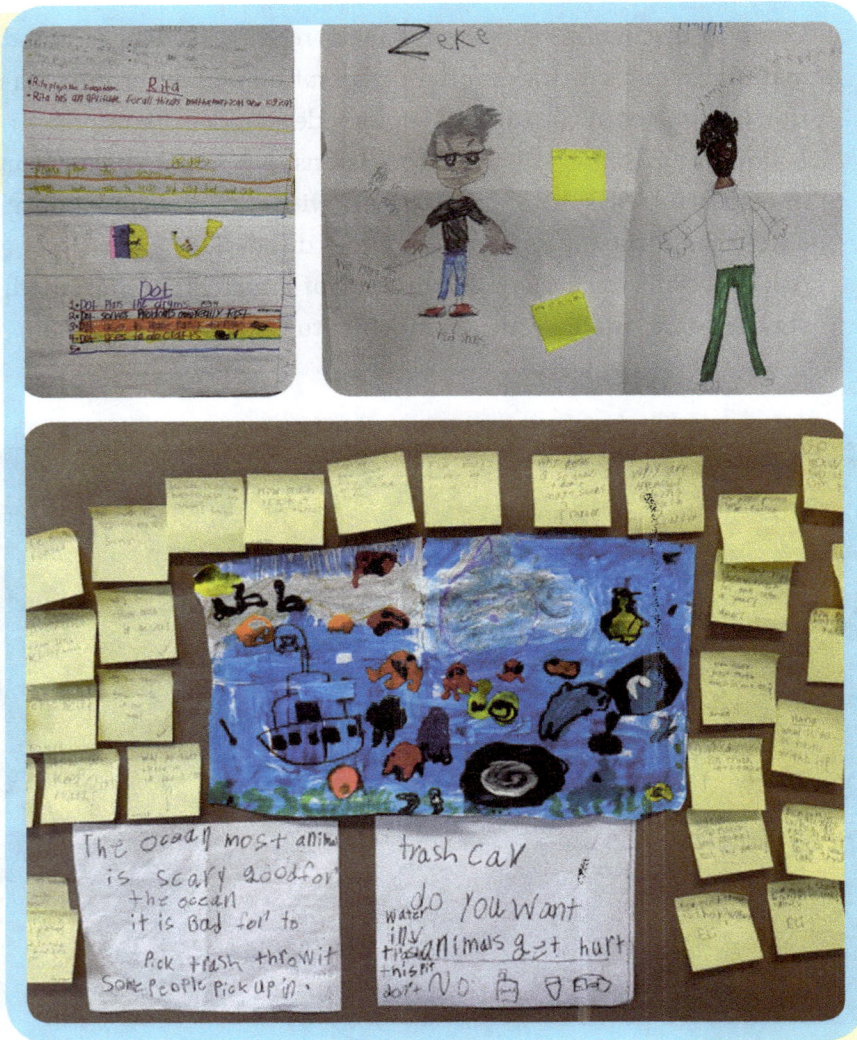

Figure 8.27 *The class slows down to practice ways of jotting down notes during whole-class instruction by creating charts together, using sticky notes, and practicing ways to organize thinking using chart paper.*

232

variety of ways so children have experience talking in a big circle, talking with the text being centered, turning and talking and figuring out ways to share thinking without raising hands. We also use the first eight weeks for children to get comfortable jotting down thinking as they read. For some readers, they need to have a pause in the reading to jot. Other readers can capture their thinking while the reading is occurring. We want students to get to know themselves in this classroom space and we want them to practice active engagement with the text and with the community in many ways.

What Really Matters in the First Eight Weeks

There is nothing like the start of a new school year. We know that eight weeks is a lot of time, but we take a great amount of pleasure in setting up our classrooms and establishing community routines. The first eight weeks of school is such a sacred time of getting to know one another and fostering new relationships. We know that slowing down during these first eight weeks is well worth it. We love watching the fruits of our patience as we witness the work of agentive students working together in a beloved community. But that isn't to say that the first eight weeks are easy.

We have to personally commit ourselves to building this culture year after year. We have to let go of our own traditional expectations of what it means to be the teacher in a classroom. We have to catch ourselves when we feel bothered that a child took something in a different direction or when a child gets up in the middle of read-aloud to write something on the board. We have to realize how deeply ingrained the power structures of a traditional classroom are and consistently push against those during the first eight weeks of school.

Essentially, we have to trust that the children will teach us and that our main role these first eight weeks is to listen and learn. It is easy to worry that this class will never be able to do what last year's group did, but when we think that way, we find that we are always wrong. We must commit to trusting that with time, this group of children will show their brilliance in new ways and that we will be able to teach from that brilliance.

As our children are learning a new way to be in school these first few weeks, so are we. We too are becoming part of this new community that is growing together.

Final Thoughts

A couple of years ago, midway through the first semester of school, Franki came to visit Lynsey's third-grade class. Franki walked through the door just as Lynsey was reading *Crossings: Extraordinary Structures for Extraordinary Animals* during the whole-class reading instruction. The class was sitting in the meeting space, eyes fixed on the digital book being projected on the interactive screen. Typically, Lynsey's class isn't fazed by an adult entering the room or a visitor coming in but this time many turned to look as Franki sat down by the meeting area. Lynsey took a minute to introduce Franki. "Everyone, this is my good friend Mrs. Sibberson and she is going to spend some time with us today." The class broke out with, "Hi Mrs. Sibberson...hello Mrs. Sibberson."

Then Harper chimed in, "Is she going to spend the entire day here?"

Before Lynsey could respond, Josh spoke up, "Welcome, Mrs. Sibberson. We are family here. Come join our family." Franki smiled so big as Josh motioned with his hands to come to the meeting space.

"Yeah, we just started reading a book together," Roman added.

Lynsey then jumped in. "Speaking of family, guess who recommended this book we are reading right now when she heard you all were thinking about protecting animals? Mrs. Sibberson did. I'm so glad she is here to read it with us." The class cheered and Lynsey continued to read while Franki joined the beloved reading community.

The two of us have been on this journey together, alongside brilliant and wonderful children, for almost two decades. Along the way, we have learned from and with children and each other. We know our journey is not over and, as we continue to learn in community, we will grow and change in response to all that the children teach us. Being part of a beloved community with elementary readers and writers is a gift, and we do not take that for granted. It is our hope that you, too, enjoy a beautiful journey as part of your beloved reading community.

Appendix A

Social Identity Wheel
(Adapted from "Voices of Discovery," Intergroup Relations Center, Arizona State University)

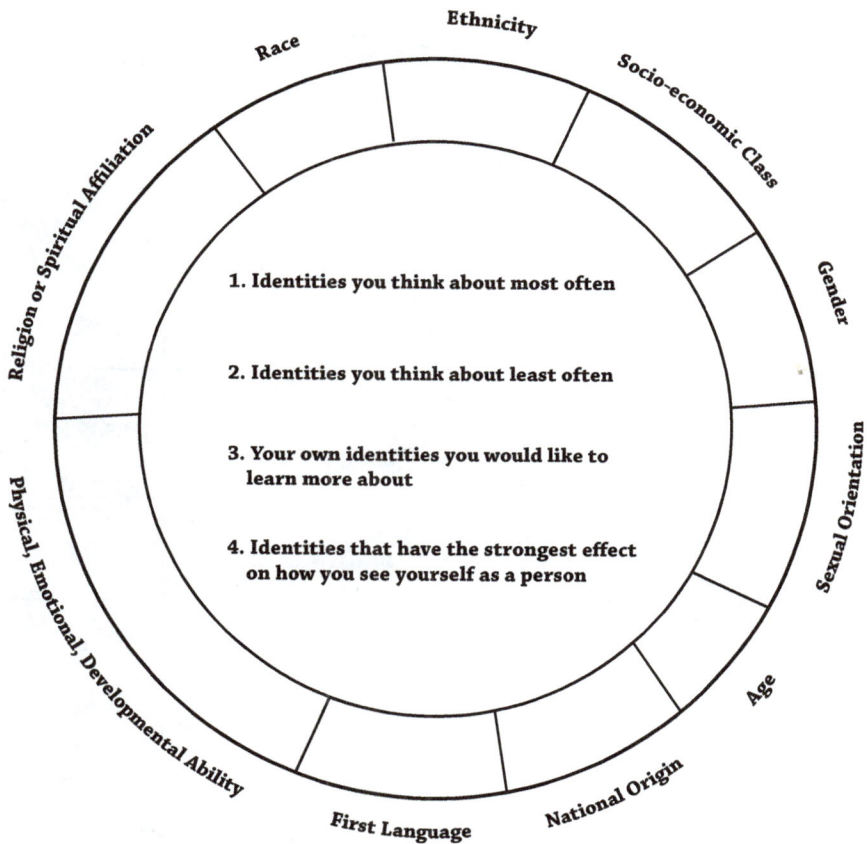

Ethnicity

Race

Socio-economic Class

Religion or Spiritual Affiliation

Gender

1. Identities you think about most often

2. Identities you think about least often

3. Your own identities you would like to learn more about

4. Identities that have the strongest effect on how you see yourself as a person

Sexual Orientation

Physical, Emotional, Developmental Ability

Age

First Language

National Origin

Appendix B

Appendix C

Unit: _____   **Week of:** _____

Focus Standard:

Focus Standard:

Focus Standard:

Focus Standard:

Document Recording Sheet

References

Bennett, Samantha. 2007. *That Workshop Book: New Systems and Structures for Classrooms that Read, Write, and Think*. Portsmouth, NH: Heinemann.

Bishop, Rudine Sims. 1990. "Mirrors, Windows, and Sliding Glass Doors." *Perspectives: Choosing and Using Books for the Classroom* 6 (3): ix–xi.

———. 2016. "A Ride with Nana and CJ: Engagement, Appreciation, and Social Action." *Language Arts* 94 (2): 120–123.

Burkins, Lynsey, and Franki Sibberson. 2023. *Classroom Design for Student Agency: Create Spaces to Empower Young Readers and Writers!* Champaign, IL: NCTE.

Ebarvia, Tricia. December 12, 2017. "How Inclusive Is Your Literacy Classroom Really?" Heinemann blog. https://blog.heinemann.com/heinemann-fellow-tricia-ebavaria-inclusive-literacy-classroom-really.

Ebarvia, Tricia, Lorena Germán, Kim Parker, and Julia Torres. 2021. "What is #Disrupt Texts?" https://disrupttexts.org/lets-get-to-work.

Ferlazzo, Larry. 2020. "Eight Strategies for Engaging in Culturally Relevant Teaching." *Education Week*. https://www.edweek.org/leadership/opinion-eight-strategies-for-engaging-in-culturally-relevant-teaching/2020/12.

Freire, Paulo. 2000. *Pedagogy of the Oppressed*. 30th Anniversary Edition. New York: Continuum.

Ginott, Haim. 1993. *Teacher and Child: A Book for Parents and Teachers*. New York: Scribner Paper Fiction.

Hahn, Mary Lee. 2002. *Reconsidering Read-Aloud*. Portland, ME: Stenhouse Publishers.

Hijabi Librarians. 2023. *Hijabi Librarians*. https://hijabilibrarians.com/.

hooks, bell. 1994. *Teaching to Transgress: Education as the Practice of Freedom*. New York: Routledge.

———. 1996. *Killing Rage: Ending Racism*. New York: Henry Holt and Company.

Jiménez, Laura M., and Carla K. Meyer. 2016. "First Impressions Matter: Navigating Graphic Novels Utilizing Linguistic, Visual, and Spatial Resources." *Journal of Literacy Research* 48 (4): 423–447.

Johnston, Peter. 2004. *Choice Words: How Our Language Affects Children's Learning*. Portland, ME: Stenhouse Publishers.

Landrigan, Clare, and Tammy Mulligan. 2013. *Assessment in Perspective: Focusing on the Readers Behind the Numbers*. Portsmouth, NH: Stenhouse.

Lee & Low Books. 2017. "Classroom Library Questionnaire." https://www.leeandlow.com/educators/grade-level-resources/classroom-library-questionnaire.

———. 2019a. "How to Choose the Best Multicultural Books for Your Collection." https://blog.leeandlow.com/2019/04/02/how-to-choose-the-best-multicultural-books-for-your-collection/.

———. 2019b. "Tackling the Challenges of Implementing Diverse Libraries at Your School." https://blog.leeandlow.com/2019/01/28/tackling-the-challenges-of-implementing-diverse-libraries-at-your-school/.

McNair, Jonda C. 2021. "Surprise, Surprise! Exploring Dust Jackets, Case Covers, and Endpapers in Picture Books to Support Comprehension." *Reading Teacher* 74 (4): 363–373.

McNair, Jonda C., and Hoover, Hayley J. 2021. "Design Elements in Picture Books." *YC Young Children* 76 (3): 14–23.

NCTE. 2023. "Build Your Stack." https://ncte.org/build-your-stack/.

Miller, Donalyn, and Colby Sharp. 2018. *Game Changer!: Book Access for All Kids*. New York: Scholastic.

Nieto, Sonia. June 15, 2016. "Language Is Never Neutral." Heinemann blog. https://blog.heinemann.com/language-never-neutral.

Ohio Department of Education. 2017. "Ohio's Learning Standards: English Language Arts." https://education.ohio.gov/getattachment/Topics/Learning-in-Ohio/English-Language-Art/English-Language-Arts-Standards/ELA-Learning-Standards-2017.pdf.aspx?lang=en-US.

Parker, Kimberly N. 2022. *Literacy is Liberation: Working Toward Justice Through Culturally Relevant Teaching*. Alexandria, VA: ASCD.

Reese, Debbie. 2022. *American Indians in Children's Literature.* https://americanindiansinchildrensliterature.blogspot.com/.

Shalaby, Carla. 2017. *Troublemakers: Lessons in Freedom from Young Children at School.* New York: New Press.

Vasquez, Vivian Maria. 2004. *Negotiating Critical Literacies with Young Children.* Mahwah, NJ: Lawrence Erlbaum Associates.

Credits

Chapter 2

FIGURE 2.3 Cover of *The Teachers' March!* by Sandra Neil Wallace and Rich Wallace. Illustrated by Charly Palmer. © 2020 Astra Books.

FIGURE 2.3 Cover of *Child of the Civil Rights Movement* by Paula Young Shelton and Raul Colón. Illustrated by Raul Colón. © 2013 Penguin Random House.

FIGURE 2.12 From *FRONT DESK* by Kelly Yang. Cover art © 2018 by Maike Plinzke. Reprinted by permission of Scholastic Inc.

FIGURES 2.13, 2.14, AND 2.15 From *The Girl Who Drank the Moon* by Kelly Barnhill, copyright © 2016. Reprinted by permission of Algonquin Young Readers, an imprint of Hachette Book Group, Inc.

FIGURE 2.16 Cover of *Dragons in a Bag* by Zetta Elliott. Illustrated by Geneva B. © 2019 Random House.

Chapter 4

FIGURE 4.3 Social Identity Wheel used by permission of Arizona State University Intergroup Relations Center staff.

Chapter 6

OPENER PHOTO, UNNUMBERED FIGURES 1–2, FIGURE 6.7 Cover and interior of *Blue* by Nana Ekua Brew-Hammond. Illustrated by Daniel Minter. © 2022 Penguin Random House.

FIGURE 6.5 cover of *Whale Fall* by Melissa Stewart. Illustrated by Rob Dunlavey. © 2023 Penguin Random House.

FIGURE 6.5 cover of *A River's Gifts* by Patricia Newman. Illustrated by Natasha Donovan. © 2022 Lerner Publishing.

Chapter 7

· · · · · · · · · · ·

Index

Note: Page locators in *italic* refer to figures.

Alexander, Kwame (*Crossover*) 99
annotations, student: evolution of
    reading notebooks 60–62;
    planning whole-class instruction in
    response to 128–129; power shift
    56–62; as routine 124–129;
    of standards *51, 52, 140, 144*;
    student ownership of 59–60;
    tools for 125–127, 179; while
    reading 128; whiteboard 179–180
Applegate, Katherine (*Odder*) 28, 173
asset-based approach to listening 114
audiobooks 100
Auxier, Jonathan (*Sweep*) 64–65

Barnhill, Kelly (*The Girl Who Drank the
    Moon*) 56–59, 60
Bathe the Cat (McGinty) 212
beloved community 6, 234;
    building and developing 169–171;
    defining 16–17; glimpse into
    12–15; listening in 113–115
Bennett, Samantha 115
bilingual students 100
Bishop, Rudine Sims 88, 100, 109
*Blue: A History of the Color as Deep
    as the Sea and as Wide as the Sky*
    (Brew-Hammond): choosing to use
    134, 146–150; curating resources
    around 150–151; minilesson cycle
    151–163; using planning and
    documentation tool with 48–50

book displays 204
book lists, ready-made 97
book previews *60*, 177, *178*, 184–185;
    to center student thinking 228–229;
    posters 126; power shift 53–56
book talks 122, 220–221
books, getting to know 85–109;
    being responsive to students 88–90;
    commitment as teacher readers
    109; keeping track of reading 108;
    knowing standards and 172–175;
    personal reading identities 90–93;
    reading with a teacher's lens 104–108;
    reflecting on personal social identities
    93, 94–97; resources 98–102;
    teacher-of-reading identities 97–108;
    tips for reading widely 98
Brew-Hammond, Nana Ekua (*Blue*):
    choosing to use 134, 146–150;
    curating resources around 150–151;
    minilesson cycle 151–163;
    using planning and documentation
    tool with 48–50
Bruchac, Joseph (*Rez Dogs*) 217
Build Your Stack 98–99
Butt or Face (Lavelle) 213
Button, Lana (*Raj's Rule (For the
    Bathroom at School)*) 215

character development, Menu of
    Mentors 44
charts *55*, 126, 224, 225, *226*

classroom library 100, 201–203, *204*, *205*

Classroom Library Questionnaire 101

co-intentional education 32–33; lens 34; viewing standards through lens of 68–72

Cole, Henry (*Forever Home*) 214

collective thinking 24–26, 39, *71*, 224

complex texts, skills for reading more 18–19

connected cycle of lessons 46–47

conversations, invitations and 42, 69, 192–193; around books beyond first weeks 215–220; around books in first weeks 211–215; whole-class instruction as 13, 29–30

critical lens 34; reading standards through 72–78

Crossover (Alexander) 99

culturally responsive listening 113–114

daily schedule 28–29

digital shorts 45

digital tools 125, 126, 157, 208–209

Disrupt Texts 99

diversity: books representing 100–103; culturally responsive listening and 113–114; incidental 102–103

Dragons in a Bag (Elliott) 41, *60*, 216

Ebarvia, Tricia 99, 102

Elliott, Zetta: *Dragons in a Bag* 41, *60*, 216; *The Phoenix on Barkley Street* 173

Faruqi, Reem (*I Can Help*) 214

Faruqi, Saddia: *Mayra Khan and the Incredible Henna Party* 173; *Yusef Azeem Is Not a Hero* 217

felt tip pens 125

Ferlazzo, Larry 33, 67

Forever Home (Cole) 214

free children 83

Freire, Paulo 32–33, 34, 201

gaps in reading, addressing 92–93, 97, 99–100

Ginott, Haim 92

The Girl Who Drank the Moon (Barnhill) 56–59, 60

goals for first eight weeks 192–197

Goodreads 108

Google Classroom 209

Google Slides 125

graphic novels 86, 174, 221

Gray, Gary R., Jr. (*I'm From*) 4–5

Hahn, Mary Lee 53

Harbor Me (Woodson) 14, 54–55, 216

highlighters 125

highlighting text 178–179

Higuera, Donna Barb (*The Last Cuentista*) 217

Hijabi Librarians 100

Holi colors 88–89

hooks, bell 6, 16, 113, 170, 192

I Can Help (Faruqi) 214

I'm From (Gray) 4–5

incidental diversity 102–103

independent reading, whole-group instruction and 17, 23–24

invitations and conversations 42, 69, 192–193; around books beyond first weeks 215–220; around books in first weeks 211–215; whole-class instruction as 13, 29–30

Kindle annotation tools 126, 179
Kindle app 178, 179

Langley, Kaija (*When Langston Dances*)
106–107
language, shifting 41–43
The Last Cuentista (Higuera) 217
Lavelle, Kari (*Butt or Face*) 213
Lee and Low Books 100–101
Lee, Hannah (*My Hair*) 5
Leon the Extraordinary (Nicholas)
174
library, classroom 100, 201–203, *204*,
205
Lin, Grace (*The Ugly Vegetables*) 184
Lin, Grace (*The Year of the Dog*): book
preview 177, *178*, 184–185;
deciding to choose as a read-aloud
174, 175; pairing with standards 176,
176; read-aloud 166–169, 177–189
The List of Things That Will Not Change
(Stead) 218
listening, teacher 195; creating
conditions for 113–115; creating
predictable routines and structures
for 115–129; in culturally responsive
ways 113–114; developing and
utilizing listening skills 131–132;
minilessons 151–157;
read-aloud 178–180, 186–188;
rethinking routines for 129–130;
taking a researcher stance 114–115;
tips on 196–197; using an asset-based
approach 114

Mahin, Michael (*Muddy*) 151
Maizy Chen's Last Chance (Yee) 218
*Mayra Khan and the Incredible Henna
Party* (Faruqi) 173

McGinty, Alice B. (*Bathe the Cat*)
212
Menu of Mentors: on character
development 44; moving from
text sets to 37, 43–45; planning
minilesson unit of study 145–151;
reading to create 172, 211–221
Miller, Donalyn 87
minilesson cycle 133–163; Days 1 to 3:
standards 140–145; Days 4 to 6:
reading text and listening 151–157;
Days 7 to 10: moving forward in
response 159–163; recording
student thinking 157–158; starting
with standards 135–139; studying
student thinking 158–159; text sets
as Menu of Mentors 145–151
minilessons 18; comparing read-aloud
and 19–20; connected cycle of
lessons 46–47; fitting into daily
schedule 28–29; length 135;
planning follow-ups to read-aloud
181–184; shifting of thinking on
43–47; working together with
read-aloud 20–21
*Muddy: The Story of Blues Legend Muddy
Waters* (Mahin) 151
Muslim characters 100
My Hair (Lee) 5

name grids 82, *83*, 210; template
236
National Council of Teachers of
English (NCTE) 98–99, 199
Nicholas, Jamar (*Leon the Extraordinary*)
174
noticing and naming 194; to center
student thinking 225; as a routine
122–124

Odder (Applegate) 28, 173

Operation Frog Effect (Scheerger) 107–108, 216

Ortega, Mirelle (*River of Mariposas*) 213

The Other Side (Woodson) 12–13

Padlets 126; tips on using 157; use in *Blue* minilesson 152, *153*, 157

Parker, Kim 21, 99

The Phoenix on Barkley Street (Elliott) 173

picture books in first eight weeks 212–215

planning: connected lessons 46–47; minilesson cycle 135–139; minilesson follow-ups to read-alouds 181–184; read-aloud 172–177; text sets as Menu of Mentors 145–151; whole-class instruction 25, 121, 128–129

planning and assessment tools, setting up 210–211

planning and documentation tool 48–50, *50*, 81–83, 157–158, 211; template 237

planning for first eight weeks 191–234; active engagement in whole-group instruction 232–233; building routines 221–231; designing classroom space 197–205; goals for first eight weeks 192–197; reading to create a Menu of Mentors 211–221; sharing student voices 228; tools for teacher planning and assessment 210–211; tools to support student agency 205–209; what really matters 233–234

power and control, shifting 15, 31–62; evolving physical space 37–41;

an example 35–37; how it happens 47–52; language shifts 41–43; minilessons 43–47; read-aloud time 52–62; tips 42

power of whole-group instruction 18–23

Powwow Day (Sorell) 213

previews, book *60*, 177, *178*, 184–185; to center student thinking 228–229; posters 126; power shift 53–56

questions: to ask yourself 9–10; for students to ask themselves 21

Raj's Rule (For the Bathroom at School) (Button) 215

read-aloud 18, 165–189; building and developing a community 169–171; comparing minilessons and 19–20; an example 166–168; fitting into daily schedule 28–29; at a glance 184–189; planning beyond first weeks of school 215–220; planning minilesson follow-ups to 180–184; planning process 172–177; power shifts in evolving 52–62; reflecting on a year of 96–97; space for 169–170; starting the new school year with 219; teaching 177–184; using reading notebooks 207; working together with minilessons 20–21

reading identities: addressing gaps in personal 92–93, 97; growing and changing 86–87; personal 90–93; sources to help fill gaps in 99–100; teacher-of-reading identities 97–108

reading interviews and conferences 119–122, 159; tips for 122 reading notebooks 125, 180, 206–207, 227; evolution 60–62

reading with a teacher's lens 104–108

recording sheets *176*, 177, 180, *181*

Reese, Debbie 100

researcher stance, developing 114–115

resources 98–102

Reynolds, Jason 18, 221; *Stuntboy, in the Meantime* 218

Rez Dogs (Bruchac) 217

River of Mariposas (Ortega) 213

routines: building routines in first eight weeks 221–231; creating predictable routines and structures for listening 115–129; rethinking listening 129–130

A Rover's Story (Warga) 218

Ryan, Pam Muñoz (*Solimar*) 217

Scheerger, Sarah (*Operation Frog Effect*) 107–108, 216

series books for book talk 220–221

Shalaby, Carla 24

Sharp, Colby 87

Shihab, Naomi (*Turtle of Oman*) 68

skills: developing and utilizing teachers' listening 131–132; for reading more complex texts 18–19

social identities, reflecting on personal 93, 94–97

social identity wheel 94–95; template 235

Solimar (Ryan) 217

Sorell, Traci (*Powwow Day*) 213

Souto-Manning, Mariana 33, 67

space, designing classroom 197–205; book displays 204; to center student thinking 224–225; classroom library 201–203, *204*, *205*; space for conversations around room *198*, 199; teaching from back of whole-group space *40*; wall space 199, *199*, *200*, 224–225, *226*; for whole-group meeting 37–41, 169–170, 197–199

Srinivasan, Divya (*What I Am*) 212

standards 63–83; anchoring student learning with 78–80; and deciding what to teach next 45–46; keeping track of students' learning in relation to 80–84; knowing the standards 66–67; Ohio speaking and listening standard 231; pairing books with 176, *176*; planning and documentation tools 48–50, *50*, 81–83, 157–158, 211, 237; planning minilesson cycle with 135–139; planning read-aloud with 172–175; power of 67; reading through a critical lens 72–78; recording sheets *176*, 177, 180, *181*; role in whole-class reading instruction 66–80; understanding standards together 50–52, 140–145; viewing through co-intentional lens 68–72

Stead, Rebecca (*The List of Things That Will Not Change*) 218

sticky notes *65*, 125, *223*, *223*, *232*

student thinking: recording *55*, 157–158, 180, *181*, 222; rethinking routines for listening to 130; routine to visibly center 223–231; sharing student work and 222; studying 158–159, 180–184; valuing thinking over right answer

193–194; whiteboard as a space to hold *40*, 41, *116*, 166, *166*, 224–225

student voices: amplifying 41, 194–195, *196*; centering 39–41, 158; responding to 88–90, 122–124; sharing 228

students, getting to know 111–132; creating conditions for listening 113–115; creating predictable routines and structures for listening 115–129; developing and utilizing teachers' listening skills 131–132; rethinking routines for listening 129–130

Stuntboy, in the Meantime (Reynolds) 218

Sweep: The Story of a Girl and Her Monster (Auxier) 64–65

Talking Circles 88, 112–113, 116; to center student thinking 229–231; tips for 117

teacher-of-reading identities 97–108

The Teachers' March (Wallace) 35, *36*

text pairs 151

text sets and Menu of Mentors 37, 43–45, 145–151

Thought Partners 119

tips: all book talk counts 122; on listening responsively 196–197; for reading widely 98; on shifting language 42; for Talking Circles 117; on using Padlets 157

tools: digital 125, 126, 157, 208–209; planning and documentation tool 48–50, *50*, 81–83, 157–158, 211, 237; for student annotations 125–127, 179; to support student

agency 205–209; for teacher planning and assessment 210–211

tracking systems for books read 108

turn and talk partners 117, 179

Turtle of Oman (Shihab) 68

Vasquez, Vivian Maria 34, 67

visual maps 127

wall space 199, *199*, *200*; to center student thinking 224–225, *226*

Wallace, Sandra and Rich (*The Teachers' March*) 35, *36*

Warga, Jasmine (*A Rover's Story*) 218

What I Am (Srinivasan) 212

When Langston Dances (Langley) 106–107

whiteboard: annotations 179–180; positioning of interactive 208, *208*; space to hold student thinking *40*, 41, *116*, 166, *166*, 224–225

whole-group discussions 179

whole-group instruction 11–30; active engagement in first eight weeks 232–233; beloved community, defining 16–17; as culturally responsive 113–114; frequency and timing 27, 28–29; glimpse into beloved community of 12–15; goals 27; independent reading and 17, 23–24; as invitations and conversations 13, 29–30; physical space for 37–41, 169–170, 197–199; planning and implementing 25, 121, 128–129; power of 18–23; role of standards in 66–80; rooted in collective thinking 24–26; visual of *22*; why it matters 15–16

Woodson, Jacqueline: *Harbor Me* 14, 54–55, 216; *The Other Side* 12–13; *The Year We Learned to Fly* 214

The Year of the Dog (Lin): deciding to choose as a read-aloud 174, 175; pairing with standards 176, *176*; previewing 177, *178*, 184–185; read-aloud 166–169, 177–189

The Year We Learned to Fly (Woodson) 214

Yee, Lisa (*Maizy Chen's Last Chance*) 218

Yusef Azeem Is Not a Hero (Faruqi) 217

For Product Safety Concerns and Information please contact our EU
representative GPSR@taylorandfrancis.com
Taylor & Francis Verlag GmbH, Kaufingerstraße 24, 80331 München, Germany